ANA

'A remarkable piece o̶̶̶̶̶̶̶̶̶̶̶...̶̶ṵalism' Ed Moloney

'Cobain delves forensically into the murder [and] does a superb job of uncovering the facts, the context and the aftermath . . . without veering towards either side . . . A compellingly brilliant book' *Dublin Sunday Business Post*

'Though scrupulously even-handed, Cobain doesn't shy away from telling a good story, using deft lyrical flourishes and narrative teases, he expertly marshals both quotidian detail and the broad social backdrop as he builds up to the shooting itself' *TLS*

'By homing in on one man's violent death, Ian Cobain tells a riveting and tragic story but, while doing that, he has also written a precise, compelling history of the Troubles. It's one of the best I've read' Roddy Doyle

'His description of the killing is as compelling a piece of non-fiction as I've read for a while . . . This is a useful contribution to our understanding of the conflict in Northern Ireland and an interesting – in places fascinating – read' *Mail on Sunday*

'*Anatomy of a Killing* is meticulously researched and the results are arresting. For anyone who grew up in the Troubles, this will be a valuable reminder of just how dark a shadow we lived under. For many others, it will be shocking to discover what people in one part of the British Isles had to endure in recent times' Timothy Phillips

'A concise and gripping history of the Troubles, revealing the people behind the pain and violence' *Vice*

'A superb piece of journalism that avoids any moralising or analysing from [Cobain's] own perspective and that has a powerful impact, forcing the reader to consider the humanity of the players but also leaving space for the reader to make the final judgment' Malachi O'Doherty

'A compelling narrative account of the human cost of the Conflict . . . This book is both a valuable contribution to preserving the memory of the Conflict and to the continued out-workings of the fragile peace (in) process in this Northern Ireland' *Village Magazine*

'*Anatomy of a Killing* is a fine book, very much the product of serious research and prodigious analysis' *Fortnight*

Ian Cobain

Anatomy of a Killing

Life and Death on a Divided Island

GRANTA

Granta Publications, 12 Addison Avenue, London W11 4QR

First published in Great Britain by Granta Books, 2020
This paperback edition published by Granta Books, 2021

Copyright © Ian Cobain, 2020

Map copyright © John Gilkes, 2020

Ian Cobain has asserted his moral right under the Copyright, Designs and
Patents Act, 1988, to be identified as the author of this work.

A CIP catalogue record for this book is available from the British Library.

1 3 5 7 9 10 8 6 4 2

ISBN 978 1 84627 642 2 (paperback)
ISBN 978 1 84627 641 5 (ebook)

Typeset by Avon DataSet Ltd, 4 Arden Court, Arden Road, Alcester,
Warwickshire B49 6HN

Printed and bound by CPI Group (UK) Ltd, Croydon, CR0 4YY

MIX
Paper from
responsible sources
FSC® C020471
www.fsc.org

For Alan Harding and Ian McGinnity,
with thanks for a lifetime of friendship

'Look at Ireland. There we have the great failure of our history . . . I am inclined to regard it as the one irreparable disaster of our history; and the ground and cause of it was a failure of historical perception: the refusal to see that time and circumstance had created an Irish mind; to learn the idiom in which that mind of necessity expressed itself; to understand that what we could never remember, Ireland could never forget.'

G. M. Young, *Portrait of an Age*

'But now, for the first time, I see you are a man like me. I thought of your hand-grenades, of your bayonet, of your rifle; now I see your wife and your face and our fellowship. Forgive me, comrade. We always see it too late. Why do they never tell us that you are poor devils like us, that your mothers are just as anxious as ours, and that we have the same fear of death, and the same dying and the same agony – Forgive me comrade; how could you be my enemy?'

Erich Maria Remarque, *All Quiet on the Western Front*

Contents

Preface	xi
A Note on Language	xiii
Acronyms and Abbreviations	xv
Map	xvii
1. The People	1
2. The Time	32
3. The Place	77
4. The Killing	121
5. The Consequences	162
6. The Far Side of Revenge	213
A Note on Police Interview Records and Other Sources	235
Acknowledgements	238
Notes	241
Bibliography	249
Index	261

Contents

Preface

This is the story of one particular event that took place on 22 April 1978 in the Northern Ireland market town of Lisburn. Early that afternoon an off-duty policeman was shot dead at his home and shortly afterwards six people were arrested, several of them members of an IRA Active Service Unit. The killing was covered by the local press at the time, as were the trial and prosecution of some of those who were arrested. But in this book I wanted to re-examine this single event from the perspective of history. I wanted to explore what forces, ideas and actions caused these people's lives to intersect on that day – both their personal circumstances and the wider context in Northern Ireland – and to consider the long repercussions of the killing. It was of course a profoundly traumatic event for the family and friends of the dead man. It was also just one of more than 3,700 deaths that occurred in Northern Ireland during the Troubles. But this one act offers us a way to reflect more broadly on this turbulent period: to examine the reasons why some people become involved in political violence, the means by which governments and security forces attempt to overcome those people, and the way in which individuals and communities try to live with the consequences.

A Note on Language

Words are rarely neutral in Northern Ireland. Or, if you prefer, they are rarely neutral in the six counties. So often, the use of one term – Derry, say, rather than Londonderry – appears immediately to place the writer or speaker on one side of the divide, or the other.

Samuel Johnson was doubtless correct when he declared that 'language is the dress of thought', and I have thought about these two traditions and attempted to remain sensitive to them, but not hobbled by them. I believe that understanding why so many men went to prison during the Troubles, for example – and attempting to comprehend something of their experiences of incarceration and resistance – is more critical than the question of whether that prison should properly be called Her Majesty's Prison Maze, or Long Kesh. It was both.

As a consequence, I have employed the term that appeared to me to be most apt within the context in which it is being used. So the north-east corner of the island is at times the north of Ireland, most frequently Northern Ireland, and occasionally Ulster.

This is a book that focuses on the actions of members of the IRA. They will be described as both gunmen and volunteers. They were prosecuted as terrorists. Some members of the IRA were, of course, thugs; some were idealists, dedicated to progressive political change.

They, like the men and women of the Royal Ulster Constabulary and the British army, were also husbands and wives and sons and fathers. I have attempted to be fair to all of them. More important to me than the language I have used to describe them is my belief that we should not lose sight of the fact that they were all ordinary men and women.

Acronyms and Abbreviations

ASU – Active Service Unit
BMH – Bureau of Military History, Dublin
CQA – close-quarter assassination
INLA – Irish National Liberation Army
IRA – Irish Republican Army
IWM – Imperial War Museum, London
NAM – National Army Museum, London
NIO – Northern Ireland Office
OIRA – Official Irish Republican Army
PIRA – Provisional Irish Republican Army
PRONI – Public Record Office of Northern Ireland, Belfast
Provos – Provisional Irish Republican Army
PSNI – Police Service of Northern Ireland
'Ra – IRA
RIC – Royal Irish Constabulary
RUC – Royal Ulster Constabulary
SAS – Special Air Service
SDLP – Social Democratic and Labour Party
TNA – The National Archives, Kew
UDA – Ulster Defence Association
UDR – Ulster Defence Regiment
UVF – Ulster Volunteer Force

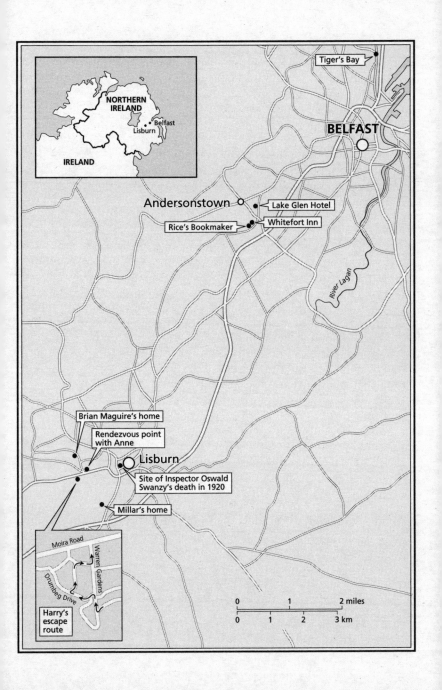

NORTHERN
IRELAND

Belfast
Lisburn

IRELAND

Tiger's Bay

BELFAST

Andersonstown

Lake Glen Hotel

Rice's Bookmaker

Whitefort Inn

River Lagan

Brian Maguire's home

Rendezvous point
with Anne

Lisburn

Site of Inspector Oswald
Swanzy's death in 1920

Millar's home

Moira Road

Warren
Gardens

Drumbeg Drive

Harry's
escape
route

0   1   2 miles

0   1   2   3 km

1

The People

In early winter, as a boy, all wrapped up in his mittens and his duffel coat, Millar McAllister could gaze skywards as formations of birds winged their way south, flying first across the flat farmland towards Belfast, and then over the sea; down to France and Spain and who knew where? As he watched, Millar knew that the following spring would bring the thrill of the songs to be heard from the trees and hedgerows around south Antrim. So often, animals are among a child's first true loves, and encounters with them cast a life-long spell, one that binds the child, and then the adult, to the wider world.

By the time he was a teenager, Millar was learning how to handle racing pigeons, how to gently pick them up and whisper into their ears, hidden below their eyes; before long he would be photographing them, and writing about them too.

Millar had been born in 1942 in one of a row of two-up, two-down terrace houses in Cogry, a tiny village half an hour's bus ride from Belfast. He was christened Laird Millar, but known always by his middle name. When Millar was born, more than two years into the Second World War, his father Hugh was serving as a corporal in a British army infantry unit, the 45th Regiment of the Reconnaissance Corps, which spent years fighting in the jungles of the Far East.

After the war, Millar's father worked at the nearby flax-spinning mill, which employed many of the menfolk in Cogry, and several of the women. Within a minute or two of the narrow street of terrace houses at Cogry there were fields and brooks and boreens, and Millar was a country boy at heart. One of his neighbours was a well-known figure in Northern Ireland's pigeon-racing circles. He would let the boy spend time in his pigeon loft, and after Millar had helped out with a bit of scraping and cleaning, he would be allowed to feed the birds. Millar loved those birds. Before long, he became familiar with the country lanes by training this neighbour's pigeons from a hamper strapped to the back of his bike. Soon he acquired a few birds of his own.

Millar's generation did not have the choice that his father's did, of working for life in the linen industry, which stumbled into steep decline during the post-war years. The mill at Cogry closed just as Millar was leaving school. So, in December 1961, at the age of nineteen, he joined the Royal Ulster Constabulary – the police.

The Troubles in the north of Ireland were barely visible on the horizon, and Millar would not have been taking *sides*, as such: it was just a good, steady job. Nevertheless, his neighbours in Protestant Cogry may well have approved.

Initially, he served in uniform in north Belfast and at the RUC Barracks at Carryduff, a quiet town in County Down, south of the city. In April 1965, while serving at Carryduff, he married Nita Corry, a farmer's daughter, in a Baptist church south of Belfast. Millar was twenty-three and Nita was twenty-two. In September the following year the couple's first son, Mark, was born. In May 1970 Nita gave birth to another boy, Alan.

Millar transferred to the RUC's administration branch at its headquarters in Knock in east Belfast. He soon wanted another move: through his love of pigeons he had become a skilled photographer, and not long after arriving at Knock he made a successful application to join the RUC's Photography Branch.

Here, his duties including recording scenes of crimes; this was 1971 – two years into the Troubles – and there was no shortage of carnage to be photographed.[1]

As his police role became more demanding, pigeons became even more important to him: a source of respite. Sometimes, he confided, when on duty on a Saturday he would find a loft, and wait there, watching for the birds.

By this time, he was breeding and racing his own pigeons. Such was his expertise that since 1968 he had been the Northern Ireland correspondent for the *Pigeon Racing News and Gazette*, sending monthly reports of racing and breeding news in the province to the magazine's offices in Weybridge, south-west of London. Those reports appeared under the byline 'The Copper'. They were not quite anonymous, however: each month, appearing alongside the byline, would be a picture of Millar.

Early in 1977, Millar and Nita and the boys moved from Newtownabbey, north of Belfast, to Lisburn, nine miles south-west of the city, bringing them closer to Nita's family.

The town of around 70,000 people had witnessed comparatively little violence during the Troubles. There had been a handful of sectarian killings, a number of car-bomb attacks in Bow Street in the town centre – the local paper dubbed it Bomb Alley – and several RUC men from Lisburn had died elsewhere in the province. But by 1977 not a single member of the security forces had lost their life in Lisburn. Many police officers and prison officers had settled in Lisburn. It was a good place for them to raise their families. It seemed not only safe, but impregnable.

Millar, however, had been spotted by the other side. He'd been 'dicked', as the security forces in Northern Ireland would say at that time. He'd been clocked by IRA suspects at Castlereagh in east Belfast – a place that the RUC euphemistically referred to as a 'holding centre'.

Because he had always been in plain clothes they had assumed, incorrectly, that he was a detective with Special Branch, the intelligence-gathering section of the RUC. They had also come to believe – again, incorrectly – that Millar was an Orangeman, a member of the Orange Order, a Protestant fraternal organisation.

In the late 1970s, a seemingly endless stream of men and women accused of terrorist offences – both Republicans and Loyalists – were being brought to Castlereagh, where teams of police interrogators would work around the clock, extracting confessions that could be deployed before the juryless criminal hearings known as Diplock courts. These suspects were routinely denied lawyers. Some were subjected only to threats and a little rough handling. But many say they were treated appallingly, and in time some of their complaints would be confirmed by an Amnesty International investigation and an official inquiry by an English judge.

In the late 1970s, any IRA volunteer who had been interrogated at Castlereagh for any length of time held in his or her heart a particular abhorrence for the police officers who worked there. And Millar had been dicked.

Harry Murray's early life was not so very different from that of Millar. He too had been born into a working-class Protestant family, in Belfast, in March 1948. His mother Margaret and his father Henry, a labourer, christened him Henry Harrison Murray, but he was always known as Harry.

The family home was a terrace house in Mervue Street in the Tiger's Bay area of north Belfast. The road rises up a hill, and from the top Harry and his mates could see the docks on one side of the Lagan and the sprawling Harland & Wolff shipyards on the other. It was a close-knit, cousins-around-the-corner, front-door-never-locked kind of place. Many of the houses in Tiger's Bay had been built for the dockers and the shipbuilders. They were poorly constructed, however, and the area had been truly battered during the Luftwaffe's air raids of early 1941. When the raids began, local people discovered to their distress that their homes were so flimsy that a single German bomb could bring half a street crashing down. Fires then raged out of control, despite the arrival of fire crews from across the north, and even from across the border in the Republic.

Harry and the other kids of Tiger's Bay grew up in a landscape that had been shattered and shaped by the violence of this global conflict: bomb sites, neatly piled rubble, terraces that ended abruptly, with the wallpaper still flapping on the final wall, and fireplaces suspended from the first floor of what had become end-of-terrace houses.

Growing up, Harry needed to survive the routine, indigenous violence: the casual slaps and kicks that could be all too common in districts like Tiger's Bay. He soon learned how to look and sound hard. Although a short youth, he was brawny, and he was proud that he hailed from a neighbourhood with such a tough reputation. In later life, however, friends nicknamed him 'The Crab'. 'He might have appeared hard on the outside,' explains one, 'but on the inside, he was soft.'

At seventeen, Harry escaped the knocks of north Belfast by joining the Royal Air Force. The RAF was as good as the promises of the advertisements on its recruiting office walls, and posted Harry to exotic foreign climes: in his case it was Aden.

By the time Harry arrived, the British military was steadily losing a desperate and ruthless counter-insurgency campaign. By mid-1967, not long after his arrival, the British were staging a fighting retreat, falling back within an ever-shrinking defensive perimeter, before finally withdrawing from south Arabia in November 1967.

By his own account, Harry did not have a particularly good war. At one point he was disciplined for an ND, as the RAF called it at the time: the negligent discharge of a round from his rifle. Mercifully, the bullet did not hit anyone. The following

year Harry was kicked out of the RAF for good. He would later
tell friends that he had sold his rifle to one of the insurgents,
but escaped arrest for weeks by going into hiding on his RAF
base. Today, he does not like to dwell on the particulars of the
incident that led to the end of his RAF career. 'I just couldn't
take orders,' he says.

Back in north Belfast, Harry was soon embroiled in a few
more scrapes, ones that seemed always to involve beer and
knuckles. In January 1968, having travelled to Scotland, he
appeared at Aberdeen Sheriff Court, where he was fined £30
for breach of the peace and resisting arrest. Nine months later,
in Belfast, he was jailed for two months for assault, disorderly
behaviour and malicious damage: he had punched a police
reservist, a member of a notorious quasi-military force known as
the B Specials. 'I had no idea he was a B Special,' he says. 'How
could I? I was drunk.' In 1970 there was another three-month
sentence in Belfast for an assault on a police officer. 'He hit me
first. So I hit him back.'

By now, Harry and Millar were following divergent paths.
In 1971, as Millar was applying for a transfer to the RUC's
Photography Branch, Harry was working as a steeplejack – not
a job for the faint-hearted. He had his arms tattooed with a
number of symbols to show that he was a Protestant and a loyal
subject of the British Crown. There was a fourth appearance
in court that year, when Harry was fined £15 and received a
three-month sentence, suspended for two years, for obstructing
the military. He cheerfully acknowledges that all these offences
'were drink-related matters'.[2]

By this time, he was also dating Kathleen Kelly, a twenty-
year-old woman from the Cliftonville area, a few hundred yards
from Tiger's Bay. Kathleen was a worker at the enormous
Gallaher's tobacco factory that towered over north Belfast.

On 2 October that year, Harry and Kathleen were married
in a non-religious ceremony at the city Register Office. The

witnesses were Harry's father, by now working as a lorry driver, and Kathleen's father, Matthew Kelly, a docker.

It was a low-key affair: the city had been engulfed in yet deeper violence following the introduction of internment without trial eight weeks earlier. During the week before the wedding, two men had been killed when an IRA bomb exploded without warning in a Protestant pub in west Belfast; the night before the wedding, a 22-year-old British soldier on patrol in north Belfast, a short walk from the couple's family homes, had been shot dead by an IRA sniper; and on the night of the wedding, a teenage IRA volunteer from Andersonstown in west Belfast was killed in Lisburn, by his own bomb.

Everyone wished the happy couple the best, but feared the worst: for Harry was a Protestant and Kathleen was a Roman Catholic. Mixed marriages were fraught affairs in 1971. Some Protestants regarded the Provos' campaign of violence as a Catholic declaration of war. Harry was bullish about crossing the divide, but some couples in mixed marriages had few friends on either side and enemies on both, and even if not to his face, some of Harry's relatives and friends would inevitably have objected. Furthermore, it was far from clear where the couple could safely live. And it was about to get worse.

The following year, 1972, was undoubtedly the worst year of the Troubles. Almost five hundred people died, half of them civilians. Harry and Kathleen were living in Tiger's Bay, and this corner of north Belfast had become even more solidly Protestant and Loyalist after the few Catholic families had been driven out. The couple was about to be caught up in yet more violence. One night, Harry travelled across the city to Andersonstown, to have a drink with Kathleen's father and brother in a couple of bars in the area. 'In one of them I saw a Protestant man that I knew from prison, drunk, with a couple of Catholics. He was very drunk, and I thought perhaps he hadn't seen me.'

He had. A couple of days later, two members of the Loyalist paramilitary organisation, the Ulster Volunteer Force (UVF), approached Harry in north Belfast, and said that they had heard he had been going to Catholic churches on Wednesday evenings.

'I said no, I hadn't. I didn't know then that Wednesday night was supposed to be the night that converts went to Catholic churches. A little while later they told me I had been seen in a couple of bars in the Andersonstown Road. I said yes, I was with my brother-in-law and father-in-law, so what? What am I supposed to do?

'They had a social club around the corner, and they said: "Why don't you come upstairs and we'll sort it out?" I knew they had a kangaroo court planned.'

Harry feared the encounter would end with him being shot dead. There had been an attack on the flat he shared with Kathleen. His anxieties were well grounded: in 1972, week-in, week-out, men, women and children were being killed on lesser suspicion.

'I said to them: "OK, I'll come and see you." Then I went straight home and said to my wife: "Right, we're going. Now." We moved straight out and we moved in with my mother-in-law.' That, Harry likes to joke, was the worst part of this entire episode. 'It was hell, in fact.' Eventually, the Housing Executive found the couple an end-of-terrace house in the Lenadoon Avenue area of west Belfast. In jarring contrast to the way he and his wife had been driven out of Tiger's Bay by his 'own side', Harry was impressed by the warm reception they received in Lenadoon.

'I encountered absolutely no hostility in that area, no bigotry at all. Not at that time.'

After moving across the divide, Harry says he could see that Nationalist areas and Unionist areas were policed in an entirely different fashion. In Tiger's Bay he was accustomed to encounters with RUC officers on the streets. Some of them were aggressive individuals, some of them were reasonable, but most were familiar with the local population. In Nationalist west Belfast, he encountered fewer police officers, and a lot more British soldiers; many of them young, some of them frightened and sullen, others frightened and bullying. All of them gave the impression that they felt they were a long way from home.

Harry found work in local factories. Whenever the work dried up, which it frequently did, he went on the bru, as they say in Belfast – signing on for unemployment benefit. Harry and Kathleen had two boys born in 1972 and 1975, and twins – a boy and a girl – born in May 1976.

Over the years Harry became increasingly sympathetic to the argument that only armed Republicanism could bring the British presence to an end – a presence that he believed at best to be clumsy and, at worst, to amount to an oppressive military occupation. Harry was considering whether to volunteer to join the IRA, and the thought of volunteering appealed to the rebel within him. In time, he would admit that he was desperate to 'get back at the Prods' and that he would 'continue fighting until he was either dead or the war was over'.[3] Furthermore, having been exiled not only from his home, but also from the north Belfast neighbourhood where he had grown up and lived among family and friends, while living in Andersonstown he wanted dearly to fit in, to *belong*.

When he wasn't working, he spent a little time in the local bars and bookies and – critical to his future trajectory – he started playing football for a local side. Harry was a very good footballer, and a few of the young men with whom he played also enjoyed Gaelic football. Through their shared love of the game Harry came into contact with a number of leading local Republican figures, including a number of senior local Provos.

Harry says that his first act in support of the Provisional IRA was to agree to store weapons in his garden shed. One day, he says, he returned home and, seeing that his house was being searched by RUC officers, tried to pre-empt arrest by going straight to Andersonstown police barracks to confess that he had been hiding IRA guns. He says he was driven to Castlereagh for interrogation, where he was very badly beaten.

Appearing at Crown court before Mr Justice John MacDermott, Harry pleaded guilty to a charge of possessing weapons. Harry's counsel said in mitigation that he had been intimidated by the IRA; he was, after all, a Protestant living in the heart of Nationalist west Belfast. As such he was a vulnerable man. MacDermott was an unfailingly courteous person, but had a reputation for handing down some extremely lengthy prison sentences; he was known around the courts as Long John. In this case, he took sympathy on Harry, and handed down a short suspended sentence.* Harry was set free and, still shocked at the severity of the beating he says he had received at Castlereagh, immediately volunteered to join the IRA. 'I knew I couldn't keep weapons at my home any more. The only way that I could help was to volunteer.'4

Despite the risk of arrest and lengthy imprisonment, there was never any shortage of young people wishing to join the IRA. By the end of 1977, the supply of would-be volunteers is said to have outstripped the demand for recruits to such an extent that it could take up to three months for an individual to be admitted. At this time, would-be volunteers to the IRA living in Belfast were routinely told that they should consider their decision carefully, as they would be active for around three months, six at best, at the end of which they would be in jail; 'offside' – on the run in the Irish Republic; or 'in Milltown' – buried in the vast Catholic cemetery in the west of the city. As one volunteer put it: 'When you join the 'Ra, you're told straight up, you'll

---

* Although Harry's account of this conviction for firearms offences has been corroborated by others, it does not feature in the police record that was later included in the court files. This details eight minor convictions for assault, disorderly behaviour and resisting arrest.

either spend a lot of time in jail or you'll die.' Volunteers who operated in rural areas tended to remain active for longer.[5]

The way the IRA handled would-be recruits was described by a member of the organisation's headquarters staff in an interview in 1981:

> The IRA does not engage in an actual or active recruitment campaign and very rarely, except on a person to person basis, approaches people to join the organisation. The lectures and recruiting process, once people have indicated that they want to join the IRA, are aimed at whittling down the numbers and making sure people coming in are aware of all the points posed in the question. The people who end up as IRA volunteers are fully conscious of all the dangers that are before them and are prepared for a life of self-sacrifice.

Unlike locally recruited members of the security forces, this man stressed, there were no financial rewards.* 'Essentially, since the 1969 situation there have been no problems at all with getting people to join the IRA. The problem has been in fact ensuring that those who wish to join are people who come up to the standards that the IRA lays down for its volunteers.'[6]

Like the handful of other Protestants who joined the IRA, Harry says he came across very little prejudice from his fellow volunteers, or indeed from Catholics in general. In the 1980s, a Protestant IRA man from east Belfast told the American sociologist Robert White that while he had 'never, ever been

---

* According to former IRA volunteer Gerry Bradley, married prisoners' families received £5 a week during the 1970s, and the families of single prisoners received £3. During the 1980s, he says, payments of £20 a week were introduced for active volunteers. This was around a third of an industrial wage in 1980, and the sum remained the same until the Good Friday Agreement in 1998. (Bradley, *Insider*, pp.197–8.) However, many volunteers say that they never received a penny.

the victim of sectarianism from Republicans', he believed Loyalism to be sectarian, and even fascist 'by its nature', adding that he was quite disgusted at the way some Protestant para-militaries slaughtered their victims.[7] This was an opinion that Harry would echo – up to a point.

The IRA did engage in vicious sectarian murders, of course. Protestant farmers were killed on their lands along the border; workmen were ordered out of their vans and massacred at the side of the road; bombs exploded in Protestant towns and neighbourhoods.

Harry says that when he volunteered, he made it clear that there were two acts he would not carry out:

> I said that I would never kneecap anyone, I thought that was plain wrong. And I wouldn't shoot anyone because they were a Protestant. I would shoot a Protestant if they were a Loyalist, but I wouldn't ever shoot anyone just because they were a Protestant.
>
> There were a couple of young lads who did that, in the Ardoyne [in north Belfast], places like that – they were told to do it, when Loyalists were killing Catholics. And the number of Catholics being killed did go down for a while. But those boys would get a bit older, a bit wiser and a bit more political, and they were very upset by what they'd done.

Unlike many volunteers from urban areas at that time, Harry was sent by the IRA for training. 'I was put in the back of a van with six other lads. I hadn't met them before, although from the way they talked I could work out where a few of them were from. We were driven for about eight hours and then let out, outside a barn in the middle of the countryside. I've no idea where it was.' He glances over his right shoulder. 'It could have been on the other side of that hill for all I know.'

The training was brief. 'In the barn we were taught how to strip down, clean, assemble and load various firearms. I had already had experience of handling SLRs (self-loading rifles) from my time in the RAF. We were also taught how to mount foot patrols. It was very, very intensive.'

The new volunteers were discouraged from exchanging personal information with each other, and Harry never set eyes on most of them again. 'I did see a couple of them some time later,' he says. 'In prison.'[8]

In the months before Harry joined the IRA, the organisation rewrote its 21-year-old training and induction manual, known as the Green Book. It was a manual that included a statement of military objectives and instructions on personal conduct, and it stressed the need for complete secrecy.

Being 'green-booked' became a term that described the process of induction into the IRA. Green Book training would be given in living rooms, back rooms of pubs, even school classrooms. Even today, some former volunteers are reluctant to talk about this most clandestine moment of their initiation into the secret army.

One former volunteer who was green-booked around this time – and who has written about the process – had been a young boy when his father was shot dead by British soldiers, along with twelve other unarmed protesters, on Bloody Sunday in Derry. As soon as he was old enough, Tony Doherty joined the IRA.

At school, Tony had heard a rumour that his form teacher met new recruits in his classroom. 'I didn't really believe it, though, as I still couldn't square up the connection between his apparent obsession with Shakespeare's *Macbeth* and fighting the Brits out of Ireland.'

For his Green Book training Tony was sent to a different school, and wandered around the grounds in the dark until he found a classroom with its lights on. He was greeted by a teacher who shook his hand, gave him a copy of the manual and told him to read the first few pages. The teacher asked Tony if he understood what he had read and whether he had any questions. The meetings were repeated one evening a week for five weeks.

On the final session Tony was warned that informing was a crime punishable by death. He was then told to memorise an address in Derry, where a week later the teacher and another man were waiting for him. He entered a room where, on one wall, was a framed copy of the 1916 Proclamation of the Irish Republic, while opposite was a Sacred Heart, lit by a red bulb. The two men swore Tony into the IRA as they stood around a table draped with the Irish tricolour.

Shortly after this, Tony discovered that the rumours about his form teacher had been correct. He was then sent across the border to Donegal for firearms training.[9]

The version of the Green Book that was used to induct Harry, Tony and others at this time began by stating:

> The army shall be known as Óglaigh na hÉireann* . . .
> enlistment in Óglaigh na hÉireann shall be open to all
> those over the age of 17 who accept its objects as stated
> in the constitution and who make the following pledge:
> 'I . . . (name) . . . promise that I will promote the objects
> of Óglaigh na hÉireann to the best of my knowledge and
> ability and that I will obey all orders and regulations issued
> to me by the army authority and by my superior officer.

The book went on to explain the objectives of the army as being to 'guard the honour and uphold the sovereignty and unity of the Irish republic as declared by the First Dáil'; to support the establishment of an Irish socialist republic based on the 1916

---

* The Irish Volunteers.

Proclamation; to establish a government across all thirty-two counties of Ireland; to defend the civil and religious liberties of all on the island; and to promote the Irish language.

The newly updated version of the Green Book reflected not only concern that RUC interrogators were breaking young volunteers in the 'holding centres', but also widespread paranoia being generated by the recruitment of informers and fears of widespread surveillance.

One section included the exhortation 'whatever you say – say nothing' and warned:

> The most important thing is security. That means you don't talk in public places; you don't tell your family, friends, girlfriends or workmates that you are a member of the IRA. Don't express views about military matters. In other words, you say nothing to any person. Don't be seen in public marches, demonstrations or protests. Don't be seen in the company of known Republicans, don't frequent known Republican houses. Your prime duty is to remain unknown to the enemy forces and the public at large.

After a paragraph that warned against drinking too much alcohol, this version of the Green Book stressed the 'moral and legal' justification for attacks on what are described as foreign occupation forces: 'The army are the legal and lawful army of the Irish Republic which has been forced underground by overwhelming force.'

Life would be harsh, the Green Book warned, and at times volunteers would be disillusioned. Nevertheless, commitment was expected to be absolute: 'The army . . . enters into every aspect of your life. It invades the privacy of your home life, it fragments your family and friends, in other words claims your total allegiance.'

By the time Harry was being green-booked in late 1977, Michael Culbert had been a member of the IRA for some time. At a glance, Michael may have appeared as unlikely a volunteer as Harry. Although a Catholic, he was a quiet, bespectacled young man who had worked as a tax inspector before becoming a social worker, a job he loved. Unlike Harry, his commitment to Republicanism was deeply rooted in long traditions; but he too was shaped partly by violence.

Michael was born in July 1949 at his family's home in west Belfast: number 43 Bombay Street. An unremarkable-looking street lined with modest terrace houses, Bombay Street was situated in a highly volatile location: it sat on one of those unmarked borders where the tectonic plates grind and where explosions can be expected; places where communities in conflict – living sometimes just a few yards apart – attempt to stare each other down and come frequently to blows, and possibly always will. These places exist in Cyprus and Jerusalem, in Kashmir and eastern Ukraine. And in the north of Ireland.

Bombay Street was in the Catholic Clonard district. But only just. The undeclared border with the Protestant area centred on the Shankill Road was just feet away, so close that in winter you could exhale and see your breath drift away into an alien land. The area had enjoyed a fragile peace for some years by the time Michael arrived, but the older people, on both sides of this undeclared border, had no illusions about how brittle that truce could be. This was a ceasefire, they knew: not an area engaged in community cohesion.

Michael was a bright boy and at school lessons appear to have come easy to him. He was also a first-class sportsman: a strong footballer and an even better Gaelic footballer; a physical young man. In 1969 he was a wing-back in the Antrim team that won the Ireland Under-21 championship.

In August that year, during the sectarian rioting that engulfed much of the province, a Loyalist mob attacked Bombay Street.

Families like Michael's were forced to flee. They had next-to-no notice that their lives were about to be turned upside down. Everyone lost something; many lost everything.

The police simply stood by. This inaction later faced muted criticism from an official inquiry established by the Northern Ireland government, under an English judge, which concluded in 1972 that the RUC was not a partisan force – a number of its members had by that time been killed by Loyalists – while also reporting that it was viewed by Nationalists as the 'strong arm' and 'an offensive weapon' of a 'hostile Protestant ascendancy'. But by the time the inquiry concluded the Troubles were spiralling out of control and the report noted that 'the fateful split between the Catholic community and the police' had already taken place.[10]

The older people had seen it all before in the 1920s, of course. But for younger people it was an unthinkable as well as terrible experience, one that some would recall as the Night the Troubles Began.

At the time, Denis Murray, who would later become the BBC's Ireland correspondent, was an eighteen-year-old witnessing events from a few miles away in Andersonstown.

That afternoon, I remember, columns of smoke were climbing, and, I swear, cinders, bits of the Catholic houses on Bombay Street being torched by Loyalist mobs, were floating by on the breeze.

There was a barricade at the end of the street, and flatbed trucks came from the Lower Falls with what few possessions were left, heading out to some kind of safety. And the smell . . . not like the autumnal bonfire, but worse: a charring, clinging smell of old roof beams, which have been in flames for hours but which, for some inexplicable reason, never burn through and go on stinking like that for days.[11]

Many of the houses in Bombay Street were burned to the ground.* Michael and his family were eventually rehoused further to the west. There was a terrible fear among many of these people, and their experiences remained etched in both memory and folklore for generations.

After studying for his A levels and working for the Inland Revenue, Michael retrained as a social worker, and for the next five years worked at St Patrick's Training School in west Belfast. Here he cared for boys who had been removed from their families or placed at the residential care home by the courts, and prepared reports on the boys for the Juvenile court.

In August 1971 Michael married Monica Higgins, a primary school teacher. Both were devout in their Catholic faith. The couple bought a house in a middle-class suburb beyond Andersonstown, and by 1975 had two sons. Michael was also an IRA volunteer. He joined not in reaction to the events of 1969, he says, but as a consequence of Britain's historical colonial role in Ireland, and his belief that political change was not possible at that time through any other means. Over the following years, he rose steadily through the ranks and, in time, the police would conclude that he served as an intelligence officer.

Intelligence officers had a reputation within the IRA for extraordinary secrecy. People in Nationalist areas sometimes described them simply as 'spies'. A number of boys from St Patrick's Training School also went on to join the IRA, and some were amazed to later discover that Michael had been an IRA officer. 'I was quite shocked when I found out,' one

---

* During two days of rioting seven people were killed in Belfast alone, 745 were injured, including 154 with gunshot wounds, scores of houses were torched and 1,800 people were driven from their homes. Some 1,300 were Catholics, and many fled across the border into the Republic. The BBC, which had teams of journalists in Belfast, decided against informing the British public about what was happening, transmitting only material that had been slightly sanitised, 'in a way designed to avoid extreme provocation'.

explained. 'We had no idea, when he was teaching us.'[12] Michael had taken to heart the Green Book injunction to say nothing.

Like Michael, Phelim Hamill would have regarded himself as an ideological – rather than *reactive* – Republican. But he too had been shaped by events, influenced by friendships and schooled by a family tradition of IRA activism. Phelim had been born in March 1958 in the suburban semi in the Perry Barr area of Birmingham where his father Sean, a floor-layer from Belfast, and his mother Molly were then living.

His mother died when he was a young child and, back in Belfast, he and his sister were looked after by relatives before their father bought a house in the north of the city. Phelim and his family were Catholic, and in those days there were a few other Catholic families in the neighbourhood, although most were Protestant. Many of young Phelim's friends were Protestant. 'I didn't regard them as Protestants, I just regarded them as friends,' he recalled later. The only time of tension was around 12 July, when Protestants celebrate the victory of William of Orange over the Catholic King James II at the Battle of the Boyne in 1690. As a boy, Phelim had regarded the building of enormous bonfires around this time as a game. At this time of the year, some of the children would call him a Fenian, but at that age he didn't understand that this word was used by some as a derogatory term for Catholics.

A tall and slightly delicate young man, Phelim was thoughtful and naturally cautious. He was also academically gifted. In 1969, he won a place at St Mary's, a boys' grammar school in west Belfast. That summer, before starting at his new school, he spent some time with his mother's family in County Fermanagh. It appears to have been a carefree holiday. Elsewhere, the Troubles were erupting in deadly earnest: the province was being convulsed by rioting, shootings, arson, murder. Civil war loomed. On 14 August, in response to pleas from desperate Nationalists, James Callaghan, the British Home Secretary, agreed to send British troops to the province in an attempt to restore order.

When he returned to north Belfast, one of Phelim's young Protestant friends showed him around the neighbourhood, blackened and forever transformed. It was pock-marked by the burned shells of houses, the homes of Catholic families that had been driven out. Phelim's friend explained what had happened. 'He was still friendly to me, but it just became clear that I wasn't "one of them".'

Phelim's father Sean owned a car – not common in those days – and it was repeatedly vandalised. The home too was attacked. A Catholic neighbour was shot dead in his house, just along the street, while pulling down a blind as rioting flared outside. Sean decided that the neighbourhood was too dangerous. He was unable to find a buyer for the house, but moved anyway, first into the home of another family in the Lower Falls area to the west of the city centre, and later to an end-of-terrace house on the Twinbrook estate on the outskirts of the city.

Although the family was not as vulnerable to sectarian attack in the Lower Falls as it had been in north Belfast, the new neighbourhood was nevertheless a battlefield, and Phelim witnessed some of the violence. Friends and relatives were being arrested. And Loyalists were killing people even here, some of them children. The UVF gang known as the Shankill Butchers had begun its murder spree, abducting, torturing and slaughtering Catholics in the city. Unsurprisingly, this became a major topic of conversation for Phelim and his class-mates. He said, 'Everyone our age was afraid of being chopped up, tortured to death.'[13]

However, he was greatly impressed – and emboldened – by one incident that he witnessed during his teenage years, in the early 1970s, when he saw an IRA volunteer open fire on soldiers nearby.

He was a grown man, in his 30s, wearing a suit and shirt. He was standing on a street corner, behind a lamp-post, with a rifle, shooting at soldiers. He was a grown man and I was a teenager, and he was taking shots at soldiers across the way. I walked past him and then the soldiers started shooting back.

More than anything else, Phelim was struck by the way the volunteer made no attempt to hide his identity. In later years, volunteers would regularly wear balaclava masks during operations. Wearing masks, Phelim later concluded, was a security measure that split volunteers from the Nationalist population in which they lived. 'But this man was just standing there, taking shots at soldiers, with no mask. We could see his face . . .' It made a deep impression.

Phelim struggled around this time: should he volunteer, or not? There were international influences, he says, such as the war in Vietnam, and 'the likes of Che Guevara'. He was also considering whether he should devote himself to the priesthood. 'I was very religious and the Catholic Church was telling me this was a mortal sin and that was a mortal sin, but at the same time I was very political, so it took an awful lot of time for me to weigh things up. I was torn; it was a moral dilemma.'

At one point during his childhood, while reading a comic, Phelim had come across an article headlined WHAT DID YOU DO IN THE WAR, DAD? He asked Sean whether he had fought in the war. Yes, said Sean. 'What did you do? Did you drive a tank?' Sean began to laugh. No, he said, he didn't drive a tank.

Sean had been in the IRA in the 1930s and 1940s, but as a boy Phelim knew little of this period of his father's life. He discovered, only a few years before his father died, that his father had broken out of Derry Gaol in 1943, was captured in Dublin, and interned in the Republic. One of his fellow internees had been Brendan Behan, and Sean had been one of the first to read the manuscript of *Borstal Boy*.

According to Phelim: 'He . . . would have been influenced by a lot of things – by the conditions in his local community, unemployment, discrimination.' He would have felt a sense of injustice, Phelim says, at the way Nationalists were left to fend for themselves following the creation of a Unionist state in the north, but he would also have been a socialist, and was anti-sectarian. Phelim is proud of his family's connections with leading Republican families, and when he speaks of his own father's involvement with the IRA, appears to regret not learning earlier of his family legacy.

Phelim excelled at school, passing eleven O levels before going on to take A levels. It was while studying for his final school exams and before being admitted to Queen's University in Belfast to study zoology and biochemistry that Phelim decided to join the IRA. Later, he realised that many of the boys in his grammar school class had also joined. He had no knowledge of this, however, until one by one they were jailed, went on the run, or were killed.

After Phelim volunteered, Sean took him into the kitchen of the family home. There, Sean broke down and cried.

> He said: 'I understand you've got involved. I didn't want my kids to go through this. I thought and I hoped that none of my children would have to be involved.'
>
> I think he felt guilty that I was caught up with it. There's a thing with a lot of Republicans, I think, certainly older Republicans: the notion that they hadn't succeeded and that it was up to their children to do something.
>
> I think he was afraid of what would happen to me, his only son.[14]

So who were the volunteers? Unsurprisingly, given the secrecy surrounding recruitment, there are no government estimates of the numbers of IRA volunteers. One Republican estimate suggests that more than 10,000 men and women volunteered after 1969, very roughly around 3 per cent of the adult Nationalist population. Another puts the number of volunteers imprisoned at between 8,000 and 10,000 by 1987. What is certain is that the average number of prisoners in Northern Ireland's jails was 600 in 1969; by 1979 it had risen to almost 3,000, including Loyalists. Between 1985 and 1997 the figure stabilised at around 2,000 at any one time. Given that many volunteers escaped incarceration, and others were killed, the figure of 10,000 over a thirty-year period appears to be credible, and perhaps conservative.[15]

Just as there are no precise figures on the numbers of people who joined the IRA, there have been few empirical, data-based studies of the sociological and operational profiles of those who did. One that was attempted, and published in 2013, drew upon a dataset of 1,240 individuals who came to public notice either because they were brought before the courts, or because they had been killed during an operation – while 'on active service', as the IRA would put it. The researchers examined their ages, their gender, the earliest age at which they could be said with certainty to have been involved with the IRA, their educational achievements, their occupations, their places of birth and the locations of their homes at the time that they were either arrested or killed.

Significantly perhaps, two thirds of the sample were aged between ten and twenty-two at the time of the Bloody Sunday killings in 1972, and just under a quarter were at this age at the time of the 1981 hunger strike in which ten men died. Of course, those who joined as reactive Republicans came immediately into contact with men and women with a proactive agenda.

The average age at which male volunteers could be seen to have first been active during the late 1970s was twenty-five, and twenty-six for women. This compared with an age of twenty-two for those who joined up in the early and mid-1970s, twenty-eight for those who became involved during the early 1990s and thirty-two for those who joined in the mid-1990s. The longer the Troubles continued, the older were the people attracted to joining the IRA.

Women appeared infrequently on the database, and the researchers speculated that this may have been because they were less likely to be recruited, or because they were more likely to be deployed in roles such as couriers or lookouts or in the running of safe houses, and so less likely to be arrested or killed. The involvement of female volunteers appears to have peaked in the mid-1980s, after the hunger strikes.

Unsurprisingly, 82 per cent of the volunteers on the database had been born in the north of Ireland, particularly Belfast, while 14 per cent were born in the Republic. Two per cent had been born in England and 1 per cent in the United States. The study also found that most of the volunteers operated in towns or cities. Guerrilla warfare in late-twentieth-century Ireland was a largely urban affair.

A little over two-fifths of the volunteers were married and a similar percentage were parents. Those who were most likely to be married were those operating in England. And the study found that married volunteers were likely to stay alive and at liberty for an average of sixteen months longer than their unmarried comrades, possibly because of support provided by their spouses.

This research showed the IRA to be an overwhelmingly – but not exclusively – working-class organisation. A little more than a third of the volunteers on the database worked in construction, and around 60 per cent of these men were skilled workers, such as electricians, engineers or joiners. The authors of the report speculate that this could have been a consequence of the IRA's skills-based recruitment preferences. A further 28 per cent worked in industry and services, while 11 per cent were unemployed. A little under 7 per cent were clerical workers, while less than 3 per cent were students.

Examining the volunteers' roles within the organisation, the authors found that older individuals were less likely to be involved in violent activity such as shooting and bomb planting. Front-line operations tended to be reserved for younger men and women; around 9 per cent of bomb planters on the database were women. The oldest volunteers tended to be involved in gunrunning and bomb-making. Curiously, the volunteers directly involved in violence were also more likely to be married and have children than those involved in support roles.[16]

The sociological study showed that consistently throughout the Troubles around a third of IRA volunteers became active before their twenty-first birthday. A number of volunteers cite their youth as an important factor in their decision to join. 'The motivation was that I was young,' one volunteer has recalled. 'Fuck me, somebody has given me a gun, this is great!'

Others say that romantic stories of past Irish rebellion, passed down through memory, folklore and balladry, made a profound impression upon them. 'My attraction to the IRA was not initially based on the sight or experience of any particular social injustice,' recalls one. 'It was the discoveries of the tragedies of Irish history which caused my desire to give myself to the IRA.' This man became driven by a desire for self-sacrifice. 'There could be no greater love than to lay down your life for your people or your country, I thought.'

Many volunteers – like Phelim – grew up in families with a history of Republicanism. This legacy was, for some, the key to their decision to join the secret army. 'I was so young then, I didn't know the difference between right and wrong, between Ireland and England,' one volunteer recalls. 'But I knew that my grandfather was violently opposed to British colonialism.' Another, whose parents had both been involved with the IRA, described himself as 'romantically involved with the IRA even before I joined it'.[17]

Some of the least fruitful attempts to understand those who turned to political violence in the north of Ireland and elsewhere have been those that focused on the psychology of individuals. Most studies have either failed to identify and describe the typical terrorist personality, or, perhaps more usefully, have concluded that there is not one.

Such attempts first began in Europe in the late nineteenth century, at a time when physicians were attempting to use their knowledge to embark upon pioneering psychological research. By coincidence, this was happening at the same time as the first anarchist insurrections were erupting in Lyon, Florence and St Petersburg: modern psychology and the phenomenon of bomb-throwing were emerging at the same time, and in the same places.

In the 1870s, Cesare Lombroso, a celebrated Italian surgeon-turned-criminologist, focused his mind on political violence. Lombroso believed most criminality to be an inherited condition. But terrorism, he concluded eventually, had a different explanation: a lack of vitamin B3.

Elsewhere across Europe, Lombroso's fellow pioneers in this new science offered other theories: bomb-throwing, they suggested, could be explained by barometric pressure, or by inadequate cranial dimensions, by alcoholism or by droughts. Some even suggested that terrorism was linked to the phases of the moon.

A century later, a small number of researchers were still searching for that elusive physiological explanation for terrorism. In the late 1970s, for example, one widely published psychiatrist concentrated on lengthy examination of inner-ear malfunction, while in the mid-1980s an eminent biochemist studied the inhibitory effects of serotonin on rats and then attempted, in all seriousness, to extrapolate his findings to terrorists.

These theories and experiments all chose to ignore or minimise the significance of the political and social circumstances within which individuals chose to turn to violence, and instead promoted the view that terrorists were psychologically deviant or abnormal. The theories then foundered because of the complete absence of any empirical evidence.

From the 1960s onwards, however, there were a small number of projects in which researchers actually met people who had engaged in political violence, and made inquiries about those individuals' lives. Almost without exception, these researchers found that the most striking common characteristic of terrorists was their normality.

Interviews in the 1960s with imprisoned members of the French Canadian separatist group the Front de Libération du Québec, for example, and in the 1970s with jailed members of the Red Army Faction in West Germany, led the interviewers to conclude that terrorists with unbalanced or pathological personalities were the exception rather than the rule.[18]

In 1986, two psychiatrists from Northern Ireland, Alec Lyons and Helen Harbinson, published the results of a study of 106 people who had undergone psychiatric examination after being charged with murder in the province over a ten-year period, between 1974 and 1984. Forty-seven of these people had been accused of political or terrorist killings, and 59 were accused of killing for non-political reasons.* There were 98 males and 8 females.

The two psychiatrists noted that unlike most non-political

---

* Before the Troubles erupted in 1969, murder was rare in Northern Ireland. During the previous five years, the average was five murders per annum, and most were domestic. The domestic murder rate rose during the Troubles, possibly because of the greater availability of weapons and the general atmosphere of violence.

killers, political killers tended not to be intoxicated when they struck, and rarely knew their victim. They were likely to have higher levels of educational attainment and tended to come from families with less history of personality disorder or mental illness. Significantly, only around 16 per cent of the sample of political killers who had been sent for examination were found to show some sign of mental illness, as opposed to 58 per cent of the non-political killers.

By every measure the study applied, the political killers were judged to be 'normal'.

> The political killers tended to be normal in intelligence and mental stability . . . they didn't show remorse because they rationalised it very successfully, believing they were fighting for a cause. The politicals, generally speaking, did not want to be seen by a psychiatrist; they feel there is nothing wrong with them, but they did co-operate. Some of them were probably quite bright.

And they tended not to break down on being jailed for life. 'They have clear ideals and goals, many of them: they have leadership, they get strong support from other members of the group, and that helps to keep them well. They don't need tranquilisers or night sedation.'

In 1984, meanwhile, a study by a Dublin-based psychologist found that 'the behaviour of terrorists in Northern Ireland does not differ substantially from the behaviour of men in conflict-oriented groups generally'. Young men who joined the IRA were not so very different from those who chose to join a conventional army.

A few years later, a consultant psychiatrist who had spent ten years working with paramilitary prisoners in Northern Ireland said: 'There are some suffering personality disorders or some form of mental illness. But most paramilitary killers are not mentally ill.' He concluded: 'The evidence in the main is that they are quite ordinary people.'[19]

One aspect of the psychology of terrorism that may be worth examining is the complicated psychology of vengeance. Some groups, it appears, are more likely to seek revenge than others: men tend to see vengeance in a more positive light than women, for example; the young are more positive about it than older people; those with religious faith more positive than those without.

Furthermore, a common feature of the desire for vengeance is the willingness of individuals to endure suffering and self-sacrifice in order to carry out an act of revenge. As one veteran American prison psychiatrist has written: 'I have yet to see a serious act of violence that was not provoked by the experience of feeling shamed and humiliated, disrespected and ridiculed, and that did not represent the attempt to prevent or undo this "loss of face" – no matter how severe the punishment, even if it includes death.'[20]

Only a minority of people responded by engaging in political violence. But there was never going to be a shortage of young men and women who would equate armed activism with honour and dignity, and who would risk years of imprisonment – or even death – for a chance to regain the respect that had been denied to them, and their communities, first by the Northern Ireland government, and then by British troops on the streets of their neighbourhoods.

One man who joined the IRA following an incident in which a group of British soldiers severely beat him, along with his father and his fifteen-year-old brother – and then ransacked the family home – wrote about how he was later recruited to the organisation's internal security unit, where he witnessed would-be recruits being questioned.

The most significant question was always, not surprisingly: why do you want to join the IRA?

The same simple reasons cropped up all the time: the Brits were killing our people; the army, police and legal system were biased against Catholics; they felt as Catholics they were discriminated against generally in society and nothing was ever done about it. Almost always they expressed personal experiences of harassment and intimidation from the Crown forces. In the simplicity of their answers, these young men expressed their total alienation from the state.[21]

It is always the *events*, and the desire to react to them: Bloody Sunday; the little-reported massacre in Ballymurphy by British troops of ten Catholic civilians in west Belfast in August 1971; the torturous interrogations in the police holding centres; the shoot-to-kill operations; internment without trial; the house searches and the mass surveillance; the assaults by members of the security forces. All of this resulted in some Nationalists and Catholics concluding that when those who made the law broke the law, there was no law – and that a lawless response was entirely justified. In the mid-1970s the IRA found, following an informal survey among its members in prison, that up to 90 per cent had joined primarily not through ideological conviction or a desire for political change, but in order to hit back following security force violence or harassment.[22]

In other words, it could at times be the acts of state violence – and the repeated official denial of that violence – that had, for a minority of people in Northern Ireland, untied the moorings that usually bind people into a liberal democracy. And once they had volunteered, they were members of an organisation that regarded its own violence as legitimate.

Many Protestants and Unionists – and many Catholics – saw members of the IRA as terrorists, pure and simple: 'men of violence' whose campaign was an aberrational and criminal attack on the democratic state. Pro-Unionist security forces, so this argument went, were not protagonists in a national and sectarian conflict, but men and women who were upholding law and order in the face of a concerted assault.

But the volunteers, the men and women who joined the IRA, had a strong sense that they were simply members of a violated community, which they needed to defend. Gerry Adams, the former IRA and Sinn Féin leader, chose to explain it this way: 'People . . . have an image of IRA volunteers as terrorists, but the reality is that members of Óglaigh na hÉireann are just ordinary citizens who are forced through difficult circumstances into resistance.'

Another Republican would put it slightly differently. A BBC journalist visiting Long Kesh prison noticed that one prisoner on one of the IRA wings – a young man serving life for murder – was reading Tolstoy and Hardy. Asked why an IRA man was reading such books, the prisoner replied: 'Because an IRA man's normal, like everyone else.' When the reporter commented that normal people did not go around killing other people, the young man pointed out that normal people, elsewhere, did not live in Northern Ireland.[23]

2

The Time

Towards the end of 1977, a year that had seen 113 deaths in the north, Michael Culbert was arrested and taken to Castlereagh, the RUC's interrogation centre in east Belfast. The police were anxious to question him about the murder of Hugh Rogers, a part-time corporal in the Ulster Defence Regiment (UDR), the British army's locally raised infantry unit.

Unusually for someone serving in the UDR, Hugh had been a Roman Catholic. He was fifty years old, married, and had five children, aged ten to twenty-one. He wanted to leave the army: he had not been on duty for a year, and had asked to resign.

On the evening of Tuesday 8 September, Hugh had said goodbye to his wife and stepped out of the front door of his detached house in Finaghy on the southern outskirts of Belfast, closing the door quietly behind him. He walked to his daughter's car, a few feet away, and slipped into the driver's seat. He was on his way to work on the nightshift at a nearby car component factory.

Finaghy was a pleasant suburb, close to the affluent Malone Road area, where few people cared about the religion of their neighbours. At least, not enough to mark them out for murder. But Hugh's home was no more than a couple of hundred yards from Andersonstown and Lenadoon, where members of the security forces were always at risk.

Before Hugh could turn the key in the ignition, a gunman walked over to the car, took aim, and shot him once in the shoulder and twice in the head. Then he turned and ran to a car where another man and a young woman were waiting. Hugh's wife, on hearing the noise of the gunfire, came out of the house to find him slumped across the front seats, dying. The stolen getaway car was later found abandoned in Andersonstown.

Hugh's funeral was held at the Catholic church in south Belfast where he had been a Scoutmaster for the previous five years, and where his wife and four daughters sang in the choir. He was buried in Milltown cemetery. At the Ford Autolite plant, Hugh's workmates staged a brief strike in protest at his killing.[1]

There were no immediate arrests and the IRA's campaign continued unabated. For the remainder of the year, the death toll ran at a rate of around one person killed each week: policemen, soldiers, Republicans, Loyalists and civilians. The dead included a Catholic boy of sixteen and a Protestant girl aged fifteen.

The IRA also mounted a firebombing campaign against hotels in the province, attacking ten in the space of a few days. The organisation said that targeting hotels was part of an 'economic war', although there was no tourist industry left in the province worth destroying. Unionist politicians accused the Provos of targeting Protestant-owned businesses in the hope of provoking a backlash from within the majority community.

Towards the end of the year, the investigation into Hugh's murder led to Michael's arrest. On 1 November, Michael was taken in for questioning. Once at Castlereagh he was accused of being an IRA intelligence officer and told that he was going to be charged with conspiracy to murder.

This is Michael's description of the way he was treated at Castlereagh:

Both [policemen] immediately took off their coats and rolled up their sleeves. One took my glasses off. They spoke to me for five minutes and asked me to cooperate, failing which, they threatened to beat me all night. I said I couldn't help them.

At this one grabbed me by the throat and pulled me also by the arm and ran me backwards against the wall. He then put his left forearm against my throat and squeezed it. I was choking at this and the other man had my left arm, twisting it, twisting my wrist and pressing my fingers against the sockets.

I managed to fall to the ground and one lifted my right leg and dragged me along the floor, twisting my ankle. They karate-punched me on the upper stomach and continually slapped my face and ears. I was continually shouted at directly into both ears but especially my right. I fell to the ground and rolled up.

My head was pulled back by the hair and the fair-haired one knelt on my stomach pressurising it every so often with his knee. I was wriggling on the floor but could not get up. They let me up and spreadeagled me against the wall by the fingertips. They sat down and had a smoke.

A few minutes later they started again, this time throwing me from wall to wall. One then said: 'Fuck it, we'll do it my way.' I thought he was going to start hitting me again but he got a pen and paper and wrote out a statement while calling it out. This he got the other one to sign and said: 'Thanks Mick for that verbal – it will put you away for life.'

It stated that I had admitted membership of PIRA and involvement in a murder and bombing. I said nothing but was worried. They then said if I would just admit membership they would destroy it.[2]

This was Michael's first experience of Castlereagh, but he already knew it well by reputation. In 1977, the RUC had other such centres, in Derry and Armagh, but nowhere else could strike such fear into terrorism suspects. On occasion, while driving a prisoner through the city, officers were known to yell into their ears: 'You're going to Castlereagh!'

The place had assumed a vital tactical importance to the police since the appointment of a new Chief Constable of the RUC the previous year. Kenneth Newman was an Englishman whose police service stretched back forty years, to his days as a young Special Branch detective in Mandate-era Palestine. One of his first acts as Chief Constable had been to set up a series of new Regional Crime Squads across the province. Working closely with his head of the Criminal Investigation Department, Bill Mooney, he made sure that the detectives serving in the new squads understood their roles: they were to be interrogators who would extract confessions from terrorism suspects arrested on the basis of intelligence. Those confessions would then be put before the Diplock courts and, providing a defendant could not prove that his or her confession had been extracted through force, a lengthy prison sentence would follow.

It was not long before suspects complained that they were being tortured: slapped, punched, hurled around interview rooms, deprived of sleep, forced to assume stressful positions, their arms and fingers stretched out of shape, and held out of shape for long periods. The number of complaints of assault rose from 384 in 1976 to 671 in 1977.

The allegations were dismissed by Newman as propaganda, but many of them were true. Many years later, a handful of former detectives admitted this. One former officer said he employed 'torture, inhuman and degrading treatment' – exactly what the law prohibited. Another explained how interrogators became known for the use of specific techniques, such as 'hyper-flexing' – the twisting of joints. The interrogators did not describe what they were doing as torture, however: they called it 'slap and tickle'.

At Castlereagh, Derry and Armagh, RUC interrogators were running a conveyor-belt system with several two-man teams of interrogators working around the clock. There was no training in the techniques of abuse and some went too far. 'Eventually the arm twisters were rumbled,' recalled one. 'The doctors could see signs of swelling and tenderness. They were quietly told: "Stop − your system is showing through here."' But alcohol played its part, with some of the most severe beatings being meted out after interrogators had taken a break, during which they would down a few vodkas or whiskies.

The men of the Regional Crime Squads became convinced that their methods were working. Casualty rates from attacks across the region began to fall. In 1977 the annual death toll fell from 308 to 113 and in 1978 it was 88. It would never again be as high as it had been before the interrogation squads were formed. The men of the Regional Crime Squads could justify their actions to themselves: they were using a degree of violence to suppress a far larger violence. Only later did some worry that they had exacerbated and perhaps lengthened the conflict.

The number of conflict-related incidents as a whole also began to fall. In 1972, there had been 10,682 shooting incidents, 1,382 explosions and 1,931 armed robberies, with just 531 people being charged. In 1977, that number had fallen in total to 2,739 crimes, while the number of people charged − 1,318 − remained relatively high. And now, even when a person was acquitted, they were often being held on remand for a year or more. The high attrition rates could be attributed to the policing practices that were endorsed by Newman.

'We were getting headlines every day about the number of people charged, about so-and-so getting thirty years,' one former member of the interrogation squads recalls. 'The Chief Constable was happy, Mooney was happy, the press were happy. Everything was wonderful, but there was no doubt that people were getting assaulted. There was plenty of slap and tickle.'

The number of convictions based upon extracted confessions severely rattled the IRA. At one point the organisation is said to have executed a twenty-year-old west Belfast volunteer, Michael Kearney, not because he had been recruited by the security forces as an informer, but reportedly because he was considered to be guilty of 'breaches of general army orders' when he divulged information after being beaten and abused for three days at Castlereagh. He died *pour encourager les autres.*[3]

Frequently, the Diplock courts did not examine too closely the defence lawyers' complaints that their clients' confessions were being beaten out of them at Castlereagh and the other holding centres. In October 1977, a couple of days before Michael found himself in Castlereagh, research undertaken by the Law Department at Queen's University showed that 94 per cent of the cases brought before the Diplock courts were resulting in convictions. Between 70 and 90 per cent of those convictions were based wholly or mainly on admissions of guilt said to have been made to the police during interrogation. Rarely was there any forensic or eyewitness evidence.

Within the Northern Ireland Office, officials told each other that complaints against the police were mostly 'of a trivial nature', and predicted that increased police activity, 'especially in sensitive areas', would see an even greater number of allegations being made against officers.

Newman knew that he and his interrogators had the complete support of the new Northern Ireland Secretary, Roy Mason, the British government minister responsible for the province. Mason later wrote that 'our campaign of picking up suspected terrorists in batches and subjecting them to hard questions' had resulted in the gleaning of information of immense value at Castlereagh, as well as the extraction of confessions. He was delighted at what appeared to be mounting success.[4]

This assessment was typical of Mason's habitual appearance of confidence. When he was appointed Northern Ireland Secretary the previous year, he had breezed into Stormont Castle, the seat of the Northern Ireland Office in east Belfast, fresh from the Ministry of Defence, where he had become accustomed to giving orders, and to being obeyed. He was full of bluster, spoiling for a scrap, and gave the impression that he believed he could bring the Troubles to an end by sheer force of personality. At his first press conference he declared that the IRA was 'reeling'.

One of Mason's first acts on arrival was to have a tweed safari suit made by a local tailor. He also famously designed his own flamboyant ties. Dressed like this, observed Gerry Fitt, the leader of the Nationalist Social Democratic and Labour Party (SDLP), Mason was acting as though he were in Leopoldville rather than Belfast.

The contrast with his predecessor, Merlyn Rees, could not have been sharper. Rees, a former history teacher, had become consumed by the complexity of the Northern Ireland situation, and its seemingly intractable problems; British army officers recall him roaming around Stormont, a volume of Irish history in one hand, asking whether he was perhaps being a little *too hard* on the IRA? 'He ached, and looked as if he ached with tiredness,' the Downing Street press secretary Joe Haines observed.

Unlike Rees, Mason was not going to attempt to be conciliatory. He certainly was not going to vacillate. According to one senior civil servant who worked closely with both men, 'Rees, the most likeable and honest of men, was inhibited by humanitarian instincts and an inbuilt irresolution. Few such inhibitions were to deter Roy Mason.'

Mason, a Yorkshireman who had gone to work down the mines at fourteen, was diminutive, tough and possessed of the most enormous and fragile ego. He loved telling people his pit-boy-to-Cabinet-minister tale. He appeared at times to be more military than the military, which gave him the confidence of the army's high command. A senior Downing Street aide observed that 'he also seemed more "Protestant" than the "Prods" and but for his accent might have been taken for a classic Ulsterman'.

As Secretary of State, Mason had given himself two objectives. The first was to create jobs and prosperity, not because he believed that the conflict was rooted in inequality, poverty and oppression, but rather, as he saw it, because 'the terrorists needed unhappiness and hopelessness as fish need water'. The second was to 'take on' and defeat the IRA.

Some senior civil servants in Belfast enjoyed the sense of certainty that Mason seemed to offer. Others thought him ludicrous. One senior official, Maurice Hayes, later wrote: 'He had the insecurity of many small men, the over-compensating aggressiveness and the ignorance of the truly uneducated. He was a little boy playing with toy soldiers and tanks and he was completely in the pocket of the army. He had no interest in or desire to promote political activity.' Mason, concluded Hayes, was 'a small man in every respect'.

Nationalist politicians in the north already had experience of Mason, and his hostility to them, from his time at the Ministry of Defence. On the night of Mason's appointment Fitt offered an opinion that was short and unambiguous: 'He's an anti-Irish wee get.' By the time Mason had moved on from the Northern Ireland Office, Fitt had had time to develop his assessment a little further. Mason, Fitt told his biographer, 'was an arrogant, bumptious little bastard – a nasty wee cunt'.[5]

Mason constantly attacked news organisations, particularly the BBC, for reporting on the conflict in a manner that he considered unhelpful; he appeared at times to wish that journalists would ignore it completely. Six weeks after his arrival, at a dinner hosted by the BBC, he accused the corporation of 'stirring up trouble'. Interviewing Republicans on air was 'quite appalling', he said, adding: 'Whose side does the BBC think it's on?' At one point, Mason threatened the imposition of censorship. In a clearly coordinated attack, the British army commander in the province, the Lord Chief Justice and even the vice chancellor of Queen's University joined in the post-prandial denunciation of the BBC.

Unionists, by and large, loved their new Secretary of State. He was, one said, 'like a hard wee rubber ball' that just kept bouncing. Mason was promising what they had been demanding for years: a resolute approach to security in general and to the Provisional IRA in particular.

But above all Mason loved himself. And despite his stated distrust of the news media, he simply could not keep away from the TV cameras. One of his officials described him as being 'switched on by the cameras, like being jerked into action by electricity'.[6]

Kenneth Newman, a quiet, thoughtful man with a law degree from London University, was less than impressed by Mason. He was glad to have Mason's support for the hard line he was attempting to take and knew that he would continue to back him in the face of rising numbers of complaints about the abuse of suspects, but he was deeply troubled by Mason's repeated boasts that the IRA were on the run. In a private conversation in early 1978, Newman told Charlie Stout, the United States Consul General in Belfast, that not only were the IRA not on the run, but he did not believe they could be defeated militarily.

Stout dispatched a confidential cable to the US State Department in which he wrote that Newman had always been cautious not to speak of police success, and that he had 'criticised the opposite tendency of Secretary of State Mason'. Stout added that 'Newman's statement that the police/army cannot win the struggle is striking. He did not use the phrase, but he obviously agrees with a senior army commander who told us in January the best military action could hope for was "an acceptable level of violence".[7]

Newman was not alone in feeling that Mason's bragging was dangerous. The chair of the Northern Ireland Police Federation went so far as to publicly rebuke the Secretary of State, warning that 'words can be as lethal as bullets in the unfortunate circumstances in which we work'. Senior civil servants like Maurice Hayes concluded that Mason's 'disagreeable habit of periodically claiming total victory over the IRA . . . provoked them to worse excesses'.

At one point, an adviser took Mason to one side and pointed out that too often after he made one of his bullish pronouncements a member of the security forces was shot. Mason would not shut up, however, declaring in one newspaper interview: 'We are squeezing the terrorists like rolling up a toothpaste tube. We are squeezing them out of their safe havens. We are squeezing them away from their money supplies. We are squeezing them out of society and into prison.'

But despite Newman's caution, the IRA's leadership was worried. Years later, when asked about the various Northern Ireland Secretaries who had come and gone, the IRA and Sinn Féin leader Martin McGuinness said: 'The only one who impressed was Roy Mason. He impressed some of the Unionists, because he beat the shit out of us.'[8]

In November 1977, another volatile character arrived on the scene when Lieutenant General Timothy Creasey was appointed General Officer Commanding – the head of the British army in the province. Known to his men as 'The Bull', Creasey arrived in Northern Ireland from a series of small colonial wars, and quickly made clear that he believed the situation demanded a military solution.

Creasey had joined the Indian Army as a junior officer in 1942 and had fought in Italy and Greece. In the post-war years, he had served during the bloody counter-insurgency campaigns in Kenya and Aden, as well as in Oman, where he had led the final stage of the successful war against communist insurgents in Dhofar, in the south of the country.

He appears to have had little time for the military doctrine that said the battle-space in a counter-insurgency campaign is not physical, but psychological; that it is essentially a fight for hearts and minds. He had not been in Northern Ireland too long before he began speaking of the need to 'stop messing around and take out the terrorists'. His own experience had taught him that unconventional wars needed to be fought unconventionally, and not through the patient application of some semblance of law and order. Asked how he dealt with his enemies in Dhofar, he replied that they 'just disappeared'. That might have been possible in Dhofar, he was advised, where there was endless space in which to bury evidence, but it was going to be a little tricky in west Belfast.[9]

The fourth member of the quartet with ultimate responsibility for government and security in the province in late 1977 was Sir Brian Cubbon, the 49-year-old Permanent Undersecretary at the Northern Ireland Office.

Cubbon was personally very fearful of the IRA, and with good reason: the previous year, he had been badly injured by a roadside bomb that had killed the newly appointed British ambassador to Dublin, Christopher Ewart-Biggs. Cubbon's 25-year-old personal secretary Judith Cooke, who was travelling alongside him in the ambassador's armoured Jaguar car, was also killed.

More than eighteen months after the bombing, Mason received a message from the IRA, conveyed via a representative at the World Council of Churches, suggesting that it was a good time to open peace talks. On hearing this, the Downing Street policy adviser Bernard Donoughue noted that Cubbon 'immediately looked frightened'. Cubbon not only advised that the government ignore the offer, but insisted that it was 'essential that we should not say or do anything in reply that gives any hint we have considered their message or are taking it seriously'. Donoughue said he understood Cubbon's fear, but concluded that 'his course and his attitude point straight to the political desert'.[10]

Together, these four men were expected to deliver a new government strategy for Northern Ireland. It was a programme that had been quietly developed during a truce that the IRA had called in 1975: a breathing space during which the British thought hard about the shape of the security landscape that should follow the ceasefire's widely anticipated collapse, which happened after thirteen months.

The new strategy incorporated a number of legal, policing and security policies intended to ensure that members of the IRA continued to spend long periods behind bars despite the ending of internment without trial in December 1975. At the same time, it sought to undermine the Republicans' argument that they were fighting a war, rather than committing a series of crimes.

The strategy was detailed in a classified report entitled 'The Way Ahead', completed in 1976 by a committee headed by John Bourn, a senior civil servant in Northern Ireland. Predicting that the violence would continue for many years, the report concluded that 'the best way forward is to seek to drive an increasing wedge between the terrorist and the great majority of people on both sides of the community who are heartily sick of violence'.

According to the report, putting increasing numbers of people before the juryless Diplock courts, rather than interning them without trial, had already paid dividends: 'Terrorists are increasingly seen as criminals, and not as wayward political heroes.'

The key policy within the programme was known as Police

Primacy, a strategy designed to give greater responsibility for the province to the local police, rather than the army, which was so closely connected with British rule. It required that there be more police, both part-time and full-time, improved community relations and more men and women serving in the UDR, the British army's locally recruited infantry unit. In time, according to the plan, the RUC would be 'acknowledged as the providers of impartial law and order'.[11]

On the other hand, most British soldiers in the province – other than members of the UDR – would gradually 'play a progressively less dominant role', concentrating on protecting the police, manning checkpoints and conducting searches, along with specialised operations such as bomb disposal, surveillance and intelligence gathering.

Following the introduction of Police Primacy in 1977, security force casualty figures were turned on their head. Between 1969 and 1975, 270 British soldiers were killed in the conflict, compared with 148 local members of the security forces. Between 1976 and 1984, the figures were 150 and 235, respectively. Men like Millar McAllister and his police colleagues began to be exposed to ever-greater dangers, and this was happening, in part, so that fewer British soldiers would be flown home in coffins.

The greater use of locally recruited police and soldiers was also intended to undermine the Republican narrative that it was fighting a national war of liberation that was essentially colonial in character: a narrative that resonated in many parts of the world. As the IRA attacked UDR and RUC targets, increasing numbers of locally recruited men and women were killed and maimed. This helped to reinforce the British narrative – intended for British and international consumption – that it was a matter of locals killing locals.[12]

Despite Creasey's scepticism and frustration, Newman was committed to Police Primacy because he could not see any other way. He was determined to see it through by raising the manpower, professionalism and technical abilities of his force. The only alternative, as far as he could see, to bringing terrorists before the courts – albeit after extracting 'confessions' by force – was to attempt to suppress the Republican movement through detention without trial. That had been attempted, and it had been disastrously counter-productive.

In London, ministers hailed the new strategy as a period of 'normalisation' for Northern Ireland. In truth, there was nothing in the least normal about Northern Ireland following the introduction of 'normalisation'. The ratio of police officers to members of the population was more than four times that in the south-east of England. While the army had a less visible presence on the streets, the police, for understandable reasons, became more militarised: they travelled in armoured vehicles, wore flak jackets and were heavily armed.

The Ulster Defence Regiment – a unit whose very name was offensive to Nationalists – was expanded and, despite official denials, there continued to be a high level of sectarian criminality among some of its soldiers.[13]

Meanwhile, in targeting the most visible and accessible members of the security forces – members of the RUC and the UDR – Republican paramilitaries were killing and maiming a largely Protestant foe. As a consequence of the British government's new approach, the conflict became perhaps more, rather than less, sectarian, and the prospect of power-sharing diminished.

Republicans insisted that they were targeting members of the security forces, and the fact that the people they were killing were also Protestants was coincidental. But their armed struggle was having a devastating impact upon entire towns and villages. 'We should have thought, and we didn't, about the impact we were having on Unionist communities,' one former senior IRA figure admitted many years later.

Ultimately, Archbishop Robin Eames, the Church of Ireland Primate, would write that 'it has become increasingly apparent that Protestantism perceives itself to be the victim of the Troubles. This is not always recognised by others in Ireland or people outside the conflict.'

Nor would Republicans acknowledge that Unionists' basic political heritage was their Britishness; that, as the Ulster Unionist Party would put it, 'they are simply British and intend to remain British . . . Britishness is at the heart of unionist philosophy, the feeling of belonging'.

Many Republicans, at the time, appeared not to believe that the 'Britishness' of the Unionists or Protestants had any real substance. The Green Book, for example, had nothing to say about Unionists and Protestants in the north. In one discussion paper on Loyalism, Sinn Féin declared: 'Loyalism is not British. It is a distinctly Irish phenomenon. The heritage that loyalists think they have depends on a complete distortion of history.' Having cut themselves off from Ireland, the paper went on, Protestant culture 'can reach nothing higher than a pathetic imitation of English traditions'.[14]

As the war went on, the gulf grew wider. Young Nationalist men and women developed a greater sense of 'Irishness', and some Irishmen, like Michael Culbert and Phelim Hamill, would develop a Republican ideology, becoming convinced that many of Ireland's problems had been caused by the British, and that the British would be removed from Ireland only by force. Unionists, meanwhile, refused to see themselves as people who would one day discover they were Irish.

Those engaged in the conflict remained unable to reach any agreement over its history, or over the language that should be used to describe it. Among Republicans, 'normalisation' was derided as 'criminalisation', or 'Ulsterisation'. There was little concurrence between the two communities over the purpose of the law, nor over the legitimacy of the state. Normalisation may have been a programme born out of desperation, but it was being attempted at a time, and in a place, where normality was a pipe dream.

In reality, Mason, Newman, Creasey and Cubbon were simply being expected to tread water in 1977; in London, the Labour government had decided that it was not going to attempt any new political initiatives whatsoever in Northern Ireland. It was essentially concerned with just two burdens, each of which threatened to break its back at any time: its lack of a parliamentary majority, which had forced it into a pact with the Liberals, and the sickly state of the British economy.

Both Jim Callaghan, by now the Prime Minister, and his Chancellor, Denis Healey, were familiar with Ireland and concerned about the Troubles: Callaghan had been appalled by the behaviour of the B Specials in 1969 when he visited the province as Home Secretary; his family had a cottage in the south-west of the island and he was on good terms with his opposite number in Dublin, Jack Lynch.

Healey had been brought up to be sympathetic to Ireland and the Irish: his grandfather had emigrated to England from a village in County Fermanagh and his father had regarded himself as an Irish Nationalist. But Healey would say that he saw the province's problems as 'insoluble'.

And Callaghan made clear to his advisers that he was not going to attempt to make any progress in the north, and would instead try to contain the conflict, keep the violence at an 'acceptable' level, and just get through from one year to the next. On being warned by one Northern Ireland civil servant that a lack of political initiative would, in the long term, lead to more violence, the Downing Street adviser Bernard Donoughue replied candidly that the government had time only to deal with those three issues that could be expected to be lead items on the news each day. Furthermore, were he to draw up a list of the thirty issues of most concern to the government, Northern Ireland and her Troubles would not appear on that list.[15]

Many British people appeared to share their government's indifference, thinking about the Troubles only when one of the bloodier events was reported on the *Nine O'Clock News*, or when a bomb exploded on that place that they tellingly called 'the mainland'. As the violence in the north of Ireland continued it seemed that some members of the British public preferred mockery to empathy or understanding. Between 1977 and 1979, for example, one London publisher sold 485,000 copies of three separate volumes entitled *Official Irish Jokes*.[*]

Like their government, however, the British people were deeply worried about the economy. In the years since the Yom Kippur War and the oil crisis of 1973, Britain seemed to have slipped into a deep malaise, one which threatened to smother all hope of eventual recovery. It was as if Britain was suffering a decade-long hangover following the Swinging Sixties; after the exuberance of Beatlemania and Carnaby Street, LSD and flower power, it seemed to be enduring an inevitable period of despair.

In her 1977 state-of-the-nation novel *The Ice Age*, Margaret Drabble described the miasma of weariness and foreboding that had settled over Britain. One of Drabble's characters, Kitty Friedmann, is in hospital; an IRA bomb planted inside a restaurant has taken away both her foot and her husband Max, just as he was tucking into his smoked salmon. A device planted by Palestinians, Kitty could have comprehended – 'Max had donated liberally to Israel' – but the Irish? 'The whole thing had been a ghastly, arbitrary accident.'

---

[*] Asked to review them, the anthropologist Edmund Leach found that the prototypical Irishman who emerged was 'not so much a figure of fun as an object of contempt merging into deep hostility. He is a drink-addicted moron . . . who wears his rubber boots at all times, cannot read or write, and constantly reverses the logic of ordinary common sense' (*New Society*, 20 December 1979).

Most of the other characters are suffering merely from ill health and economic despondency.

All over the nation, families who had listened to the news looked at one another and said 'Goodness me' or 'Whatever next' or 'I give up' or 'Well, fuck that' . . . all over the country, people blamed other people for all the things that were going wrong . . .

A huge icy fist, with large cold fingers, was squeezing and chilling the people of Britain, that great and puissant nation, slowing down their blood, locking them into immobility, fixing them in a solid stasis, like fish in a frozen river.

Drabble was far from alone with such doom-laden thoughts. A few days before *The Ice Age* was published, the BBC had broadcast the latest episode of the sitcom *The Fall and Rise of Reginald Perrin*, a comedy about a man driven to increasingly bizarre behaviour by the absurdity of his life. In this episode, Reggie has gone to visit his brother-in-law Jimmy, and finds he has an arsenal of rifles in a chest under his bed, 'for when the balloon goes up'.

'Come on, Jimmy, who are you going to fight when this balloon of yours goes up?' demands a sneering Reggie. 'Forces of anarchy,' replies Jimmy . . .

Wreckers of law and order. Communists, Maoists, Trotskyists, neo-Trotskyists, crypto-Trotskyists, union leaders, communist union leaders, atheists, agnostics, long-haired weirdos, short-haired weirdos, vandals, hooligans, football supporters, namby-pamby probation officers, rapists, Papists, Papist rapists, foreign surgeons, head-shinkers who ought to be locked up, Wedgwood Benn, keg bitter, punk rock, glue sniffers, *Play for Today*,

> squatters, Clive Jenkins, Roy Jenkins, Up Jenkins, up everybody's . . . !

It was a hugely popular programme. Half of Britain would have been in stitches. The other half may well have been thinking: 'Jimmy is spot-on.'

Meanwhile, the British government became utterly consumed by its attempt to halt the slump of the pound on foreign exchanges, and by a series of tortuous negotiations with the International Monetary Fund. In a moment of national humiliation, the UK was asking for a loan of £2.3 billion, the largest in the IMF's history. The IMF, in its turn, was demanding a cut in state spending of £3 billion in 1977–8 and of £4 billion the following year. It eventually settled for cuts of £2.5 billion over two years.

By the end of 1977, with the loan in place, the UK economy was showing small signs of having turned a corner. Stock markets had recovered and oil had begun to flow from the North Sea. There were fewer days lost to strikes in the UK than in Canada, Australia and even the United States. Members of the British public were feeling wealthier, buying new homes and travelling more.

In November, the BBC screened Mike Leigh's *Abigail's Party*, the comedy of manners that so excruciatingly captured the anxieties and pretensions of a society that was slightly uncomfortable with its slowly growing affluence. In the play's wake came a series of sitcoms that mercilessly depicted the ambitious inhabitants of the newly built suburbs, the men and women who found themselves handling corkscrews, discussing foreign holidays and passing around canapés for the first time in their lives.

But this was in Britain – England, Scotland and Wales. Not Northern Ireland.

*

The economy of Northern Ireland had struggled ever since partition of the island in 1921. It had been thought that it would make a net contribution to the running of the Empire through a mechanism called the Imperial Contribution, but this was abandoned during the 1930s depression. That slump hit Northern Ireland more severely than the rest of the UK as the province was highly dependent on agriculture, linen-making and shipbuilding, all of which experienced severe difficulties.

In the 1950s and 1960s the development of man-made fibres had led to widespread job losses in the linen industry, which had been a major employer in the north for generations. And then came the Troubles, which brought attacks on business premises, disinvestment by British and foreign firms and a collapse in local business confidence.

By 1977, the only sector that was expanding was security – under Police Primacy the numbers of both police and prison officers doubled. 'UDR – It's Time You Joined And You Know It' read the cut-out-and-fill-in adverts published daily in the press. The RUC's cut-out adverts, headlined A NECESSARY AND WORTHWHILE JOB, told would-be recruits: 'Once you put on a police officer's uniform, people will turn to you when they need help or guidance.' This was at a time when an average of fifteen RUC officers were being shot dead or blown up by their fellow citizens every year. Police photographers like Millar McAllister became accustomed to taking pictures of the remains of RUC colleagues, and the places where they died, and they were expected to live with the trauma that they witnessed and documented without complaint; it would be another nine years before the force established an occupational health unit.

In 1976 a report by George Quigley, a senior civil servant in the province, had warned that 'the Northern Ireland economy is in serious difficulty, and if no measures are taken, the outlook is grim'. One solution, Quigley wrote, might be to persuade foreign companies, particularly American, to invest in the province.

In December of that year unemployment in the north reached 10.4 per cent, the worst rate since the outbreak of the Second World War. The following year, in other parts of Britain, where millions were laughing at Beverly in *Abigail's Party* – 'if you want olives, would you put them out please, Laurence . . . mind you don't get oil on your suit, Tone' – unemployment was little more than 5 per cent. In Northern Ireland that year it rose to 11 per cent.

There was far higher unemployment in the mainly Catholic rural west of the province than in the mainly Protestant industrial east. But even within these regions, at the decade's end there was far higher unemployment among Catholics than Protestants.

In early 1978, the Fair Employment agency, which had been established in 1976 in an attempt to eliminate workplace discrimination, reported that Catholic men were two-and-a-half times more likely to be unemployed than Protestant men. In largely Catholic west Belfast, between 35 and 40 per cent of all adult men were without a job, while youth unemployment stood at 50 per cent. But the agency lacked powers to do anything to deal with the problem it was highlighting. And all the time, the discrimination that lay behind some of these statistics fuelled a desire for radical political change, and nudged some men and women towards volunteering to join the IRA.

The jobless invariably lived in cramped and dilapidated homes. 'The deprivation in parts of Belfast is frightening,' a *Times* correspondent informed the newspaper's readers at the end of the decade.

Anybody who feels like risking a drive through Turf Lodge, Whiterock, Ballymurphy or the Lower Falls cannot avoid being moved. There, fear is the master.

The working-class Roman Catholics and Protestants have drawn strict boundary lines during the 1970s. You can tell whose territory you are in by reading the slogans.

> But wherever you are the scene is the same: relentless
> rows of centuries-old terraces, some of them bombed
> and bricked up; Army vehicles everywhere; barbed
> wire and great walls of corrugated iron protecting vital
> installations; roads strewn with bricks and stones that
> have been hurled a thousand times at military vehicles.
> Hope, tragically, is in short supply.[16]

Even once the IMF deal had been struck and the British
economy had begun to recover, Callaghan and his government
remained disinclined to pay much heed to the savage little war
that was being waged just across the Irish Sea. Cabinet records
suggest that the full Cabinet rarely discussed Northern Ireland in
1978, and show that it made only one decision on the province:
more time appears to have been spent debating whether the
wearing of car seat belts should be made compulsory across the
UK than was spent talking about the Troubles.

During the fortnight after Michael Culbert's arrest, four more
people died. Three were killed by the IRA: a part-time soldier
fatally wounded by a bomb under his car; a Catholic civilian
caught in a bomb blast in Belfast city centre; and an off-duty
soldier shot dead in front of his mother outside their home in
Andersonstown. The fourth was a fifteen-year-old schoolgirl,
who died in an arson attack on her family home.

Within the holding centre where Michael found himself
being choked, punched, threatened and kneeled upon, others
were experiencing similar treatment. Complaints about the
treatment of suspects at Castlereagh were now being voiced not
only by defence lawyers and Sinn Féin, but by other politicians.
The SDLP accused the RUC of 'illegal, inhuman and obscene
behaviour' in their interrogation centres. Critically, police
doctors were also objecting, at first privately, and then in public.

After three days in Castlereagh, Michael was released without charge. The only evidence that the detectives had was the unsigned 'confession' that they had written themselves. The police warned him against making any complaints against them. They also threatened him with repeated arrest, and said he would be beaten again, until he made a confession.

In spite of the threats, Michael gave a statement to the Association for Legal Justice, an organisation founded in the early 1970s by a number of priests and others in order to document the mistreatment of people detained in police holding centres and army bases. One of the members of the Association, Father Denis Faul, took Michael to see the delegation from Amnesty International that arrived in Belfast at the end of November to conduct an investigation into the Regional Crime Squad's methods.

The four-strong delegation – a Dutch lawyer, two Danish doctors and a member of the organisation's research staff – met police, government officials and court staff, and took testimony from fifty-two people who had spent periods in police custody. Five were examined in detail, and thirty-nine medical reports were examined.[17] Michael also lodged a complaint against the police, but four months later received a letter from the Director of Public Prosecutions informing him that the matter was not being taken further. From the moment he made his complaint, he says, he was stopped constantly and questioned by the security forces.

Michael may have been targeted as a suspected member of the IRA, but by the late 1970s few people in Northern Ireland could escape from the Troubles; it pervaded too many corners of everyday life.

By the second half of the decade, after several years of apparent uncertainty, the novelists and poets in the north began to reflect a place that was scarred not only by economic and physical decline, but by deliberate destruction: a terrifying and confusing world in which human rights abuses were being perpetrated by the enemies of state, by militias operating in support of the state, and by the state itself; one where killers and their victims were neighbours and workmates. As the writers began to address the conflict, they soon found, according to Seamus Heaney, 'recognition and respect, including self-respect'.

Heaney said that his 1975 volume *North* 'came most intensely out of the first shock of the Troubles'. He took the title of one of the poems, 'Whatever You Say, Say Nothing', from a poster that was displayed in Republican areas at the time, and which was itself based upon the Green Book warning. It is a poem about the proximity of violence –

> Men die at hand. In blasted street and home
> The gelignite's a common sound effect

– and about the way violent sectarianism muffled frightened individuals and communities. It is also a poem that addresses the poet's previous reluctance to deal with the Troubles head-on. Above all, it should be acknowledged, it is a poem that highlights the ignorance of some English journalists and the inadequacy of their attempts to comprehend the complexities of Ireland.

Heaney later wrote widely about the Troubles, including verse that revisited the murders of his cousin and of one of his friends. But the critics were divided on some of his 'bog poems', which meditate upon the unearthing of victims of ancient tribal sacrifice. Some feared that Heaney was becoming a mystifier of political violence, a muddier of deep and ambiguous waters and, as such, an apologist for the contemporary carnage.

Some writers also sought to address the horrors of the present in a very direct fashion. In his first collection, *Sheltering Places*, published in 1978, the Belfast poet Gerald Dawe wrote of a city that had grown to live with its own sickness; he wrote about kids, as they play by a stinking river, stumbling across 'a wee lad . . . dumped shot through the head'.

In 'Memory', any place 'as man-forsaken as this', Dawe concluded,

> must carry like the trees a silent
> immaculate history.

In 'The Civil Servant', published in 1979, Michael Longley responded even more directly to the murder of his friend Martin McBirney, a Protestant magistrate and left-leaning Belfast literary figure, gunned down by the IRA five years earlier as he cooked breakfast at home:

> He was preparing an Ulster fry for breakfast
> When someone walked into the kitchen and shot him:
> A bullet entered his mouth and pierced his skull,
> The books he had read, the music he could play.

After the police had searched the crime scene and dusted the kitchen for fingerprints, they took away the corpse, leaving behind 'only a bullet hole in the cutlery drawer'. It was bleak, comfortless verse, about an act which Longley described as 'offending the gods'.

By late 1977, however, a new art form was emerging that would both give expression to the febrile energy within these traumatised communities and transform it into something joyful – and bring young people in Northern Ireland together across the sectarian divide.

On the evening of 20 October that year there was a riot in the heart of Belfast. It was just a small riot – *tiny*, actually, by Belfast standards – but it was unique in the history of the city. The rioters were music lovers, both Protestant and Catholic, and they were fighting side by side against the police.

They had arrived for a concert at Ulster Hall, the grand

Victorian venue where Enrico Caruso had sung and where Charles Dickens had read, only to be told that it had been cancelled after an earlier altercation. Some people lay down in the road and stopped the traffic, while others smashed windows. These young people were punks, and they had come to see a performance by emerging punk-rock stars the Clash. The band's first single, 'White Riot', released earlier that year, had electrified them, as had its B-side, '1977': a five-chord wonder about living on the dole and the imminent demise of Elvis, the Beatles and the Stones. The army and the police soon arrived, and a few arrests and broken heads later, order was restored.

Paul Burgess, who was the drummer with the Belfast punk band Ruefrex, recalls: 'In terms of Belfast riots, it was about a two out of ten.' Brian Young, who was there with the other members of his punk band Rudi, says the security forces completely overreacted. 'They went nuts. They were treating people who were going to a concert as if they had turned up for an ordinary Belfast riot.'

While many people who were teenagers in Britain in 1977 remember the year for the confrontational aggression of the punk explosion, those who were punk rockers in Northern Ireland recall it tenderly as a moment of deep personal and social significance: a short-lived glimmer of unity.

Young recalls how Belfast punks mimicked their counterparts in London, and 'sure, we got it ever so slightly wrong' – one girl used a kettle as a handbag – 'but in the process created something kind of unique and very special'.

The Belfast punk scene was indeed unique. While the city and the music seemed made for each other – no other place more closely reflected the elements of punk music that might be described as abject – the punk rockers themselves had no interest in embracing the hippy-hating postures of their British cousins. Instead, punk rock in the north of Ireland meant a flowering – the first for many years – of love, peace and understanding.

Jake Burns, who formed his own band, Stiff Little Fingers, in June that year, says punk can be credited for 'crossing religious boundaries, bringing kids together from both sides of the divide'. At first some were hesitant, but 'by going to see one of the bands you had become an outsider by default, so you would bond together anyway'. Paul Burgess says he had previously been 'trapped into a world of sectarian politics', and that punk rock liberated him, allowing him to develop an interest in politics 'that wasn't coloured or painted by the place where I lived'.[18]

The journalist Henry McDonald recalls himself and a group of punk friends, along with a pet dog whose fur had been dyed green, being stopped by police for a routine security check while en route to a Belfast record shop.

> When an old cop started taking our names and addresses he looked flummoxed. There were punks from the Glencairn estate, Divis Flats, Ardoyne, the Lower Shankill and the Markets. It must have been the first time since 1969 that he had encountered a large group of youths from working-class republican and loyalist areas that were not trying to kill each other.

Punk music fan Guy Trelford recalls: 'Belfast had been a dead city until punk gave it a good kick up the arse. Punk spread like a virus across the six counties. The authorities started to get worried. Punk was corrupting the youth. Ha! Like fuck it was. Other kids were out throwing petrol bombs.' Some people, it seemed, could not see beyond the zips and safety pins, and acknowledge that these young people were breaking down the barriers of sectarianism and bigotry. 'Or maybe they could. Maybe that's what they were scared of.'

The local punk bands who were snapped up by record companies were those that were thought likely to appeal to

British punks, or that were calculated to have global appeal. Stiff Little Fingers signed a deal after Gordon Ogilvie, an Englishman working as a Belfast correspondent for the *Daily Express*, and who was enormously excited by this new music, approached them after one of their first gigs with some lyrics he had written for a song about the Troubles. Jake told Gordon that he did not wish to exploit the situation, and Gordon replied that it would be no different to the Clash singing about London.[19]

The title of the song drew upon a piece of journalese that Gordon had used countless times in his dispatches from Belfast: 'Suspect Device'. The single was recorded in February 1978 and, unusually for a single, was released on a cassette – cassette boxes were a common container for small IRA firebombs. It sold tens of thousands:

> Inflammable material, planted in my head
> It's a suspect device that's left two thousand dead
> . . .
> Don't believe them
> Don't believe them
> Don't be bitten twice
> You gotta suss, suss, suss, suss, suss, suss
> Suss suspect device

It was the wail of a teenager who realised that the Troubles had turned him into a violent weapon. 'It was a pacifist song written in a very aggressive style,' says Gordon.

The following month, after playing Ulster Hall on St Patrick's night, a young man called Declan MacManus began writing 'Oliver's Army', which would become one of his most successful singles. Declan – or Elvis Costello, to use his stage name – had been struck by the sight of young British troops on patrol in Belfast. 'They looked like little kids. But they were little kids holding machine guns. You knew that they'd come from towns that looked no different from Belfast.' This third-generation member of the Irish diaspora was writing about working-class British boys being called upon, once again, to kill and be killed.

Suddenly, the music industry could not get enough of Northern Ireland's young punks. Just hours after the BBC DJ John Peel played the Undertones' effervescent first single 'Teenage Kicks' on his late-night Radio 1 programme, a man from a major record company turned up in Derry, the band's home town, to sign them. Michael Bradley, the band's bassist, recalls how the singer, Feargal Sharkey, was dispatched into town with a copy of the contract that they were being offered, to find a solicitor to run his eye over it. 'Our local solicitors were expert at representing teenagers with guns, rather than teenagers with guitars,' Bradley says. Sharkey found a solicitor, who took a close look at the document. 'He declared that yes, it was indeed a contract.'[20]

The unity did not completely last: many Protestant punks became disenamoured with the Clash after singer Joe Strummer was photographed wearing a pro-Republican T-shirt and began calling for troops to be pulled out of Northern Ireland. 'Just over a year before Joe had basked in the glory of "uniting Protestant and Catholic Kids with punk rock" and now our hero was seen to be taking sides in the conflict,' recalls Trelford. The singer's statements also made life difficult for punks living in Unionist areas, where some Loyalists suspected all punks of being Republican sympathisers.[21]

But then, punk itself did not last. Although Stiff Little Fingers and the Undertones would continue to flourish, much of the punk scene, in Northern Ireland as elsewhere, was ready to burn itself out, its energies expended too quickly: it had been a sprint, it seemed, not a marathon.

And all the while, the violence on the streets of Northern Ireland persisted, and some of the province's young people continued to be drawn to the fight.

Those who, like Harry, joined the IRA in the late 1970s were signing up at a critical juncture in its history. Just as the British had spent the IRA's 1975 ceasefire drawing up the classified 'Way Ahead' report and recalibrating their security strategy, so leading Republicans spent the following year reconsidering the IRA's organisation and tactics.

Their starting point was their conclusion that the truce had been an unmitigated disaster: a period that had often been a ceasefire in name only, during which the Provisionals had carried out a number of sectarian murders and indulged in deadly feuds with the Official IRA – the organisation from which it had split in 1969.

Incarcerated in Long Kesh, Gerry Adams had plenty of time to consider what was going wrong. Born in 1948 and raised in Ballymurphy, in the heart of working-class west Belfast, Adams was from a family that could trace its activism back to the Irish Republican Brotherhood of the nineteenth century. His own father, Gerry Snr, had been shot by the RUC and imprisoned in 1942. Gerry Jnr had joined Sinn Féin in 1964 – at a time when the party was officially banned – and was working as a barman when the Troubles erupted. After joining the Provisionals, he was soon a leading figure in the Belfast area. He had been interned in 1971, released in 1972 in order to take part in talks in London with the British government, and rearrested and interned in 1973.

Adams was initially imprisoned in what was known to the prison authorities as Compound (Internees) 6, but he was transferred to Compound (Convicted) 11 after he was caught trying to escape. To Adams and his fellow inmates, this compound was known simply as Hut 11. Here, he found himself surrounded by many of the more able thinkers of the Republican movement of the mid-1970s: men with the time and the experience to plan for the future.

Some imprisoned IRA men would refer to Hut 11 as 'the

General's Cage'; before long it became something of a think tank. Through debates with leading members of the IRA such as Bobby Sands and Brendan Hughes, and with his then friend Ivor Bell, in Hut 9 – and through a series of articles that he wrote for the *Republican News* newspaper under the pseudonym Brownie – Adams wrote about the need for the politicisation of the struggle, and began to redevelop the Republican concept known as active abstentionism.

Through active absentionism, Adams argued, Republicans could establish an alternative state and the means of administering that state, rendering British rule increasingly irrelevant in Nationalist areas. They could set up street committees to replace local authorities; people's taxis to replace the bus service; local 'civil administration' militias in place of the RUC; and their own employment agencies . . . 'All people organisations, all carrying out necessary functions, all for the welfare of the people, all divorced or easily divorced from the Brit administration, all abstaining or eager to abstain if there was an alternative.'

These ideas were developed further in an internal IRA document that talked of the Republican movement recreating community identity and politicising the population in Nationalist areas by launching newspapers, raising taxes, and establishing its own courts.[22]

Brendan Hughes recalled that Adams wanted to create a new generation of volunteers who would not in future allow the leadership to lure them into another ceasefire. 'Adams's point of view was that we must turn out a politically active, politically educated rank and file. That was the key phrase, a politically educated rank and file so that control is taken off the leadership [and put] into the hands of the fighting men.'[23]

Working closely with Bell, Adams began to draw up a blueprint for the reorganisation of the IRA. It was a document that arose out of his conviction that the ceasefire had sapped Republicans' resolve, because too little political activity had filled the void when the guns largely fell silent. 'The main problem was that the struggle had been limited to armed struggle,' he wrote in his memoirs. 'Once this stopped, the struggle stopped.' In those memoirs Adams acknowledged his authorship of the blueprint, a document that was entitled simply Staff Report. 'I wrote a lengthy paper and had it smuggled outside to the leadership,' he wrote.[24]

Adams argued that the first change needed was the creation of a Northern Command, which would prise power away from the Provisional IRA's leadership in Dublin – which had been the organisation's centre of gravity for generations – and maintain close control of those northern units that were actually engaged in the fighting. The Hut 11 think tank was unanimous: it was a northern war and it must be led by northerners. Adams and his comrades were also in agreement that the new Northern Command could not be centred upon the existing Belfast leadership: there is even said to have been some talk within Hut 11 about shooting some of these older men.

The second change involved reorganising the fighting units. Since the 1920s, the structure of the IRA had been largely unchanged. Essentially, it was modelled on the British army: there was a brigade, which was divided into battalions, and the battalions controlled the companies. The battalion commanders had adjutants, and the companies had captains and lieutenants who reported to the company commander.

By the late 1970s, this large, relatively open and easily understood structure began to look extremely weak. Amid the mass surveillance in the Republican areas, the betrayals by informers and the confessions that were being extracted at Castlereagh, a more streamlined and secretive IRA was required. It would be based around a core of around three hundred volunteers.

The Staff Report made clear that the two strands of the proposed reforms – political and military – depended heavily upon each other. If the secret army was to become even more secretive, it would become cut off from the community; this meant that overt political action would be required to maintain support for the Provisionals within the wider Nationalist community.

The difficulty lay in striking a balance between violence and politics. For generations, the central tenet of physical force Republicanism had been that only through armed struggle could the British be ejected from Ireland: many Republicans would want to be sure that increased political activity would not mean any reduction of their armed campaign.[25]

Adams's vision for the reorganisation of the secret army was specific and precise. It would involve 'putting unknown men and new recruits into a new structure. This new structure shall be a cell system.' In the urban areas, the Staff Report said, the IRA should be entirely rebuilt around this new system, with each four-person cell specialising in intelligence work, sniping, executions, bombings or robberies. The existing brigade and battalions should be dissolved over a period of months, with the existing brigade officers deciding who should join one of the cells and who should remain at brigade level.

> Cells should operate as often as possible outside their own areas; both to confuse Brit. Intelligence (which would thus increase our security), and to expand our operational areas.
>
> The breaking up of the present structure into administration sections and operational cells will make for maximum military effectiveness, greater security, a more efficient back-up structure to increase support and cater for our people's problems.

Each cell's weapons and explosives would be controlled by the brigade's quartermaster, but they should have their own hides for overnight storage. Each cell would be financed – 'for wages, running costs, financing of operations' – through the cell leader.

Lectures on resistance to interrogation were to be given at the same time as indoctrination lectures. 'The ideal outcome should be that no Volunteer is charged unless caught red-handed.' Common-sense methods of personal security were to be made clear. 'Any new recruit mixing with known volunteers should be suspended pending discipline. We emphasise a return to secrecy and strict discipline. Army men must be in total control of all sections of the movement.'

Women were to play a greater military role, with the Staff Report suggesting that the Republican women's organisation, the Cumann na mBan, be dissolved, with the most promising new female volunteers joining one of the new cells. Similarly, the boys' youth wing, Na Fianna Éireann, should once again become an underground organisation whose recruits would be prepared for transfer to the new IRA cells, once of age. The girl's youth wing, the Cumann na gCailíní, was to be dissolved and merged into the Fianna.

Auxiliaries – members of a back-up force first established during the Second World War, who were not formally inducted into the IRA, and not on 24-hour call – should continue to be recruited, but should be used mainly for defence and policing: the IRA should make less use of them.

More Republican clubs should be opened, as a source of funding and cultural activities, and there should be an expansion into services for youths, mothers and pensioners.

Finally, Adams's blueprint for change stated:

> Sinn Féin should come under army organisers at all levels. Sinn Féin should employ full-time organisers in big Republican areas. Sinn Féin should be radicalised (under Army direction) and should agitate about social and economic issues which attack the welfare of the people.

SF should be directed to infiltrate other organisations
to win support for, and sympathy to, the movement. SF
should be reeducated and have a big role to play in
publicity and propaganda, complaints and problems . . .
it gains the respect of the people which in turn leads to
increased support for the cell.*

One of the most telling sentences in the Staff Report was the
admission that the new cell system was needed because the IRA
must gear itself 'towards long-term armed struggle'. Adams and
his Hut 11 think tank were confirming that previous promises of
imminent victory had been delusional: there was to be a war of
attrition, waged on a broader political and military battlefield,
for many years to come. The IRA's supporters must come to
understand the need for patience and resolve, and its enemy
must understand that armed Republicanism was not a passing
phase. Within the IRA, this new doctrine became known as the
Long War Theory.

The theory was correct: it was going to be a very long war
indeed.

Even before Adams had been released from prison, the
reorganisation had begun on the basis of the copy of the Staff
Report that he had smuggled out.

In February 1977, Adams was released from Long Kesh. His
wife and young son were waiting for him at the gates; the boy
had been born while Adams was in jail. The family drove to
Ballymurphy for a reunion at his parents' house. Adams had
planned to spend some time with his wife and son at a house in
County Meath, but waiting at his parents' home was a man with
a message from Seamus Twomey, the IRA's Chief of Staff.

* The content of the Staff Report was disclosed in open court when
Seamus Twomey was sentenced for his prison escape, and was reported in
the *Irish Times*, 13 June 1978.

Twomey had been on the run since escaping from Dublin's Mountjoy Prison, in a helicopter, more than three years earlier. He wanted Adams to come to Dublin: Adams set off straight away. After spending a day with Twomey, Adams returned to his family, but from that day on was rarely at home with them, and was usually careful not to sleep in the same house two nights running.

He is thought to have been appointed Belfast commander of the IRA shortly after this meeting, and then Chief of Staff, in succession to Twomey, before the end of the year. The exact details of Adams's upward trajectory through the upper echelons of the secret army have always been concealed from those on the outside; what is clear, however, is that he almost effortlessly brushed aside the Dublin-based old guard. The first public sign of the changes under way came just a few months after Adams's release.

Each year, on the Sunday nearest to 20 June, the Republican faithful gather at Bodenstown cemetery in County Kildare to celebrate the birth, in 1763, of Theobald Wolfe Tone, the leader of the 1798 rebellion and the founding father of modern Irish separatism.

In June 1977, the speech was given by Jimmy Drumm, a long-standing Republican. It was a remarkable speech, given that the IRA had been hailing victory as imminent for a number of years. The lessons of the disastrous ceasefire were bitter, Drumm told the crowd. There had been a series of flawed Republican assumptions and strategic failures. There was going to be no victory in the near future; if major companies were departing the north, this was because of economic circumstances, not because the Brits were about to pack their bags. 'The isolation of socialist republicans around armed struggle is dangerous,' Drumm said.

> The British government is not withdrawing from the six counties. The British government is committed to stabilising the six counties and is pouring in vast sums of money . . . to assure loyalists and secure from loyalists support for a long haul against the IRA. A successful war of liberation cannot be fought exclusively on the backs of the oppressed in the six counties, nor around the physical presence of the British army. Hatred and resentment of this army cannot sustain the war.[26]

Drumm's words signalled that Adams and his northern comrades had taken effective control of the Republican movement and were heralding a dramatic change of direction for that movement. 'Our entire struggle was at a crucial juncture,' Adams later wrote. The speech was intended to warn the IRA and its supporters that they needed to stop fooling themselves that the armed struggle was all that was needed to secure British withdrawal. There was going to be no retreat from the war, but there needed also to be political action as part of that war; and even then, it was going to be a long, hard grind.

In time, the thinking went, with the steady drip, drip of violence in the north, occasional attacks in Britain, the enormous cost and international pressure, the Brits would finally see sense and go home.

The IRA may have been preparing for a long haul – but almost immediately it suffered a setback. In December that year, a dozen detectives of the Garda Síochána raided an apartment in a rather grand nineteenth-century house in Royal Terrace, a street in Dún Laoghaire, south of Dublin, searching for an English businessman called Robert Kingsley.

At the age of fifty-five, Kingsley had founded the Progress Electro Company, operating from offices in Middle Abbey Street in central Dublin. Through Progress Electro, he had purchased two large electrical transformers at a cost of £30,000 and shipped them to an associate in Limassol in Cyprus. There, the transformers' innards were removed, and they were packed with seven RPG-7 anti-tank rocket-propelled grenade launchers, 56 rockets, 29 Kalashnikov assault rifles, 108 hand grenades, 60 machine guns and machine pistols, several thousand rounds of ammunition and around 430lbs of military explosive.

The IRA had acquired the weaponry from the Palestine Liberation Organization, through contacts made in Europe. The transformers were packed in crates marked 'defective' and loaded aboard a British-owned freighter, the 1,599-ton *Tower Stream*, for shipping from Cyprus to Antwerp. There, they were to be loaded aboard another vessel and shipped back to Dublin. The transformers had already been examined by Irish customs officers on their way out of Ireland, and the gunrunners were hoping that the 'defective machinery' would not be too closely examined on its way back in.

At Antwerp, however, Belgian customs officers opened the crates: the brisk way they went about their business suggested that they knew exactly what they were looking for. Not long after the arms were found, the Gardai was calling at Royal Terrace, where Kingsley was arrested.

Kingsley was indeed English – he spoke with a Liverpool accent – but was of Irish descent. His name was not Kingsley, however. He was found to have an Irish passport in the name of John O'Neill. But that was not his real name either: O'Neill was a long-dead Dubliner. The arrested man was Seamus McCollum, a shipping clerk, and he had been an IRA volunteer, on and off, for almost thirty years. McCollum had served a prison sentence in England in the 1950s and had also been interned in Ireland. After living quietly in Dublin on his release, he had returned to the ranks of the IRA when the Troubles erupted in the north in 1969.[27]

An even bigger catch for the Gardai than McCollum was a man the detectives found at the wheel of a car parked outside the house as they arrived, and who was captured after a short chase: it was Seamus Twomey.

Inside the apartment were a number of other prizes, including a typed copy of Adams's Staff Report, which had been rolled up and placed inside a pencil case. Now, police and government officials on both sides of the Irish border could see exactly how the IRA intended to transform itself.

After just over four years on the run, Twomey found himself back in prison. He was to complete his original twelve-month sentence for IRA membership, and was also sentenced to a further five years for the escape.* Even while in prison, Twomey could be confident that the changes outlined in Adams's blueprint had made for a tighter, stronger organisation. Twomey had been open to the idea of change, as had other figures in the leadership. In the autumn of 1976, the Army Council, the IRA's decision-making body, had given its permission for the creation of a Northern Command, which would be responsible for operations in the six counties in the north and the five in the Republic that ran along the border. The reorganisation had started first in Belfast and then continued across the north and the border areas of the Republic. Before long the new cells became known as Active Service Units, or ASUs.

The importance of ASUs operating outside their local areas was spelled out in an interview given by one of the Provos' leaders:

> The old system came close to identifying those respon-
> sible for different operations, for if a car was hijacked in,
> say Turf Lodge, and used in a bombing expedition or
> such like, the British knew that the unit which carried
> out the expedition was one based in Turf Lodge. Then
> all they had to do was arrest all the known or suspected

---

* McCollum was jailed for ten years for gunrunning.

activists in that area, torture them, and eventually they would get a confession from at least one implicating the others.

'Quite clearly,' the interviewee added, 'the gloves are off and that now goes for both sides. We don't have as many volunteers now as we did five or six years ago and this is no bad thing. Now we have a much more politicised volunteer corps, it is a much tighter knit organisation and far more effective.'[28]

In reality, many people operating within the new ASUs were aware of the identities of IRA members with whom they had operated under the old structure. In addition, the ASU leader would take orders from the brigade's operations officer – or the Double O, as these officers were known – and guidance on targets and security force dispositions from the brigade's intelligence officer. There could also be contact with the quartermaster and an explosives expert. Far from being watertight, therefore, one person in each ASU could have contact with up to four outside the cell.

Furthermore, the new structure brought its own dangers. These have been identified by Tommy McKearney, who was commander of the East Tyrone Brigade of the IRA at the time that the reorganisation was being implemented: 'The system often appeared better in principle than it proved in practice,' McKearney says. 'Insurrectionary cells are only as secure as their component parts are impervious to outside identification and penetration, something that rarely if ever happened in the IRA. Moreover, a cell is always vulnerable when making contact with others outside its membership.'

The new Northern Command penetrated every crevice of the IRA in the north, in a way that the old Dublin leadership had not attempted, 'in an effort to better coordinate the activities of various poorly coordinated rural units . . . raise morale and create a greater sense of coherence.'

But, McKearney points out, this also created opportunities for British intelligence and the RUC's Special Branch: 'It . . . facilitated the work of those agents inside the organisation bent on doing damage to the IRA.'

In some rural areas, volunteers are said to have paid only lip service to the reorganisation plans. In parts of south Armagh, for example, where the IRA had proved to be all but impenetrable to the police and the army, and where British troops could travel only by helicopter, local volunteers saw no reason to tamper with a winning formula. Some would declare that they were going on holiday whenever commanders from Belfast ventured onto their patch.

In Belfast, however, some of the reorganisation plans became quite extravagant. Tommy Gorman, who was an Operations Officer in west Belfast until his arrest in 1978, recalls a plan to recruit academics and intellectuals from the south, to develop greater political consciousness among the volunteers. 'Marxism and all that there,' as he puts it.

> That was very quickly discounted because of the security implications, and volunteers got on with it themselves. We had people that would take on tanks and think nothing of it, but with very little political thought in their head. Having said that, you were politicised as a republican every three or four weeks when the Brits would come to your house and beat the shite out of you.

Inside Long Kesh, the new system was explained to the inmates, one small group at a time, during lecture courses that would last a couple of days. Outside, not all the volunteers were happy with the changes. Gerry Bradley, who had joined the IRA in 1970, recalled the way senior figures emerging from Long Kesh were told they were no longer required. 'Senior republicans were being given the elbow. Guys who were not "yes men" were being got rid of. Bottom line, BB [Belfast Brigade] and Northern Command . . . were eliminating local notables. They didn't want any middle management, like battalion OCs or company OCs. It was central control.'

Furthermore, being an IRA volunteer was no longer considered a full-time occupation. Men who had not worked for a number of years were having to learn new trades and find jobs. Bradley himself retrained as a French polisher. In all, hundreds of volunteers, many of them ex-prisoners, are said to have been demobbed, mostly because they were thought to be too easily monitored.

The IRA's grassroots' members were not the only ones to be disconcerted by the changes. The reorganisation soon exacerbated the tensions between Newman and Creasey too: The Bull was eager to charge at the enemy and was increasingly frustrated by Newman's more patient approach. Cubbon wrote to Mason to inform him that relationships between the RUC and the British Army 'are at present in a delicate state' because Creasey was not convinced that Newman and his force had a sufficient grip on the situation. Cubbon was concerned that the army, with its greater manpower, and its 'traditions and organisation [that] thrust them into a commanding role', might be tempted to mount operations that would be a challenge to the Police Primacy policy.

In particular, Cubbon expressed concern that the army would resort to the use of 'executive action against terrorists, rather than action through the courts'; he was worried that soldiers would begin to kill suspects, rather than attempt to arrest them. 'The message which we have to put over to the Chief Constable and the Army,' Cubbon advised Mason, 'is that PIRA's change in tactics and organisation must not unbalance us.' He added, however: 'The change no doubt calls for a change in our tactics, which must be worked out with maximum speed.'[29]

★

It was into this changed IRA that Harry was initiated. He was assigned to one of the new ASUs of the First Battalion, or One Batt, as it was known among its volunteers. One Batt operated from Andersonstown police station in the east, to Twinbrook in the south-west. It was also responsible, nominally at least, for operations in Lisburn, nine miles to the south-west of the city. For all the structural changes, a number of the new ASUs in Belfast continued to operate largely in line with the city's long-established battalion areas.

There were ASUs covering the old Second Battalion area around the Lower Falls, densely populated neighbourhoods just to the west of the city centre, where engagements with the security forces were often at close quarters, and intense. The Third Battalion's ASUs operated in north and south Belfast, and in the small nationalist enclave of Short Strand in the east of the city.

Harry's ASU had four members, and answered to an operations officer from outside the unit, a Battalion Double O. 'On the day of an op, the operations officer would become more-or-less a member of the ASU,' one former member recalls. There would also be contact with the battalion intelligence officer, who would pass targeting information to the ASU.

Harry's ASU was based upon an IRA Company that, prior to the Staff Report reorganisation, had been designated as F Company of the First Battalion of the Belfast Brigade. Members of this new unit named themselves F Troop, after a popular 1960s American television sitcom of that name which told the story of an incompetent US army unit and its Wild West encounters with equally clownish American Indians. 'Where Indian fights are colourful sights and nobody takes a lickin',' went the theme song. 'Where pale face and redskin both turn chicken . . .' The ASU's members were lampooning themselves. But their intentions were deadly serious.

The cell's initial leader was a man working as a public servant in Belfast. He had been a member of the IRA since around 1970, but left shortly after Harry was green-booked. 'Seven years was a very long time to be active,' Harry says, admiringly. By and large, former IRA members say, being a volunteer meant just that: an individual could decide when to leave, could spend time recuperating, and then could ask to rejoin.[30] This man is said to have returned to active service in an intelligence role. 'He was arrested a couple of times, but never charged,' Harry says. He is said to have remained a public servant until recently, much elevated, occupying an important and influential position in Northern Ireland life.

One of the people to whom Harry's ASU answered was Michael. Soon, Harry found that he was forming close friendships with the IRA men and women he met; emotional bonds that remain strong to this day.

If the IRA as an organisation was smaller and tighter by now, so too was its cache of arms. Such was the shortage of weapons at that time that ASUs spent a great deal of time and energy attempting to protect those that they did possess. Entire days would be spent moving weapons from A to B, from hide to hide.

It was very intense. Sometimes we would go out at about 6 a.m. and get home about 10 p.m. We would be moving arms around, hijacking, sometimes just go out driving around looking for targets.

Each member had their own arms dump, known only to them. Then there would be two dumps known to the ASU as a whole. If a person was arrested, they would get word back about the location of their dump. If they were killed, the people in whose homes the dump was located would come forward. The dump was almost always in a home. Usually it was buried under floor boards, or within a wall or a false wardrobe. There

was a lot of local support, neighbourhood support for
the ASUs. You couldn't have done it without community support.

Harry's wife did not volunteer to join. 'But she was arrested
once or twice,' Harry says. 'And she was very supportive.'

Before long, Harry was widely regarded, despite his Protestant
background, as a committed Republican activist: a hardened
IRA man. Or so it seemed. Despite his commitment to the
cause, Harry the Crab could not help but look after a few of his
old Protestant mates: 'I had a number of friends who joined the
RUC. One worked at Castlereagh – his wife told me – but I
didn't mention it to anyone in the IRA. And I knew the home
address of one man in the RUC,' he says. It would have been an
easy hit. 'But I chose not to disclose it.'

As a result of the Staff Report instruction that 'cells should
operate as often as possible outside their own areas', volunteers
from One Batt's area would be expected to carry out attacks in
Lisburn, the Unionist town where many members of the security
forces lived and raised their families. Harry's ASU would have to
travel there whether its members wished to or not. Harry, with
his complete commitment to the cause – not to mention the
Loyalist tattoos on his arms – seemed to be an obvious choice for
any operations in the town.

'Lisburn may be just eight or nine miles away but it seemed
like a long, long way in those days,' Michael says. 'It may as well
have been a thousand miles away. There was only one road in
or out. It was a garrison town: home territory.' He pauses. 'It
was the Citadel, it really was.'[31]

But if the IRA could kill a policeman at his home in Lisburn,
it would send a powerful message: that nowhere was safe.

3

The Place

The new home in Lisburn to which Millar and Nita McAllister moved in 1977, at 106 Woodland Park, was a bungalow with an ornamental cherry tree in the front garden and plenty of space at the back for a pigeon loft for Millar. It was also just off the M1 motorway, so it was an easy drive to work at the police headquarters at Knock. The couple already knew many people in the town. Many of Millar's RUC colleagues lived nearby, as did many prison officers and soldiers serving in the UDR.

The British army's Northern Ireland headquarters, Thiepval Barracks, was located in Lisburn, at the end of a quiet street of Victorian villas. The army had chosen to base itself in an overwhelmingly Protestant and Unionist town: Union flags fluttered from many of the lamp posts, kerbstones on the housing estates were painted red, white and blue, never orange and green: the town's Catholic minority was small and quiet.

Lisburn sits astride the Lagan, a river that begins life 12 miles to the south as a trickle of water near the summit of Slieve Croob – the Mountain of the Hoof – and then grows steadily in size. It follows a fold in the land that was created by a great earth movement, far back in geological time; a fold that runs from the central plain of Ireland, crosses the sea to Girvan on the Firth of Clyde, then cuts across Scotland to Dunbar on the North Sea coast. Before reaching Lisburn, it runs across some low-lying land, *logán* in Irish, giving it the name *Abhainn an Lagáin*.

The water that it carries from the hills was key to the growing of the flax that had enabled Lisburn to produce linen of the finest quality for hundreds of years. The river then runs out into open countryside, passing occasional chapels and cottages and the remains of old dye works before entering south Belfast, cleaving the city's suburbs in two as it heads for the centre. Finally, fifty-odd miles from its source, it flows into Belfast Lough.

Though the town was relatively peaceful in 1977, it had been the scene of no end of conflict since the early seventeenth century and the earliest days of the Plantation – as the colonisation of Ireland is euphemistically termed – when Sir Fulke Conway, a Welsh nobleman, built a chapel in the area, rebuilt an old castle, and erected an imposing brick manor house, which he called Lisburn.

Within a few years, when the Irish rose up against the English, Scots and Welsh who had taken their lands, there was a fierce battle in the area during which the castle and chapel that Conway had built were torched. There was more fighting less than a decade later during Oliver Cromwell's reconquest of Ireland during the civil wars that were being waged across the British Isles.

By now, the population of the north-east of Ireland was divided, sharply, between the settlers, or Planters, and the Gaels. It is a distinction that has persisted. One community could never forget that it had been usurped, and believed this to have happened at the hands of a people who were unsubtle and less cultured, and whose role was to preserve a British presence on the island. 'We knew and were given to know that Ulster wasn't meant for us,' Seamus Heaney said a few years before his death, 'that the British connection was meant to displace us.'[1]

The other community developed a parallel narrative: it was

proud of its work ethic, and told itself that it was resilient, loyal and disciplined; altogether a superior breed. It revered those Ulstermen and women who died in the service of the Crown. And while many members of this community were aware that some of their fellow Britons across the water never regarded them as full partners within the United Kingdom – or, worse, never paid them any heed at all – they suppressed any anguish that this might bring, and instead pledged full loyalty to the Crown.

Both communities appeared to believe they had an almost mystical right to this small piece of ground on which they lived and chafed. The roots of their animosity bored deeper over the years; as each generation came and went, they could readily recall the hurts suffered, but not always the injuries inflicted. Each complaint from one community about an injustice endured could be met with a retort of 'Yes, but what about . . . ?'

After visiting in 1825, the Scottish novelist Sir Walter Scott described both the land and the enmity of those who contested it: 'I never seen a richer country, nor to speak my mind, a finer people.' But, he added: 'The worst of them is the bitter and envenomed dislike which they have to each other. Their factions have been so long envenomed, and they have such narrow ground to do their battle in, that they are like people fighting with daggers in a hogshead.'

Lisburn could also be a place of goodwill and great friendship. When a Catholic church was built in the town in 1786, its foundation stone bore the inscription: 'This chapel was built by donations from people of every religion in the country. To preserve in grateful remembrance such Christian concord this stone was erected.'

The town was also united by its industry. By the early twentieth century, with Lisburn's linen valued across the world, its population of around 10,000 included many families, Protestant and Catholic, who had been lured to the area by the

houses that mill owners offered to their workers. Members of
both communities lived in the same neighbourhoods, and mixed
marriages were common.[2]

When war came in 1914, the mills were kept busy producing
material for the army's webbing and knapsacks. Wages were
good, and there was little religious discrimination in employment.
The big mills were run by Protestant and Unionist interests,
while many of the smaller concerns – the pubs and shops – were
owned by Catholics. All appeared to wish to put aside differences:
work hard, play hard; profit and prosper.

But after the war, as Britain and Ireland began to slip into
recession, working hours in Lisburn's linen industry were cut.
Demobbed soldiers were returning home and were finding little
work. Men of both communities who had served in the army
had become accustomed to handling firearms, and some were
sensing within themselves a willingness to handle them again. It
would not be long before they were given an opportunity.

After the general election held at the end of 1918, the seventy-
two men and one woman elected as Sinn Féin MPs did not
take their seats at Westminster and instead convened an Irish
assembly in Dublin; the Irish war of independence began the
same day.

Over the months that followed, a pro-independence militia
– which increasingly became known as the Irish Republican
Army – mounted one guerrilla attack after another. The fighting
was most intense in the south-west of the country, but as the
war edged northwards, it ignited a terrible sectarian conflict,
with rioting, street battles, strikes and ambushes. Ireland was
clenching itself, preparing for a terrible fissure.

As the war gathered pace during the first months of 1920, the
Royal Irish Constabulary (RIC) suffered a series of casualties.
In Cork, three RIC officers were gunned down during the first
three weeks of March. Pluggings, the local IRA called such
killings. The dead men's colleagues suspected – correctly, as it

turned out – that the Lord Mayor of the city, Tomás MacCurtain, was also the head of the local brigade of the IRA, and in command of the killers.

On 20 March, a few hours after the latest RIC casualty had been shot dead, a group of armed men with blackened faces forced their way into MacCurtain's home in the north of the city and shot him dead. Soldiers arrived to search the premises, but missed MacCurtain's revolver, which was hidden under the mattress of a baby's pram.

An inquest jury returned a verdict of wilful murder, which its members said had been 'organised by the Royal Irish Constabulary, officially directed by the British government'. They then named a number of suspects, from David Lloyd George, the Prime Minister, through to Oswald Swanzy, the local district inspector of the RIC.

Many people in Cork believed that MacCurtain's killers had been led by Swanzy, who immediately fled the city under an assumed name. However, his destination was discovered by a young IRA man, Sean Culhane, who found a hatbox in the parcel room of the city's main railway station marked 'Swanzy, Lisburn'.

The policeman's mother and sister lived in Lisburn, in a house a few yards from the police barracks, as police stations in Ireland are frequently known. Swanzy, aged thirty-eight and a single man, was moving in with them.

The jury's verdict and the discovery of the hatbox had signed Swanzy's death warrant: the Cork Brigade of the IRA decided that the policeman 'should pay the penalty for his crime'.[3]

This in turn would spark days of rioting that would change for ever the physical face and demography not only of Lisburn, but of west Belfast. And almost six decades later, the murder of Swanzy would lead directly to the killing of another policeman in Lisburn; the first security force casualty in the town since the Troubles began.

★

Sean Culhane later recalled* that he and four other Cork IRA men were given permission by Michael Collins, the IRA's director of intelligence, to travel north to hunt Swanzy down. They carried with them Tomás MacCurtain's own revolver, the firearm that had been hidden under the mattress of the child's pram.[4]

In Belfast they planned the assassination with the help of a man called Roger McCorley who, at the age of nineteen, was one of the city's leading Republicans.

The first attempt failed when a taxi they had hijacked broke down. The second attempt was made on 22 August, a Sunday; the hit squad were dressed for the occasion in their best suits. McCorley arrived in the town early, and watched the target make his way from the police barracks in Railway Street to Christ Church, the Church of Ireland cathedral overlooking Market Square.

Swanzy's family had historical links with the cathedral, which had been built in 1707, in what is known locally as Planters' Gothic style. It had been erected on the site of Sir Fulke Conway's burned-down chapel. Swanzy's ancestor, Henry Swanzy, had been baptised in the old chapel in 1666, shortly after Henry's father came over from England.

Other members of the hit squad arrived in a taxi, which was parked 200 yards from the cathedral, facing east towards Belfast. As Swanzy emerged from the cathedral and crossed the road, McCorley pointed him out to Culhane and a second man, Dick Murphy. As Swanzy walked past the entrance of a branch of the Northern Bank, Culhane pulled MacCurtain's revolver from his jacket pocket and took aim at a point behind Swanzy's right ear. 'I fired the first shot getting him in the head and Dick fired

---

* Along with other Republicans, Culhane gave a series of statements about his experiences during the war of independence to the Bureau of Military History, an oral history project that was established in the late 1940s.

almost simultaneously into his body.' McCorley also opened fire. The men ran back to the taxi and sped off towards Belfast.

Swanzy had been shot five times in the head and body. His sister Irene heard the shootings from their home, and rushed down the road to find him lying at the entrance to the bank; she was cradling his head when a doctor arrived. Swanzy was carried into the bank, where the doctor pronounced him to be dead.

Culhane and Murphy did not linger in Belfast; they left by train that evening for Dublin. 'Passing through Lisburn we noticed a number of houses on fire,' Culhane later recalled.[5] The destruction of Catholic Lisburn had begun.

A large crowd gathered in Market Square after Swanzy was shot, clamouring for revenge. The police mounted a baton charge in an attempt to disperse the mob, but were hopelessly outnumbered.

The people fell upon the first Catholic target they could find: a confectionery store next to the entrance to the cathedral, which was ransacked and set ablaze. Other Catholic-owned businesses in the square were torched: an ice-cream parlour, a shoe shop, a bar in nearby Bridge Street where the owner was shot and wounded.

But by now there were thousands of people on the streets, many fortified by beer and spirits stolen from ransacked bars. Troops from the Somerset Light Infantry arrived to protect the Sacred Heart of Mary convent but were unable to protect other buildings from being attacked.

Local clergymen, including the Rev Henry Swanzy, a cousin of the murdered policeman, tried to reason with the mob, but failed. The crowd turned its attention to local Catholics' homes, which were also torched, their inhabitants fleeing. When darkness fell, the fires could be seen nine miles away in Belfast.

The following day the mayhem continued. There were attacks on homes, shops and bars and a boot factory was burned down. The council cut off gas supplies to the town. That evening,

Catholics began to flee: at first a trickle, and then a mass exodus. The town's railway station was crowded with refugees; others simply walked, sometimes pushing carts laden with their belongings. Some families were attacked by Loyalists at Lambeg, in the Lagan valley, and took the hill roads to the north. Others slept in the open along the banks of the Lagan. A number fled south, to Dundalk.

The following afternoon, the rioting flared up again. More Catholic-owned bars were stripped and set ablaze. The mob prevented the fire brigade from reaching the burning buildings, and the few soldiers in the town were compelled to fix bayonets to protect the fire engines from the rioters.

The Sacred Heart of Mary convent was evacuated; some of the nuns fled across the Irish Sea to Liverpool. The home of the parish priest – who had died three weeks before Swanzy's murder – was ransacked and his vestments and parish records set ablaze.

There were many Protestants in the town who did not join the mob, and there were instances in which Protestant residents, armed with shotguns, threatened to shoot anyone who attacked the homes of their Catholic neighbours. But after three days of riots – or The Burnings, as they came to be known locally – the *Belfast Telegraph* published a number of pictures of the devastation. The newspaper felt compelled to publish them under a headline that read THIS IS LISBURN, NOT YPRES, a reference to the Belgian town that had been razed during the war that had ended two years earlier.

A reporter from the Belfast *News Letter* described how the night sky above the town was lit up by the flames. 'In Bow Street several large establishments were a seething mass of fire, while great clouds of red tinted smoke hung overhead, and as roofs and floors fell in the air was filled with sparks falling to the ground like thick showers of crimson snow, it looked like a veritable inferno.'

An army officer noted, on visiting the still-smoking ruins of the town: 'Lisburn is like a bombarded town in France.' This man was also a senior figure in the UVF, which had been formed as a militia before the war in order to physically oppose Home Rule for Ireland.

'All this is done by Unionists as a protest against these cold-blooded murderers and the victims are Rebels or their Sympathisers,' he wrote, adding with some satisfaction: 'It has been stated that there are only four or five R.C. families left in Lisburn; others say this is wrong that there are far more. Be that as it may there certainly are practically no shops or places of business left to the R.C.'[6]

On the Sunday following the murder of Swanzy, the 29th, it is estimated that only nine Catholics attended Mass in Lisburn. The refugees – and many of the newspapermen who reported their flight – turned to the Russian word that had arrived in western Europe at the end of the previous century, borne by waves of Jewish refugees; it had been a *pogrom*, they said: a moment of utter devastation.

A newspaperman from London who witnessed the refugees pouring into Belfast reported:

> Since the early days of the German invasion of Belgium . . . I have seen nothing more pathetic than this Irish migration. I found two mothers who each with a family of five small children had tramped the nine miles from Lisburn to Belfast coming by the solitary road over the black mountain, for safety's sake. They had slept on the hill and gone without food from Friday afternoon to Saturday midday.[7]

When the scale of destruction in Lisburn became known, there were reprisals against Protestants across Ireland. In Dundalk, 40 miles to the south, four policemen were shot, one fatally, and a Protestant-owned drapery business was set alight. Three shop assistants who were sleeping above the store perished in the blaze.

Only five people were convicted for their roles in the Lisburn riots, but their short prison sentences were set aside after a large crowd gathered in Market Square once again and threatened to organise attacks on Catholics in other towns.

Two people were prominent in expressing their sorrow at the mayhem and trauma that Lisburn and its Catholic population had suffered. Swanzy's sister Irene and their mother Elizabeth placed a notice in the *Lisburn Standard*, in which they said that they were 'grieved beyond measure at the destruction and loss which has befallen Lisburn' and that they were 'sorry that any person should have suffered any sorrow or loss on account of him'.

In time, some families returned to those homes in Lisburn that remained standing. Many had been stripped of furniture, and for weeks afterwards Catholic homes could be identified by the sacking that was nailed over gaping windows. But many families remained in Belfast, crammed into homes in the west of the city that were already severely overcrowded.

In 1921, the year after The Burnings, the island was divided. The year after that, the Irish Free State and the statelet of Northern Ireland came into being amid continuing bloody conflict between Catholics and Protestants, particularly in Belfast.

Patrick Shea, arriving in the city in 1926 as a young civil service trainee, and also as the Catholic son of a former RIC officer, later recalled:

The violence had come to an end but the signs of it – burned buildings and bullet-scarred gable walls – were there to be seen and feeling was still high in the most densely populated parts of the city.

The Catholics, large numbers of them crowded into

the streets along the Falls Road, were cowed and
dispirited; they had seen riots and death, the burnings
of homes and business premises, the violent expulsion of
their men from shipyards and factories and building
sites. They feared their Protestant neighbours with the
anger of people who had been subdued by force and left
without any means of retaliating against their persecutors.[8]

Almost six decades later, the consequences of the murder of
Swanzy were still playing out. The fact that there hadn't been a
security force casualty in Lisburn since the Troubles began made
the killing of a policeman in the town a key target for the IRA.

Lisburn's character in the late 1970s, its proud and confident
Unionist sense of itself, cannot be separated from the pogrom
of 1920 and the impact that that had on the town's demo-
graphics. It was not just members of the IRA who saw it
as a Protestant and Unionist stronghold: in Belfast, Nationalists
who were not involved in the conflict also tended to avoid
going to the town.

Between the town and the outskirts of west Belfast, the
Lagan Valley was farmed by Protestants, and on the boomerang-
shaped range of hills overlooking the valley to the north, and
all along the Mullaghglass Road, which runs along the hills,
Union flags fluttered from every telegraph pole, a clear marking
of tribal territory.

By 1977 the divide between Lisburn and west Belfast was
severely exacerbating the serious housing problems in that
part of the city. A confidential report for the Ministry of
Development at Stormont had warned earlier in the decade
that as pressure on housing in Belfast grew more intense,
Protestants from the east and north of the city had been able to
find homes outside its boundaries, usually moving to nearby
commuter towns such as Bangor, Newtownwards and Antrim.

But Catholics in the west of the city felt unable to move to their nearest commuter town: it was Lisburn, and it was beyond the pale.

'The Troubles have caused a particular problem in West Belfast,' the author of the report noted. 'At present because of widespread intimidation most Catholics are only prepared to live in West Belfast or in a limited number of other clearly identifiable Catholic areas. Meanwhile existing pressure on housing suitable for Catholics in the urban area is increasing and is expected to continue to do so.' Most of the families on the housing waiting lists were Catholic, the author added.

The housing problems were truly dire. In Westminster, government ministers believed that Belfast's housing problems were probably the worst in Europe; Roy Mason wrote in his memoirs that up to 30 per cent of homes in west Belfast were overcrowded, and that in some areas up to 90 per cent of homes lacked basic amenities.

Off the lower Falls Road, and around the Protestant Shankill Road, families were crammed into tiny, crumbling terrace houses. Where new properties had been built, they frequently had prefabricated walls that were prone to damp, and flat roofs that were guaranteed to leak in Belfast's wet weather. Further west, some developments around Andersonstown and Lenadoon were so badly designed that pedestrian underpasses were regularly inundated with rainwater, a problem that the local newspaper, the *Andersonstown News*, highlighted by photographing children inside the underpasses paddling in canoes.[9]

Many of the people living in the outer areas of west Belfast had moved there in the early days of the Troubles, when around 60,000 people had been forced to flee their homes as a result of intimidation or fear. At that time, it was perhaps one of the largest enforced movements of people that Europe had witnessed since the Second World War.

Areas like Lenadoon, for example, became almost uniformly

Catholic and Nationalist as Protestants moved a few hundred yards to the Suffolk area in 1971 and 1972. 'At that time you could have seen the exodus of Protestants,' one Protestant woman recalls, adding that Methodist church ministers had appealed in vain for families to stay put.

But those families arriving in Lenadoon had been driven out of their own homes in their turn. 'My wife's family had been burned out and they just arrived up with a lorry containing wee picks of furniture and it was just a case of grabbing the nearest vacant house,' recalls one resident. Another remembers moving into a house in which the bath and kitchen sink had been smashed by the family that had fled from it. 'For six months, if you were cooking something downstairs you had to bring all the dishes up to the bathroom to wash them.'[10]

The last hopeful housing estate to be constructed in the province had been Twinbrook, built in the late 1960s on the far outskirts of south-west Belfast. Its labyrinthine lanes are set around a slightly boggy 21-acre park; some of the housing is solidly built, some less so. It may have derived its name from the planners' desire that the twin brooks of Protestant and Catholic life could merge into a single peaceful river. Residents of the local village of Dunmurry appear to have opposed the construction of the estate not on sectarian grounds, but on class grounds: they feared that the incoming residents, regardless of religion, would be of a lower order.

Initially, the Catholic and Protestant families who moved in were determined that it would remain non-sectarian and, as far as possible, untouched by the Troubles. In 1972, when Catholic families who had been forced out of their homes elsewhere in Belfast began to arrive at the estate, looking for a place of refuge, local people of both traditions were less than welcoming, with Catholic residents fearing they would drive the Protestants away.

Some Housing Executive officials advised the new arrivals to select an empty property, put up some curtains, and then come back and inform them where they were living. The arrival of squatters was said to be the cause of bitterness and bad blood between the settled residents, both Catholic and Protestant, and the new Catholic arrivals. Soon Protestant families were moving out.[11]

Like Lenadoon and Andersonstown, Twinbrook was, as far as the IRA was concerned, One Batt's territory. Like the Lower Falls to the east, this was an area where the population was under constant observation by the police and the army. There were endless stop-and-searches on the streets, searches of homes and businesses, surprise vehicle checkpoints, telephone intercepts, surveillance photography, paid informers and covert army observation posts.

The data that was gathered was entered on card indexes and carefully collated, sifted and analysed. By late 1977 the security forces had built up an entire parallel census for Nationalist areas, with a street-by-street register of the population, containing the details of terrorism suspects, their families, friends, neighbours and habits, all of it cross-referenced to incident reports, intelligence summaries and photographs. A computer system code-named Vengeful had also been created to help the security forces track the movements of vehicles. The British army and the RUC had concluded that the main problem they faced in their attempts to defeat their enemy was identifying who that enemy was, so an extensive dossier existed for every person of potential interest.[12] As a consequence of the security force apparatus and presence required to advance these operations, Nationalist areas of west Belfast appeared to resemble open prisons.

However, unlike the ASUs based in the Lower Falls, which operated in an area where the streets were narrow and alleyways and back entries plentiful, One Batt lived and fought in an environment that was unfavourable to the IRA. The roads were wider, there were more parks and open spaces, and the soldiers in their fortified watchtowers known as sangars could observe the movements of people and vehicles far more easily. Few insurgencies or terrorist campaigns can have taken place in such open view as One Batt's war in the parks and wide avenues of outer west Belfast.

Across the province as a whole, many people had no direct experience of violence: the Troubles killed relatively few and involved only a minority. A survey published in 1978 found that just 4 per cent of Protestants and 6 per cent of Catholics had witnessed a member of the public being shot, for instance, while 64 per cent of Protestants and 51 per cent of Catholics had never witnessed a violent incident of any sort.[13] But in Andersonstown, Lenadoon and Twinbrook, the IRA could rarely mount an operation without it being witnessed by a number of local people.

Targets, meanwhile, were few and well protected. Operations needed painstaking planning, with several alternative escape routes considered. A sniping attack on an army patrol, for example, might involve one volunteer concealing the rifle at the firing point the night before the attack, the sniper arriving the next day to fire the weapon, a third volunteer being on hand to drive the sniper from the scene, a fourth taking the rifle away to be concealed, and a fifth, a sixth and a seventh volunteer acting as lookouts. All risked being killed, or jailed for life.

Being an urban guerrilla in the inner city was difficult enough; in the suburbs it seemed, at times, to be near impossible.

That is not the way it seemed to potential targets, however. The police officers and soldiers serving in One Batt's area of operations felt it to be an area that was anything but unfavourable to the IRA.

When Johnston Brown, a 27-year-old RUC detective, volunteered in late 1977 to serve at Andersonstown police barracks, he was given some clear advice. Never stop at a red light in west

Belfast if it was safe to drive on; he should assume that any pedestrians who wanted to cross the road may be part of a trap: members of the security forces had lost their lives this way. Nor should Johnston ever indicate that he was turning into a police barracks: he should approach with the flow of the traffic and then swerve suddenly in through the gates, both to reduce the risk of being shot, and to make it harder for anyone to make a note of his registration number.

And if he were unfortunate enough to fall into the hands of gunmen, he must attempt to shoot his way out: never try to talk himself out of trouble.

> I remember clearly one older detective sergeant, a man in his late forties, telling me sternly: 'This is not Newtownabbey, nor is it Bangor, son. Here you have at most between five and eight minutes at the door of any house you may call at on an enquiry. You have that much time to conduct the enquiry and get the hell out of those areas, because five to eight minutes is all the time it takes for the Provos to get hold of a weapon and a volunteer who will be only too keen to kill you before you conduct your enquiry and leave.'

At that time, the RUC's B Division was responsible for policing the whole of west Belfast: an area that its officers knew as the Wild West. The barracks were not always well equipped: one was prone to flooding; a second had no women's toilets, so women officers had to travel by armoured car to use the facilities at another.

Movement was difficult for B Division officers as the entire area was, in Johnston's words, 'in the grip of PIRA terrorists', and there was very little public support for the RUC. While there were some people who tried to provide information – 'there were still an awful lot of decent people living in those areas who wanted us there' – those who were seen to help the police were at risk of being killed.

For an RUC officer, simply staying alive every day was a task that required considerable planning. Millar, when working as a police photographer in a Republican area, would need to be careful and watchful. 'I cannot overstate the enormity of the pressure we faced as we went about our task of trying to afford a police service in the most difficult of circumstances,' Johnston says. 'I knew that we were not alone in our endeavours. Many other frontline RUC stations faced difficulties of the same nature. Every move we made out of our secure barracks had to be weighed up. A balance had to be struck between affording the locals a policing service and protecting ourselves from the constant threat of attack.'

Despite the pressure and the risks, morale was high. 'The constant threat to all of us of a sudden and violent death at the hands of republican terrorists doubtless created a strong bond between us. There was little, if any, backbiting or in-fighting. The uniformed branch was almost over-protective of us when we were called to investigate serious terrorist incidents in the area.'[14]

Brian McKee, an RUC constable who had been a soldier for six years, serving with the Royal Engineers in Germany and the Middle East, was one of the officers at Andersonstown police barracks who liaised with the army units on tour in the area, including the battalion based a short drive away at the army base called Fort Monagh, on the southern edge of the Nationalist Turf Lodge estate. He too thought outer west Belfast was a relatively easy place for the IRA to operate. As he drove between the police barracks and army bases, Brian was expected to use his own car, a red 1750 Austin Allegro, and he kept his 9mm Walther PPK semi-automatic pistol tucked under his thigh. He said:

I enjoyed it. I volunteered for it. Some army units

thought they were a law unto themselves, and there were some real headaches. And then there were good units, like the Royal Marines: they were brilliant.

You felt that the big problem was the IRA, and you felt you were doing your bit to try to defeat them, albeit not very successfully. But you weren't like a policeman at Andersonstown, you were like a paramilitary police-man. Rather than upholding the law of the land you were very much a military police service. You were more soldier than policeman.

A lot of police in Northern Ireland at that time would have seen themselves as protectors of a Protestant people rather than being there to protect the public. But at Andersonstown, the first instinct of the police was to protect themselves, literally.

First of all, you had to protect yourself and your colleagues. Then you had to protect the public and prop-erty. And then, lastly, your job was to investigate and solve crime. But investigating and solving crime was way down your list of priorities.

Not everyone appreciated Brian's efforts: even those he assumed to be allies could be deeply hostile. Brian had been standing close to Neil Bewley, a nineteen-year-old Royal Marine, when Neil was shot dead on the Turf Lodge estate in August 1977. This was an estate where the IRA enjoyed 'a considerable degree of credibility' as well as the 'extensive and vociferous support from the inhabitants', according to a subsequent report by a Marines officer.

Neil had joined the Royal Marines not because he wanted to serve on Turf Lodge but, in part, because he wanted to indulge his love of skiing. After he was shot, the Marines fired scores of baton rounds and searched 105 houses on the estate.

Brian went to Neil's funeral in Shropshire a week later.

His parents, I thought they were incredible people. They saw him as doing his duty. But I remember he had two uncles, and they would have choked me. 'What was this Irish bastard doing anywhere near us?' They didn't distinguish me in any way from the people who killed him. As far as they were concerned, I was part and parcel of the problem that shot their nephew.[15]

From his base at Fort Monagh, Private Jonathan Tompkinson, a new recruit to the 2nd Battalion Queen's Regiment, was experiencing Northern Ireland and west Belfast for the first time. Tompkinson had grown up in Sweden and his comrades, inevitably, nicknamed him 'Swede'. The base was cramped, the soldiers slept on bunks and had little privacy. The rifles, the same SLRs that Harry had learned to handle in the RAF, were long and cumbersome, having been designed for use against the Soviet army on the plains of northern Germany, rather than the streets of Northern Ireland. 'The posting proved to be one long bad dream and sometimes worse,' Swede later recalled, 'such hatred from the locals and the tension on every patrol around Turf Lodge.'

During Swede's battalion's six-month tour of duty, troops mounted 118 searches of houses on the relatively small estate, engaged in 122 chases and made 176 arrests. Throughout the Troubles, army searches of houses could be extraordinarily destructive: furniture dumped in gardens, kitchen units dismantled; floorboards and stairs ripped up. It was not unknown for soldiers with power hammers and generators to dig holes through concrete floors until they reached the soil. On occasion, new foundations would need to be constructed. Such searches could bring short-term success. But the destruction of property, and the humiliation of families, ensured that they lingered as long-term defeats.

On patrol, Swede was sometimes expected to be the last man

in line, 'and the feeling of being in the sights of a potential sniper preyed on my mind'. Rioting was an almost nightly occurrence. Before long, Swede was depressed and exhausted.

The level of hostility came as a shock to Swede and his comrades. Abuse and bottles of urine were hurled at them. 'I was a fresh-faced soldier raised in Uppsala who had previously never had a bad word said to me. It was hard to cope with. The constant banging of dustbin lids, whistling and other noises kept me on my toes, waiting for the next "contact" – of which we had many.'

Another soldier serving in Northern Ireland at that time recalls how sad he was after being spat upon. 'That was the greatest shock, just being spat on, by an extremely pretty girl. If you're being shot at, it's detached . . . there's no personal contact. But if someone spits at you it's hate, pure hate.'[16]

The hatred for the British soldiers sometimes translated into support for the IRA, both tacit and active. As a classified British military intelligence report of the time noted, there were plenty of areas 'where the terrorists can base themselves with little risk of betrayal and can count on active support in an emergency'. Nor was there ever a shortage of high-calibre recruits. The same report concluded that for the foreseeable future the IRA would 'still be able to attract enough people with leadership talent, good education and manual skills to enhance their all-round professionalism'. Gerry Adams, for his part, wrote that 'it is obvious that the IRA exists and operates with the active consent of a sufficient number of people to finance, arm, clothe, feed, accommodate and transport IRA volunteers'.[17]

Cultivating this active consent was also part of the IRA's strategy. Having grown up on the Twinbrook estate, Bobby Sands came to the conclusion that this support should be a two-way street, in much the way that Adams's Staff Report would come to prescribe: IRA volunteers, he argued, must become involved in local community affairs. He helped to organise a pre-school playgroup and a Friday-night youth disco, and encouraged the Provisionals' supporters to join the tenants' association. He even produced two thousand copies of his own local newspaper, entitled *Liberty*, which was typed or written by hand, set with stencils and printed on a duplicating machine, and distributed door to door. The underlying purpose was to turn the estate into a consciously rebellious and Republican area.

Phelim Hamill lived with his father in a cul-de-sac a few streets away from Bobby Sands and – like many other young people on the estate – came to completely idolise him, not just because he was a local IRA leader, but because he saw in him a true revolutionary spirit. Phelim helped with the production of *Liberty*, and together they painted Republican slogans on walls around the estate.

Phelim later said that his friend's subsequent arrest had an enormous impact on the group that had formed around him: 'I looked upon him in the same way I have looked at a Jesus Christ figure.'[18]

Despite the level of local support in places like Twinbrook and Andersonstown, arrest was a constant risk; there were many convictions, and sentences were long. Each week the *Andersonstown News* carried personal messages from the families of prisoners, marking the anniversaries of their incarceration and urging them to stay strong: 'Let me carry your Cross for Ireland Lord . . . we salute you and your comrades' courageous stand, from Joe and Betty, Jim and Maura, Harry and Kathleen, Paul and Sandy . . .'

There were casualties too: Laura Crawford, from the Lenadoon area, was killed in the city centre by the bomb she was transporting. When passers-by pulled her from the wreckage of her car, she was still alive, but on fire. She died within minutes. Brendan O'Callaghan, an IRA volunteer who lived in the next road to Laura, was shot dead by the army at the foot of

Lenadoon Avenue. The IRA said he had been a member of a three-man patrol that had been attempting to protect the area 'after recent bombings by British and loyalist elements'.[19] Laura was twenty-five. Brendan was twenty-one and left two sons. There were large turnouts at both funerals.

Not all the people living in Nationalist areas like One Batt's patch were supportive of the IRA, of course.

In 1976, the Republican movement had been severely rattled by the way a spontaneous public protest against the conflict had ignited suddenly in west Belfast and spread rapidly across Northern Ireland.

It was born in tragedy, after soldiers opened fire on a car carrying two IRA men across Andersonstown, fatally wounding the driver. The vehicle crashed into a young mother, Annie Maguire, who had been walking along the road with her sons Mark, six, and John, two. Annie was pushing her six-week-old baby, Andrew, in a pram. Her eldest child, eight-year-old Joanne, was a little further ahead on her bicycle. Andrew and Joanne were killed instantly. John died in hospital a few hours later. Annie was seriously injured and traumatised: three years later she would take her own life by cutting her wrists.

The day after the incident, up to a thousand women, many of them pushing pushchairs, had come out onto the streets of Andersonstown demonstrating against the violence. As the protest spread, Annie's sister Mairead Corrigan and a second woman, Betty Williams, found themselves at the head of a burgeoning working-class women's movement which became known as the Peace People. It captured imaginations across the north and headlines around the world, and became a serious threat to the IRA. By the end of the month, 20,000 people from across the divide were marching up the Protestant Shankill Road, where local people embraced Catholic nuns.

It was to be a short-lived movement, however. The Republican movement launched an intense campaign to discredit the two women, and they severely damaged their reputations among Nationalists by urging them to inform on IRA volunteers and their plans. At the end of 1977, Betty and Mairead were awarded the Nobel Peace Prize, which brought with it a substantial amount of money: £80,000. Betty decided to take her share of the money and start a new life in the United States. Mairead stayed in Belfast and continued to campaign, but too many people felt her work had been tarnished by the money, and her campaign fizzled out.

While the Peace People failed to have a lasting impact, Gerry Adams would acknowledge that, even among those people whom the Republican movement regarded as its natural constituency, 'there is no doubt that on occasions genuine war-weariness did surface, and it is very understandable that it should'.[20]

There was more than just war-weariness in Nationalist areas, however: there was always a significant number of people who resented the IRA and its methods. In 1978, an opinion poll conducted among 1,277 people, from a sample that was thought to be reasonably representative of the population of Northern Ireland, included a number of questions about the IRA. It found that while 46 per cent of Catholics in the north believed that members of the IRA were motivated by 'patriotism and idealism', and 71 per cent believed there would never be peace as long as the partition of the island remained, 55 per cent agreed with the proposition that 'the British government should take a tougher line with the IRA'. Some 23 per cent said they agreed strongly with the proposition that 'the IRA are basically a bunch of criminals and murderers'.

The writer Malachi O'Doherty, who grew up in Andersonstown, and who feared and detested the British army, had concluded that the quickest way to see off the soldiers was to not shoot at them. 'I have a long annoyance with the IRA for the way they treated non-members like me in the housing estates of west Belfast,' he wrote. 'I resented wee lads of sixteen, moving into a safe house near me, taking me out of a car at night, sometimes with a gun in their hands, to demand to know where I lived and who was with me.'

O'Doherty also resented the pressure to become engaged in the conflict. After the army raided his home, and a British soldier with an automatic rifle and a blackened face stood in his living room screaming at his mother, who was standing in her nightie, screaming back, a local IRA man told him: 'Some people here are saying you're not pulling your weight.' O'Doherty felt that his decision not to join the IRA at that point was not entirely to his credit. On the other hand, he 'loathed the thought of entering hierarchies in which gruff people could tell me what to do'.[21]

For decades, the countryside that separated Unionist Lisburn from One Batt's area of operations in outer west Belfast had been farmland, and many of those farms had been in Protestant hands. In the late 1970s, all that was about to change, in a way that would further exacerbate tensions between the two communities.

With housing waiting lists in west Belfast remaining stubbornly long and with Lisburn beyond the pale for many Catholics, it had been agreed by 1977 that new homes would be built on the land between the city and the town, at a place called Poleglass. This might entail the compulsory purchase of farmland. As the new homes would lie within the borough of Lisburn, the town's Unionist council would be expected to take responsibility for services such as education and refuse collection.

It was always clear that this was going to be a Catholic housing estate. But building it on the outskirts of Lisburn was considered unsafe, and instead it was built next to Twinbrook. Catholic west Belfast was spreading towards Protestant Lisburn, and some of the people of the town were far from happy: it was only a matter of time, they argued, before the new estate became dominated by the Provisionals, as had happened on Twinbrook.

The original plan for 4,000 new homes was halved under pressure from Unionist MPs at Westminster, where Jim Callaghan, without a parliamentary majority, was dependent on their support. But Lisburn Borough Council would still not cooperate, and an Anti Poleglass Action Committee was formed, with its leader, the Rev William Beattie, a Democratic Unionist Party councillor, vowing that 30,000 Loyalists would 'fight to the bitter end' to halt the construction of the estate.

When the Action Committee staged a rally at the scene of the proposed development, the Housing Executive had a covert observer in the crowd of several thousand, who reported that Beattie and Elsie Kelsey, the Mayor of Lisburn, 'spoke with considerable vehemence'. The observer made a careful note of what was said – 'a full record of the speeches is attached'.[22]

Reactions in the press were as polarised as they were between the people of west Belfast and Lisburn. The *Andersonstown News* called for the estate to be expanded as quickly as possible to house 50,000 people; the pro-Unionist *News Letter* asked: WHO WILL ENFORCE THE LAW INSIDE POLEGLASS?

But in January 1978, Roy Mason ruled that the development should go ahead, and it was given planning permission without Lisburn Council's consent. When councillors threatened to refuse to arrange for bins on the estate to be emptied, an order compelling them to do so was issued under local public health laws.

As with other parts of the city, the security forces ensured that architecturally designed counter-terrorism measures would be built into the very fabric of the new estate. From the earliest days of the Troubles, the army and police had been quietly consulted about any town-planning proposals that might be expected to have an impact upon the interface areas between the Protestant and Catholic communities, or upon the security forces' movements or lines of vision.

Unlike the sangars, the anti-mortar nets strung above the police stations, and the concrete emplacements at the entrances to the locked-down area of the city centre known as the Control Zone, the defensive town-planning measures that the security forces recommended were largely unobtrusive: they were intended to be invisible to the uninitiated eye.

But they were far-reaching: many new roads were able to bear heavily armoured vehicles, and housing estates were built with access routes that could provide fields of fire. As early as 1970 there were suggestions from planners that a major new highway dividing the city centre from west Belfast might be a 'prudent . . . cordon sanitaire'. That road, the Westlink, opened in 1983.

The military's recommendations could be highly imaginative: early in the 1970s, under a scheme code-named 'Operation Playground', the Royal Marines designed and constructed children's play areas in Belfast with access streets that were intended to 'counter IRA and UVF activity'.[23]

Often, the interests of the military and those of the local residents would coincide. People who lived in a block of flats on the Turf Lodge estate, for example, were delighted to be offered new homes at Poleglass; they were not told that the army wanted their current block demolished so that the IRA could not use it for sniping attacks.

There was considerable official anxiety about uncontrolled movements of the population, with the result that at the end of 1977 a body called the Security Committee on Housing was established, unannounced, at the Northern Ireland Office. Sitting alongside officials from the Belfast Development Office was Jack Hermon, the Deputy Chief Constable of the RUC, while a lieutenant colonel represented the army.

The following January the committee prepared a number of confidential papers about the steady depopulation of Protestant areas, and the impact that this was having upon security. One official expressed concern about the long-term implications of

Catholics moving into vacated housing along the main routes into the city centre from the north and the south. He wrote in a draft minute:

> If we reach the situation in which . . . approaches to Belfast are 'in Catholic hands', are we not increasing the risk that in any future period of violence, access to the city centre and the major industrial areas will be prone to control by Republican extremists? We are effectively encouraging moves towards a situation in which the Laggan [sic] becomes a division between two separate cities and in which the main industrial [and] commercial areas lie in potentially hostile territory.

A second official responded to this doomsday scenario by suggesting that population movements might need to be micromanaged in order to avoid west Belfast coming 'under virtual Catholic occupation'.

At a subsequent meeting of the committee, the army produced a paper written by Dr Philip Haskell, the Deputy Scientific Adviser at headquarters in Lisburn. Haskell reported that wealthier Protestants were moving east of the Lagan, and homes in less desirable Protestant areas west of the river were falling vacant. He also concluded that in the long term Protestants and Catholics would live peacefully alongside each other only within prosperous areas.

Haskell recommended that a programme of research and mathematical modelling be established in order to produce estimates for the amount of housing that would be required in each of three areas: 'Hard Protestant, Hard Catholic, and Mixed Prosperous.' Noting that unrest and dereliction were generated by those barriers that were manned by the security forces, Haskell suggested that greater use should be made of motorways and railways to divide the two communities.

The minutes of another meeting of the committee early in 1978, marked Secret, recorded that it had agreed that a study would also be conducted 'to assess the likelihood of a green wedge' emerging in north Belfast. 'DCC Hermon was most interested and contributed a good deal to the discussion,' the minutes record. 'He was particularly interested not only in "colour" trends but in changes in the class structures in various parts of Belfast.' If middle-class Catholics were to move into private housing in any particular area of the city, Hermon predicted, 'this would in the long term draw in working class Catholics behind them'. And that, the Deputy Chief Constable was no doubt thinking, would open new doors for the IRA.

In the years to come, the Northern Ireland Office's secret defensive planning committee would acquire more staff, some of them based at police stations, as well as the power to review all planning proposals for housing, health, education, social services and roads.[24]

When Poleglass was built, in the valley below the Mullaghglass Road with its fluttering Union flags, it had four points of entry. Two main roads crossed the estate, from each of which ran a series of cul-de-sacs, roads from which a car being pursued could not escape. Much of the estate is pedestrianised, but the footpaths are ten feet wide and reinforced to carry the weight of army vehicles. While the estate was being planned, the army suggested the new residents be provided with pubs, not because it wished to encourage drinking, but because it wanted to reduce the demand for Republican social clubs.

When the first thirty families from the Lower Falls moved to Poleglass, they did so in what one local Sunday newspaper described as a 'secret dawn operation'. It was not long before Irish murals started to appear on the terrace ends: '*Ar Aghaidh Linn*' and '*Fáilte go Gleann Ban*' – 'Let's Go!' and 'Welcome to Glenn Ban'.

Many of the Unionists of Lisburn felt that their worst

nightmare had come to pass: west Belfast and its inhabitants – its seditious Roman Catholic denizens – were creeping steadily towards their town and their homes; in Poleglass and Twinbrook, meanwhile, many people still thought of Lisburn as another planet.

With Roy Mason convinced that the IRA fed off social alienation and economic deprivation, some attempt was made to improve community relations and promote integrated education, and provide new jobs. A young peer, Lord Melchett, was appointed as a junior Northern Ireland minister and given responsibility for improving community relations, and for establishing new leisure facilities.

Melchett, an Old Etonian, was horrified at the social and economic conditions he encountered, especially in Nationalist areas. 'I had had a fairly sheltered background. I felt a burning sense of injustice at the poverty and deprivation: there were families who lived in Catholic west Belfast with three, four generations unemployed. I hadn't seen that before. It was a shock.'

His fellow ministers were less moved, however. 'All four other ministers were of the view that Northern Ireland was being treated as a special case and was being given privileges, and didn't really deserve it, compared to the north east and the north west of England.'

However, Mason's senior civil servants were convinced that only economic progress could create a more receptive climate for an attempted political settlement in the future, and so attempts were made to create new jobs alongside the building of new homes. In Andersonstown, for example, the government wrote off the £4-million debts of Strathearn Audio, a state-owned local factory that manufactured hi-fi turntables and speakers.

But Mason and his advisers believed that the real key to job creation lay not in direct government investment, but in attracting greater investment from overseas, particularly from the United States and Japan. The US State Department was wary, however, with some of its diplomats warning that too much investment from the United States might be seen as a direct challenge to the IRA.

There was good reason for such caution: a few weeks after Strathearn's debts were written off – and at a time when the government was looking for a Japanese purchaser for the plant – James Nicholson, an English public relations consultant who had been offering marketing advice to Strathearn, flew to Belfast for a meeting at the factory. Afterwards, as he drove back to the airport, he was shot dead, a victim of the IRA's 'economic war'. James left two children.

Eventually, despite the economic risks and physical dangers, Mason's efforts began to pay off: a tyre company announced a £3-million investment in a research laboratory in Belfast, and a US electronic components corporation announced that it too was opening a small plant. They were followed by General Motors, which announced plans for a £16-million seat-belt manufacturing plant to the east of the city.

During the summer of 1977, the Queen paid her first visit to Northern Ireland for eleven years as part of her Silver Jubilee celebrations. Mason was determined that the event should pass off without serious incident: he wanted the visit to send a message to potential overseas investors that terrorism was on the wane.

At Stormont, there was a great deal of anxiety about the visit and the endless number of things that could go wrong: it was to be the first major test of Police Primacy. The IRA, which had promised 'a visit to remember', mounted a series of shootings and firebomb attacks in an attempt to force its cancellation. Nine prison officers and members of the security forces were killed between the start of the Jubilee celebrations and the Queen's visit, along with two IRA volunteers.

On 11 August, the royal yacht sailed into Belfast Lough to a 21-gun salute. The Queen came ashore only twice during her stay, however, both times by helicopter, and it would be another fourteen years before she returned to Northern Ireland.

Later that Jubilee year, there was a further boost to Mason's spirits. As part of the plan to promote industrial development on land between Belfast and Lisburn – creating new jobs for both Catholics and Protestants – the Northern Ireland Development Agency persuaded the DeLorean Motor Company, a Detroit sports car manufacturer, to build a plant there. This was where it would manufacture its DMC-12 sports car, a futuristic-looking model with gull-wing doors, for export to the US market.

The company's founder, the charismatic former Ford executive John Z. DeLorean, was well aware that this deal was about more than just creating jobs – he was being enlisted in the war against the IRA – and bartered hard, eventually securing government grants and subsidies worth around £106 million.

In time, the entire enterprise would become a textbook disaster: the company went into bankruptcy, taking with it more than 2,000 jobs.[25] But for the time being, it provided Mason with some very useful headlines, as he continued to claim that mounting overseas investment was evidence that the IRA was being beaten.

One of the first tasks given to Harry Murray, after he returned from his training camp and joined his ASU, was to stand at a bus stop not far from the entrance to Andersonstown police barracks and watch the unmarked cars that came and went. He did this for seven or eight days, noting on a piece of paper, or on the back of his hand, the colours, makes and registration numbers of the cars entering the barracks between 8.45 and 9.10 a.m. One of the cars recorded in this way was a red 1750 Austin Allegro.[26]

Meanwhile, the IRA had made the link between the plain-clothes police officer who was sometimes to be spotted at

Castlereagh and the man who was the Northern Ireland correspondent for the *Pigeon Racing News and Gazette*. Somebody
who had been brought in for interrogation at Castlereagh had
also seen the man's byline picture in the magazine.

By now, however, the reports no longer appeared below the
byline 'The Copper'. They appeared under the correspondent's
real name: Millar McAllister. So the IRA now had the plain-
clothes officer's name and photograph, and they knew of his
great passion in life. It was not going to take long for one of their
intelligence officers to make inquiries in pigeon-racing circles,
and find his address.

The war ground on. In mid-December, Paul Harman, an
undercover British soldier, was driving through Turf Lodge. He
was at the wheel of what his unit called a Q Car – in his case a
red Morris Marina whose interior had been decorated with old
newspapers, crushed cigarette boxes and other pieces of litter,
in an attempt to give the impression that it was a civilian vehicle.
He brought the car to a brief halt outside a row of neat semi-
detached houses on Monagh Road, and paused just a little too
long: a gunman walked up to the Marina and shot him in the
head. The IRA took his Browning pistol, his radio and a number
of documents. Then they torched the car.

A week later, Jim Callaghan paid one of his rare visits to
Northern Ireland. Bernard Donoughue noted in his diary that
the Prime Minister had 'enjoyed it immensely' because a bomb
had gone off nearby while he was visiting an army post.

None of this was enough to dent Roy Mason's confidence
that progress was being made. He persisted in believing
that victory could be achieved by quantifying progress. At
Christmas, despite the many warnings he had received, Mason
announced that 'the tide has turned against the terrorists and the
message for 1978 is one of real hope'.[27]

On New Year's Eve, the bars and pubs outside the Control
Zone were rammed with people who were determined to

enjoy themselves at the end of what had been another painful year for the province. There was just time, however, for one more murder before 1977 came to an end. Gordon Quinn, a member of the Ulster Defence Association (UDA), a Loyalist paramilitary organisation, had a row with some members of the rival UVF about a girl. Gordon was stabbed twenty times and his body tossed in a skip off the Shankill Road. He was eighteen.

The following day, Callaghan gave an interview to the BBC in which he made a number of predictions about the year ahead in the UK: they all concerned the economy. Northern Ireland was not mentioned.

By early 1978 it was clear that the IRA had developed a new type of bomb, one that became known as a blast incendiary device. Designed initially as a way of overcoming a shortage of commercial and fertiliser-based explosives, it was deployed at a time when firefighters across Britain and Northern Ireland were on strike. It quickly proved to be a devastating weapon in the 'economic war' that the organisation said it was waging against local business. But these bombs created an enormous risk of there being unintended civilian casualties.

They were simple devices: an electrical initiating system, a pound or so of explosive in a steel container, and a couple of jerrycans of petrol. When detonated, they sounded like a 300lb car bomb.

On 12 January, Charlie Stout, the US Consul General, heard three of them go off during the drive from his home in south Belfast to his first-floor office in Queen Street, just inside the Control Zone. As he peered out of the office window, another exploded somewhere in the north of the city. No doubt Charlie was wondering how firefighters could be permitted to go on strike in a place like this.

After listening to the radio news, he decided to compose a

telegram to Washington, DC and the US embassies in London and Dublin. They should know. The heading wrote itself: 'Fire Bombs in Belfast'.

What next?

Pause.

1. Poor Belfast.

2. Under a sharp wintry sky, with snow covering the hills surrounding the city, about ten fire bombs had exploded in Belfast as of drafting time at 0920 (January 12). Many went off a little after seven, including three in King Street parallel to the Congen's Queen Street, bordering the security barrier and a short block away. Smoke is still pouring from a goodsized corner building, which will be gutted. One soldier and a policeman were injured in checking this initial series of explosions.

3. Other targets downtown or in the outskirts included a furniture store, a post office, a hardware store, and one of the few inns in the area still serving a decent meal. Traffic was chaotic, particularly since soldiers continued the early morning practice of spot-checking incoming vehicles.

4. Overnight a pleasant pub in the Belfast suburb of Carrickfergus was burnt out, and bombs exploded with little damage in two smaller towns. Yesterday afternoon a fire blazed for five hours in a large warehouse just outside the security barrier about two blocks from the Congen. Silent crowds watched the fire all afternoon. Two armed men planted the fire bombs. Staff got out before they exploded, but three pensioners living nearby were taken to hospital in shock. The bombers escaped

on foot but left behind a van which had been hijacked in the Catholic Falls Road. The army blew it up, but it contained no bombs. This morning we noticed a car parked outside the police station across the street from the Congen. It had gone through controlled explosions: the tires were intact, but the chassis was a shell.

5. In Craigavon, about 25 miles west of Belfast, police yesterday found in a garage enough material to make some 60 firebombs; 36 incendiaries complete with watches, batteries and gas igniters, and in addition 25 stereo cassette cases, 18 watches, 150 feet of electrical cable, Scotch tape and insulating tape, soldering irons, 63 gas igniters, 63 bulbs, batteries, rubber gloves, and ignition pins.

6. Comment: we note that except for Christmas Day there has been at least one explosion in Northern Ireland every day since November 29. The number had gone down somewhat after the post-Christmas/New Year series. Probably the current spectacular is timed to make difficulties for Secretary of State for NI Roy Mason at Question Time today in the Commons. Justly or not, Mason no doubt will be reminded sharply of his recent statements on the success of the campaign against the terrorists.

Charlie then signed off: 'Stout. Unclassified.'

After lunch, Charlie walked down Queen Street to pick up a copy of the evening paper. It reported that there had in fact been eight bombs detonated in and around Belfast that morning. The targets included a textile warehouse and two furniture stores. Seven buildings had been either severely damaged or totally destroyed. Each of the bombs had large hooks attached to them, which had been used to hang the devices from protective security grilles that were in place across the city to protect windows from bricks and bottles hurled during riots.

The press dubbed the new device 'the IRA meat-hook bomb'. 'Once these bombs are planted, there is virtually nothing we can do, because they explode minutes after being left,' an army officer was quoted as saying. 'It's now a question of trying to capture the terrorists before they reach the targets.'

Charlie's newspaper offered its readers a brief round-up of the other main bombings across the province during the previous twenty-four hours. Two stores had been blown up, and an incendiary device had been tossed into the offices of the *Tyrone Democrat* newspaper in Coalisland, 40 miles west of Belfast. It had only partially exploded.

Elsewhere, Charlie noted, the news was unremittingly grim. The Belfast coroner, James Elliott, had been busy, as usual. The previous day he had recorded an open verdict in the case of a man found shot in the head on a piece of waste ground. Police told Elliott that they suspected the dead man had been targeted because he was from Fermanagh, and had a rural accent, leading his killers to believe, mistakenly, that he was a Catholic. 'People have been shot quite mistakenly for less than an accent in the past,' Elliott observed. He also recorded misadventure verdicts in the case of two Loyalist paramilitaries who had blown themselves up while trying to burn down an empty house.[28]

The only good news, as far as Charlie could see, was that the leaders of the Fire Brigades Union had voted to end their two-month-old strike. On the other hand, there appeared to be a fuel crisis looming as tanker drivers threatened industrial action.

That evening, at home with his wife Laura, Charlie switched on the television to catch the evening news. At Newry, near the border with the Republic, a 56-year-old man had been shot three times in the head as he drove home from work. Cecil Grills had been ambushed after leaving the timber yard where he had been a sales manager. The IRA said they had killed him

because of his 'service with the British war machine': he had
been a part-time corporal in the UDR. Cecil left a son aged
nine and a daughter aged seven.

At the end of January, the Provisionals claimed responsibility for forty-six bomb attacks since New Year's Day.
They pledged to continue the bombing campaign, and branded
Mason 'a fool for his fundamental mistake of predicting the
defeat of the IRA'.[29] Five more bombs then exploded in Belfast
and Derry.

At this time, the police and army's penetration of the IRA
remained sufficiently effective for them to be able to closely
follow the reorganisation prescribed by the Staff Report. Some
British military strategists were tempted to see the restructuring
efforts as an admission of weakness: a sign that the IRA needed to
be able to function with less manpower and less public support.[30]

However, one man who viewed the reorganisation differently
was Brigadier Jimmy Glover, the head of military intelligence in
the province. Glover was a clear-eyed soldier who could see
that there could be no purely military solution to the problems
of the province, and that politicians like Mason who argued
otherwise were deluding themselves. Glover had been arguing
privately for some time that heavy-handed army operations
would always be counter-productive when conducted among
civilian populations. He could also see that the Staff Report
was going to reinvigorate the IRA.

Early in 1978 he warned in his monthly briefing that 'the
hooligan element has been rooted out' of the IRA during
the reorganisation, and that 'the cell structure and better training
has led to improved coordination, tighter security and higher
quality operations'. Shooting incidents had seen gunmen opening fire from three separate firing points against a single target,
while near the border in south Armagh men in uniform had
been seen moving in formation.

Glover was preparing a classified British army assessment of the strengths and disposition of the IRA following the Staff Report reorganisation. Entitled 'Future Terrorist Trends', Glover's report was intended to predict the tactics likely to be adopted by the IRA over the next five years, as well as the weapons that were likely to be used, so that the security forces could be ready with a range of new counter-measures.

Glover's assessment was stark: for the foreseeable future, he predicted, the Provisional IRA would have 'the dedication and the sinews of war to raise violence intermittently to at least the level of early 1978'. By 'sinews of war', Glover meant that the IRA had the men and women, the money and the weapons that it needed to prosecute its Long War. It no longer needed large numbers of recruits. He went on:

> PIRA's organisation is now such that a small number of activists can maintain a disproportionate level of violence. There is a substantial pool of young Fianna aspirants, nurtured in a climate of violence, eagerly seeking promotion to full gun-carrying terrorist status and there is a steady release from the prisons of embittered and dedicated terrorists. Thus, though PIRA may be hard hit by Security Force attrition from time to time, they will probably have the manpower they need to sustain violence during the next five years.

Turning to the IRA's leadership, Glover noted that the IRA was essentially – although not exclusively – working class. Many middle-class people were deterred from joining by 'the Provisionals' muddled political thinking' as well as by the inevitable loss of their middle-class ways of life. 'Nevertheless there is a strata of intelligent, astute and experienced terrorists who provide the backbone of the organisation,' he wrote.

The ASU structure meant the IRA was less dependent on

public support and less vulnerable to penetration, Glover warned. On the other hand, the new cellular organisation slowed down command and control systems, as messages were passed to the cells through a limited number of people.

There was no shortage of capable bomb makers, the brigadier noted, or of equipment, workshops and laboratories, and there was every likelihood of greater exploitation of modern technology. The IRA was enjoying an income of around £950,000 and had an expenditure of around £780,000 per annum, according to Glover's best estimates, and was thought to possess around 440 handguns, 40 sub-machine guns and 330 rifles, as well as mortars, armour-piercing explosive munitions and rocket-propelled grenades.

Glover's appraisal was not entirely uncritical of the IRA's capabilities. The fundamental political differences between the Provisionals and the Official IRA were exacerbated by 'bitter animosity between individuals and family groups', he reported, and the British army had clearly been surprised – if relieved – by the poor marksmanship of many Provo snipers, who appeared to make little effort to 'zero in' their weapons – that is, to align the sights to ensure accuracy.

But Glover's description of the rank-and-file membership was intended to be a revelation to any readers in Whitehall who had fallen for the British government's own propaganda about the nature of IRA terrorists. 'The evidence of the calibre of rank and file terrorists does not support the view that they are merely mindless hooligans drawn from the unemployed and unemployable,' he wrote. 'PIRA now trains and uses its members with some care. The Active Service Units are for the most part manned by terrorists with up to ten years of operational experience.'

Finally, Glover concluded: 'The Provisionals' campaign of violence is likely to continue as long as the British remain in Northern Ireland.' There was little prospect of political progress, and the IRA would continue to be able to recruit 'enough people with leadership talent, good education and manual skills to enhance their all-round professionalism'. The organisation would continue to enjoy popular support in the traditional Republican areas. And the most effective arm of the IRA over the next few years would be 'the increasingly professional' ASUs.[31]

Glover had no doubt about that popular support: he could see that British propaganda about the way so-called godfathers of violence intimidated the law-abiding residents of places like Nationalist west Belfast was to a great extent just that: propaganda. He also sensed that Irish Republicans had a different sense of timing from their British adversaries. They were, through their Long War plans, thinking much further than five years into the future.

The British state and British army must adopt a similar time frame, he argued. In a speech that he gave around the time he was finalising his report, he warned: 'Northern Ireland is not within decades of a political solution to its problems. The IRA has destroyed all prospect of Irish unity for at least a generation, but can still make the country ungovernable for "a Protestant Parliament for a Protestant people".' Meanwhile, he argued, 'obdurate Unionists have destroyed the practical compromise of power sharing, but will never persuade any Westminster government to restore their monopoly of power'.

Extraordinarily, Glover's report fell into the hands of the IRA and was published in *Republican News*. The official account was that a copy had gone astray in the postal system. It seems more likely that senior military figures – knowing that a general election could not be far away, and sensing that Labour would lose – wanted an incoming Conservative administration to be under no illusion about the prospects for military success in the province, and decided to leak it. In later years, Glover spoke of his satisfaction that a realistic assessment of the IRA and its members was 'paraded in front of [the government] in such an overt and, I hope, persuasive way'.[32]

Some in the RUC Special Branch saw Glover's assessment as inaccurate and excessively pessimistic. The IRA leadership, on the other hand, saw it as confirmation that the British military had accepted that the key element of Roy Mason's strategy – the military suppression of their organisation – could not be delivered. In time, it was shown to be quite prophetic.

If one took the word 'terrorist' out of Glover's report and substituted it with 'soldier', his assessment was of a highly professional, committed and resourceful enemy, one that was going to be at war for many years to come. It was certainly not, as Mason would have the public believe, an enemy that was being rolled up like a tube of toothpaste.

In February 1978, events of one evening brought the glare of international attention back to Northern Ireland, and forced the IRA to rethink its deadly tactics.

The 17th, a Friday, had begun rather well for the IRA: its volunteers, armed with an American M60 machine gun, had brought down a British army Gazelle helicopter near Jonesborough in County Armagh. One of the occupants, Lieutenant Colonel Ian Corden-Lloyd, the commanding officer of an infantry battalion, was killed. It was an episode that reflected the way the IRA liked to see itself: an army, out in the field, bravely fighting a well-armed foe.

That evening, more than four hundred people were gathered at the La Mon House, a restaurant, dance hall and hotel complex set in the rolling Castlereagh hills east of Belfast. The two largest groups were from the Northern Ireland Collie Club, many attending with their well-behaved dogs, and from the Northern Ireland Junior Motor Cycle Club.

Shortly before 9 p.m. a small IRA team from west Belfast arrived in a hijacked Fiat. They hooked two of the new blast incendiaries to the security grilles of the windows of the Peacock

Room restaurant, and then went in search of a telephone box from which to convey an advance warning. All of the public telephones in the area had been vandalised. The warning call to the police was eventually made nine minutes before the bombs were due to detonate, but when the police rang the hotel, the man who picked up the phone shouted: 'For God's sake get out here, a bomb has gone off.'

When the devices exploded, a fireball rolled through the crowded building. Those caught in the flames were burned alive. Others fled from the flames and the choking fumes, and staggered from the building with their clothes, hair and flesh alight. A waitress said later: 'People were on fire, actually burning alive. I could smell the burning flesh. I didn't realise at the time what I was smelling but I realised later what that dreadful stench was.'

On arriving at the scene, Chief Constable Kenneth Newman described the bombing as 'the ultimate in inhumanity'. One journalist asked him how the IRA could carry out such an attack if they were, as Mason continually asserted, beaten. 'I haven't talked about success,' Newman snapped back.

Twelve people, including three married couples, died in the blast. All were Protestants. A further twenty-three people were seriously injured. The dead were so badly burned and shrivelled by the flames that firemen thought initially that some were children. A radio reporter at the scene described them as resembling charred logs of wood. Many were identified from their dental records; one was identified only by a process of elimination. At the inquest later that year, James Mills would describe how his brother-in-law Joseph Morris pulled him away from the blaze. They could hear their wives, Carol and Sandra, screaming. 'We tried to get back in, but could not because of the intense smoke.'

The day after the bombing, the RUC issued 10,000 leaflets bearing the word 'murder', twelve times, in red capital letters. In the centre of each leaflet was a black-and-white photograph of one of the charred corpses, just about recognisable as a woman. She had only one leg. Beneath the picture, a caption read: 'This is what the bombers did to a human being.'*

Charlie Stout dashed off a telegram to Washington, DC: 'The Provisional IRA February 17 pulled off a spectacular massacre of NI innocents – one of the worst during the Troubles.' Along with the bodies, Stout noted, police had found in the debris a number of dogs' paws.

In the Commons, Mason faced calls for the restoration of the death penalty, while one Unionist leader demanded that 'the Republican ghettos' be bombed by the RAF, on the grounds that 'there were no innocent people in them'.[33]

After the surge of energy brought about by the restructure, the IRA was now at one of its lowest ebbs. An organisation that regarded itself as an army was, at this point, seen by most people around the world as a gang of despicable terrorists. At Castlereagh, police doctors noted that even more suspects appeared to be receiving beatings. The IRA issued a statement which acknowledged that its warning had 'proved totally inadequate', but which added: 'We accept condemnation and criticism from only two sources: from the relatives and friends of those who were accidentally killed, and from our supporters who have rightly criticised us.'

In his memoirs, Adams wrote that he was deeply shocked and despondent. 'I was depressed by the carnage and deeply affected by the deaths and injuries. I could also feel two years of work going down the drain.'

That evening, Adams broke with his usual practice of sleeping in a different house each night, and stayed with his wife and son

---

* One man received twelve life sentences after pleading guilty to manslaughter. A second man was acquitted. In 1991, while standing in a Belfast city-centre newsagent's, he was shot several times by a Loyalist gunman. He survived after surgery.

in a house off the Falls Road. Police arrested him there the following morning. A further nineteen people were arrested across the province. During questioning, police showed Adams photographs of the bodies at the La Mon House. After seven days he was charged with being a member of the IRA.*

There were to be no further blast incendiary attacks for the time being, and the IRA leadership instructed its units that there were to be no further bomb attacks of any kind on hotels, buses or trains.

Before long, British military intelligence was noting that there was 'a marked trend towards attacks against security force targets and away from action which, by alienating public opinion, both within the Catholic community and outside the Province, is politically damaging'.

Bombs were to be used more sparingly in urban locations. Instead, IRA volunteers would be expected to fall back on a tactic that the British army called CQA: close-quarter assassination.

A few weeks later, an IRA volunteer was driving around Lisburn, making a mental note of potential escape routes around the south side of the town, and paying particular attention to the bungalow at 106 Woodland Park.

---

* Seven months later the charge was dismissed when a judge ruled that there was insufficient evidence that he was a member.

4

The Killing

After the La Mon House firebombing a tide of shock and revulsion flowed rapidly across the world, but it was not long before that tide ebbed; tales of the carnage disappeared from the front pages, the evening news bulletins moved on.

Thirty-six hours after the bombing, Jim Callaghan invited his Cabinet ministers and their wives for Sunday lunch at the Prime Minister's country residence, Chequers. (Only one Cabinet minister, Shirley Williams, the Education Secretary, was a woman.) Before lunch, while the wives swam in the heated pool, there was a brief Cabinet meeting. Ministers discussed the budget, but the subject that most enthralled and worried them was the way the Conservative leader Margaret Thatcher was leading her party sharply to the right, and mounting increasingly accomplished attempts to alarm the public about matters such as defence and law and order. Thatcher was going to be a troublesome adversary. Despite this, Tony Benn, the Energy Secretary, noted in his diary that Callaghan was 'avuncular, calm, quiet' during the meeting. La Mon House appears not to have been raised; nor was there any wider discussion about the conflict in Northern Ireland.[1]

Early the following month, when the Commons finally debated politics and security in Northern Ireland in the wake of the bombing, only fifteen MPs were present. In Belfast, however, the IRA's leadership remained mortified. They hoped that, by issuing instructions that the ASUs were to concentrate on targeting members of the security forces up close, they would avoid the unintended casualties that were so damaging to public opinion, both among the Nationalist population in the north of Ireland, and outside the province.

Jimmy Glover noted in his monthly intelligence assessment that 'the outcry of revulsion after the La Mon bomb caught the Provisionals on the wrong foot. They have been at pains to redress their image.' While they had 'lain low' for a while after that bombing, 'the Belfast PIRA have the capability to implement a new round of violence whenever they wish'.

The first casualty following the bombing of the hotel was Paul Duffy, an IRA volunteer killed as he attempted to move a batch of explosives from a derelict house in Washing Bay in east County Tyrone. Paul had apparently judged that the explosives were being stored too close to the home of two elderly brothers. Unknown to him, a detachment of soldiers had the area staked out: one of them shot him in the forehead. He was twenty-three. Two days later a police constable, Charles Simpson, twenty-six, a married man with three children, died after being shot in the head as he was being driven through the centre of Derry.

Three weeks after the La Mon House attack, and two days after the Commons debate, British government ministers finally came around to discussing it. The occasion was a meeting of a Cabinet committee on Ireland, held in Jim Callaghan's office at the House of Commons. Roy Mason appeared to be deeply shocked by the attack: while it had severely damaged the reputation of the IRA, it had also completely undermined his repeated public assertions that he had the organisation on the run. During the meeting he referred to Unionist politicians by their first names, while being dismissive of Catholic political leaders. 'He's confirmed all my worst fears,' Downing Street policy adviser Bernard Donoughue wrote in his diary. 'He has become a spokesman for the Protestants.'

Somehow, Mason contrived to blame the Irish Taoiseach, Jack Lynch, for the violence in the north. Callaghan was unimpressed, and reprimanded his Northern Ireland Secretary, saying he did not want to hear any further attacks on Lynch; Mason, he made clear, must achieve greater political progress in the north, and he believed Lynch to be a good man.

Three days after PC Charles Simpson had been shot dead, students at Queen's University in Belfast were enjoying the annual charity fundraising event known as Rag Week. They dressed up in costumes, rattled tins to collect money, and sold their self-published joke books. In other British and Irish universities, students wandered freely around their towns and cities; in Belfast, they were halted at the edge of the Control Zone, where police officers watched through slits in concrete bunkers as people waited to be searched. On this day, troops, police officers and civilian searchers watched, questioned, patted down and then admitted a day-long procession of young students dressed as pirates, clowns, nuns and punk rockers.

At Donegall Street on the north side of the city centre, four young men dressed as Arabs approached the checkpoint where James Nowasad, twenty-one, a Scottish soldier with the Royal Tank Regiment, was on duty alongside Norma Spence, twenty-five, a civilian searcher from Dundonald, east of Belfast. One of the young Arabs approached James, who is said to have smiled at him. The Arab produced a pistol from beneath his robes and shot James through the head. There was pandemonium: the other people waiting to be searched at the checkpoint attempted to escape. The gunman took aim at Norma. She tried to shield herself. The round that he fired passed through her wrist and hit her in the neck. She began to run, but collapsed and died in a shop doorway.

Later that day, Charlie Stout sent a telegram from his office to the US embassy in London and the State Department in Washington, DC, informing them that the IRA had switched tactics after the La Mon House bombing, and was concentrating on gun attacks. 'So far this year the death toll is 22, of which 20 were in February. This number already exceeds that for the last five months in 1977.'

The following Tuesday, around two thousand Queen's students marched in silent protest to the city centre. In Nationalist west Belfast, a number of people were angered by the students' protest: correspondents to the *Andersonstown News* condemned them as hypocrites who had done nothing to protest the killing of Catholics over the previous ten years.[2] While many people were appalled by the Rag Week killings, there was a significant number who believed that the IRA was responding to the violence of the state – and striking back – in the only way that it could. The city was as polarised as ever, as was the whole of the north of Ireland.

The intimate nature of these close–quarter attacks was no doubt a challenge for some IRA volunteers, in part because of the possibility that their intended victims might shoot back. Reflecting on the moral problems of political violence in general and of CQAs in particular, Gerry Adams later wrote: 'I cannot conceive of any thinking person who would not have scruples about inflicting any form of hurt on another living being.' Even members of the IRA who were capable of acting in a 'ruthless, determined and callous' fashion would experience intellectual and emotional qualms, he said.

Adams also suggested that IRA volunteers – unlike recruits to the British army – might find CQAs more challenging.

> That difficulty would rarely lie in any sense of religious morality but would have to do with the type of struggle involved, because it is close up and it is nothing like joining a 'regular' army with a whole ethos about being

trained to kill. IRA volunteers are actually civilians, political people who decide for short periods in their lives to take part in armed action.[3]

Few people on the receiving end of these close-up assassination attempts survived to recount the experience. One who did was Swede Tompkinson. On yet another foot patrol through Turf Lodge with fellow soldiers of the Queen's Regiment, Swede once again found himself bringing up the rear as the patrol's last man.

> As we turned down Norglen Drive, I passed a concrete wall on the right when an enormous explosion threw me across the road. When I came to, lying in the middle of the road on my back, I looked up and thought, 'Fuck, is that it?' and wondering what my parents were going to say. I seemed to just lie there for what seemed like ages and then looked down the road – and through thick white smoke, two dark figures appeared.

They were fellow soldiers, who pulled Swede to his feet and into a nearby garage. A grenade had been hurled at him, a home-made affair with a hand-lit fuse and packed with six-inch nails, but he was largely unscathed. 'I sorted myself out and continued the patrol, although I felt sick and very dizzy.'

Returning to Fort Monagh, Swede noticed that a part of his rifle had been damaged in the blast. He asked for a replacement at the stores, where he received a reprimand for damaging army property.

He had begun keeping a diary, in Swedish, and that day his sober entry read: 'Search early in the morning. Then T.L. [Turf Lodge] in the morning, little agro. Cop shot in Andytown, snipe at Fort Monagh, then patrol in T.L. Nailbomb thrown at our patrol, nearly killed. Then lazed around. Mortar runs all night.'[4]

Perhaps the most vivid description given by a survivor of a CQA is that offered by Glen Espie. In the spring of 1978, Glen was a plumber with the Northern Ireland Housing Executive, which managed the social housing in the province. He was also a part-time soldier in the UDR.

Each morning, before setting off for work, Glen would scour the road outside his home before opening the front door. He would then check that a bomb had not been placed under his car overnight. On arrival at the depot from which he worked, he would park each day in a different location within the car park and, after clocking on, check his work van for under-vehicle explosive devices. While Glen did this, he would be watched closely by work colleagues: men whom he suspected of being members or supporters of the IRA; men who he assumed wanted to see him dead.

On March 22, five weeks after the La Mon House bombing, Glen's foreman told him that the depot had received a call that a copper cylinder had burst at a house in Ardboe, a Nationalist village on the western shores of Lough Neagh, west of Belfast.

Glen took the precaution he always took when called out on an emergency job: he first went home and donned his concealed body armour. Then he drove to Ardboe.

On arrival he reversed his van up to the house while watching the front door in his wing mirror. Although it was supposed to be a routine job, his heart was pounding as he climbed out of the van. He could never be sure what might happen.

> I stood to the side of the door and knocked so that if someone fired through the door they would be unable to hit me. The door was opened slightly by a male person. I advised him that I was there to repair the burst cylinder from the Housing Executive. He said: 'OK son, go ahead. It's at the top of the stairs.' I pushed the door open as the male in the house went through a door on my

right into the living room and closed the door behind him. I relaxed as it appeared to be just another burst cylinder . . . all in a day's work. I turned left and walked to the bottom of the stairs. I became aware that the curtains were pulled on the circular window at the bottom of the stairs, and the hall, even though it was about 2.15 p.m. It was very dark.

The door into the downstairs bathroom was open. It was to the right of the hall at the bottom of the stairs. As I was taking all this in a male of stocky build emerged from the downstairs bathroom in front of me. I saw he was wearing a black balaclava mask and I could see his eyes and mouth perfectly. He had a pistol in a two-handed grip pointed at my chest literally inches away.

The initial shock to the system literally stopped me in my tracks as I stared at this frightening figure. My first thoughts were: 'Fuck, this is it!' He fired and hit me on the left side of the chest – just below the nipple, in the heart area – and the force of the shot was like being kicked by a horse. It lifted me off my feet and propelled me backwards and I fell on the ground, lying against the open front door. As I looked up at the gunman, he had stepped forward and levelled the pistol at my head. In those milliseconds, my life really did pass in front of me like a cinema screen in fast-forward: my wife, children, mum and dad – all the people who really mattered in my life flashed across my brain in a fraction of a second.

I ducked and rolled out of the open front door, and getting to my feet I ran past my parked van to get away from the gunman, who fired again. I could feel rounds going past my head, and had covered about ten to 15 yards when I was hit again in the left shoulder. The impact of the bullet spun me around and down.

As I was running, I was trying to get the zip down on

my boiler suit as I had a .22 Walther pistol tucked into a holster on my left side. I was now lying on my back on the ground, looking over my head back towards the door. Two PIRA terrorists ran from the door of the house towards me to finish me off. They looked to be running in slow motion and it was only later I discovered that because of the adrenaline pumping into my system, my brain was thinking so fast that everything in real-time looked to be in slow motion.

As I lay on the ground I was able to pull my pistol from its holster, but because of the gunshot wound to my shoulder I couldn't pull back the slide to cock it in the normal manner. I pushed the pistol onto my left hand, held the slide and pushed the pistol forward with the right hand – chambering a round – and as I did this I brought the pistol up and over my head and fired at the two men. I can still see them to this day, and by this time they were about halfway between me and the house. When I fired, both gunmen hit the deck and I rolled over onto my belly and went to fire again, but nothing happened. The pistol had jammed. I couldn't clear it as they were too close, so I jumped to my feet and ran around the side of the last two semi-detached houses at the end of the square. There was a five-foot-high chain-link fence at the rear of the garden and I jumped clean over the fence. I ran behind a filling station, over a wooden fence and across an open field for about 150 yards.

Glen dived through a thorn hedge, cleared his pistol and took stock. He could see men moving around near the filling station and pointing at the hedge. His boiler suit was covered in blood, and he was bleeding from his mouth: it later transpired that the impact of the shot against his body armour had damaged his left lung. He assumed that no local person would have reported the shooting to the police, and that the gunmen would have an opportunity to make a second attempt on his life. 'I had never been shot before and was alone and wounded in this Republican area with the nearest haven of safety the Unionist village of Coagh, five miles away.'

Behind the cover of hedgerows, Glen made his way to a bungalow about three hundred and fifty yards away. He slipped in through the unlocked back door and checked out each room, finding a large-scale map of the area pinned to the wall in one bedroom. 'Luckily for me, the bungalow had a telephone.' He dialled 999 and asked for the police. The operator initially assumed the call was a hoax, intended to draw officers into an ambush. 'I told the police operator my name and that I was a part-time lance corporal with G Company, 8 UDR, based in Cookstown. I also told them that my civilian job was a plumber for the Housing Executive and I had been shot and wounded twice and needed help and medical attention.'[5]

Another who survived a close-quarter assassination attempt was Brian McKee, the former soldier turned RUC constable. Brian was the owner of the red 1750 Allegro whose registration number had been noted by Harry early in 1978 as he waited at the bus stop near the local police barracks. 'We knew the driver was a peeler,' says Harry, using the slang term for a police officer. 'We decided to do an operation.'

Brian was one of the many policemen who lived in Lisburn and viewed it as a safe place. 'Lisburn was a garrison town,' he says.

One morning, running early on his drive from Lisburn to west Belfast, Brian decided that instead of calling in to one of the army bases where he regularly liaised with units on tour in the area, he would drive into the police barracks at Andersonstown to see if there was any post waiting for him. 'I decided this on the spur of the moment: it wasn't a planned thing, it was a last-minute thing. It was a normal day.'

At the same time, Harry and another member of his ASU were requisitioning a black taxi, which they drove to the top of the Falls Road. Harry went to the rear of a petrol station where he had hidden some traffic cones that he had taken the night before from roadworks on the Glen Road, one of the area's main thoroughfares. The two men then laid the cones out on the Falls Road, to force traffic entering the city into a single file.

Brian turned off the M1 motorway and drove north up Kennedy Way, his 9mm Walther PPK pistol tucked under his thigh as always. 'Not that it would have been much use inside the car. If you'd fired it inside the vehicle, the rounds would probably have bounced back off the windscreen.' As he turned right onto the Falls Road, Harry and the second gunman were waiting, each with handguns: Harry was clutching a .38 revolver.

'The road was quiet,' Brian recalls. 'Unusually quiet: there was very little traffic on the road, and that's usually a very busy thoroughfare to Belfast.' As he approached the Lake Glen, a hotel on the left side of the road, he could see that roadworks appeared to be under way.

> There were all these cones laid out, but there was none of the usual paraphernalia of roadworks, diggers and machinery and things like that. And it just didn't ring true. So rather than follow the cones, which would have taken me to the inside lane, I took to the wrong side of the road.
>
> As I came level with the Lake Glen Hotel there were two black taxis parked. If I had taken the route the cones were directing me, the black taxis would have been blocking my path. One guy, a man in his fifties, he walked out across the road in front of me – I don't know whether he was part of the gang or not – and he put his hands up, like shouted: 'Oh Christ, it's a car.' That made me slow down. As I slowed down two guys stepped out

from between the black taxis. They were both armed. Neither of them was masked. One was very distinctive, a man with tight curly hair. The other guy I recognised, but at the time I couldn't put a name to him. They were about 25 feet away. If I had taken the road they wanted it would have been absolutely close range.[6]

Harry took aim at Brian's head.

I thought: 'They're shooting at me!' The car was hit several times. Most of the shots came through the passenger door, and I felt something hit my ear. I don't know how to describe it, but survival just kicks in. I knocked it down a couple of gears, put my foot down, and just kept down. The police station was only, what, 400 yards away? It was a place of safety, and I had to get there.

Brian screeched into the barrack entrance, around two obstacles, and blasted his horn, wanting his colleagues to immediately open the gates. They had heard the shooting, of course, but were in no hurry to open up, wanting to be sure that this was not a trap.

Once inside, Brian was examined. A piece of shrapnel was found to have hit him in his left ear. 'It was just a small wound, and I had the piece of metal taken out.' Rounds had hit the windscreen and radiator grille as well as the passenger door.

Brian joined the investigation into the attempt on his life, and worked for the rest of the day. 'It was terrifying, but not to the extent that I wanted to run away. I don't know whether it was bravado, but I just wanted to follow it up: just follow it through and get these buggers. I was working until about half twelve that night.'

The attempted assassination made just four paragraphs in that afternoon's *Belfast Telegraph*, tagged on the end of a report about the fatal shooting of a postman who had served as a part-time soldier in the UDR: this man had been ambushed in a country lane in County Tyrone while delivering mail in his van.

Brian arranged to have his car towed back to Lisburn and parked in the garage at the side of his house. He had done nothing to prepare his wife for the shock of seeing the bullet-riddled vehicle. 'I'd never thought of ringing her: there were no mobile phones in those days. The car was full of holes. My wife had heard about the shooting on the news, and then when I arrived home about one o'clock in the morning, and she saw the car, she put two and two together. She was hysterical.'

It was a further day or two before the impact of what had happened hit him. 'The shock did set in, and you're actually useless, your mind disappears, your sense of logic goes. So, you're better off getting out of the way. I think it was about three or four days I was off duty, just until I settled down.'

On his return to duty, Brian's superiors told him that he was being removed from army liaison duties and posted to a different area. He was bitterly disappointed.

> I didn't fancy anywhere else. I didn't want to go to down-town Belfast. I certainly didn't want to go up around Derry. I was quite happy with Andersonstown. It was a bad area, from our point of view. I now assume it had been so quiet as I drove down the road because people had been told to stay off the streets. But at least you knew where you stood. Every time you went out of the door of the station, you knew what you were up against. But I was told: 'Pick a station because you're being moved.' They offered me Portadown and I took it. I was resentful, but it was one of those things you put behind you.

Brian's superiors took an even harder line over the repair of his Austin Allegro. Although he was expected to use his own vehicle while on duty, an examination showed that his car tax had expired the day before the shooting. Since it was being driven unlawfully at the time of the attack, the RUC refused to pay for the repair. As well as the holes in the windscreen and the passenger door, one of the rounds had gouged a two-and-a-half foot-long track across the roof. 'I had to put vinyl over the roof to cover it up. It cost me more than £1,000 to have it patched up. That was a lot of money in those days.'[7]

While Harry and the second volunteer opened fire on Brian McKee, a young man who would soon join Harry's ASU was looking on. John Garrett Smyth, or Gary as he was known to his friends, was sitting with a group of his workmates inside the Lake Glen Hotel, having a morning coffee.

He was sitting by the front window and had a perfect view of the ambush. He had seen the traffic cones being put in place, watched the shooting and caught sight of the gunmen. He watched as the red Allegro sped away. 'A small woman got out of a car,' Gary recalled years later, 'and walked up to one of the [gun] men and started hitting him with her umbrella.'

Gary and his mates appear to have been largely unfazed by the scene taking place outside the hotel. In almost any other place, the ambush would have been a terrible and frightening event – and extremely rare. But this was Andersonstown in 1978. They finished their coffees, stubbed out their cigarettes, paid up, and left.

Gary had been born in July 1959 at Belfast Maternity Hospital and had grown up in Andersonstown, in a street of solidly built pre-war semis with well-tended lawns. In the distance, Gary's family and their neighbours could see Divis mountain, from which British soldiers, ensconced in their hilltop sangar, a structure festooned with aerials and dishes, looked down upon them, every day and every night.

Gary's father, Pat, was a bar manager, and he and his wife,

Mary, had three other children, a girl and two boys. Gary was the youngest. None of the others became involved in the Republican movement. One of his brothers had moved to England in search of work, and settled. The other had joined the Royal Fleet Auxiliary, the civilian-manned Ministry of Defence fleet that provides logistical and operation support to the Royal Navy. He served in the Falklands War.

There was no Republican tradition in Gary's family. On the contrary, he felt that some of his older relatives were overly fearful of Unionists; that they were too deferential by half. 'My parents would have been Republicans, but quiet Republicans. People of that generation, people who grew up in the thirties and forties, were very, very subdued.'

There was, Gary concluded early in life, 'a fear of the Unionist state'; it had been passed down through successive generations of many families. Gary's grandfather had – like other Catholic men – been driven out of the Harland & Wolff shipyards during the violence that had engulfed the north around the time of the killing of Oswald Swanzy in 1920.

He recalls with bitterness that one of his relatives was hired as a servant by William Lowry – who would later become the Attorney General of Northern Ireland – after she answered a newspaper advert that made clear that the post was open only to 'Christians'. The extraordinary, if unstated, message was well understood at that time: Catholics need not apply. When the young woman was discovered to have concealed her faith on her application for the job – to have made, according to the logic of the advert, a fraudulent application – Lowry is said to have shouted, in the recollection of Gary's family: 'Maria, I said that only Christians need apply. Go and get your coat.'

Gary believed it was not merely a historical problem. Now, in the late 1970s, when Gary was an apprentice plumber, he was angry about the continuing discrimination and the dispropor- tionately high levels of unemployment among Catholics in the north of Ireland. Great progress may have been made in Northern Ireland by the late 1970s – particularly in the allocation of social housing – but Gary felt that Catholics were still being systematically oppressed, in much the same way that black Americans had been in the southern states, less than a generation earlier.

> How was our situation different from that of black people in Alabama? If you were black, you couldn't get a job, you could register to vote but you couldn't vote. We were the blacks of our time and place. There's no other way I can describe it. It was perfectly legal to say you can't have a job, the [Catholic] schools weren't as good, we weren't given the equality in terms of housing, in representation, we weren't in government . . .

Gary's view was reinforced by the racist attitudes he perceived in the Fleet Street newspapers of the 1970s, particularly in the cartoons in the popular press. 'It was a kind of everyday racism. These cartoons that the *Sun* used to publish, showing Irish people as looking like gorillas. All the begorrah and the begosh – suggesting that we actually used to use that kind of language. They treated us as thick Micks.'

In Gary's opinion, there was nothing inevitable about the Troubles. Had most Unionists wished to coexist with their Catholic neighbours, on equal terms, and recognised and ended the injustice of discrimination, there would have been no need to resort to violence.

> My brothers probably would never have had to go away to sea, because they would have been able to get jobs here, and my father would have had his own bar, because he was a bloody hard worker. But he was never given a chance. We were never given chances.
>
> The only difference is that the black people in the

southern states of America didn't turn to violence the way that we did. But they didn't face the opposition from central government that we did: the federal government of the United States at least intervened, they stepped in to sort it out, whereas the British government sent 35,000 armed troops to support what was taking place.

So they came here, the army operated in a civilian setting, and they fired their plastic rounds, and their live rounds, and everything they did was excused, because it was 'exceptional'. But we weren't allowed to respond in a way that was 'exceptional'?

The British army came here for one reason only, and that was to maintain the union, to maintain the status quo. They got here just in time. If they hadn't come here there would have been a bloodbath. But here, the British government effectively decided to enforce the Jim Crow laws.

Like Phelim, who was a year older, Gary recalls clearly the fear that the Loyalist gang known as the Shankill Butchers struck in the hearts of Belfast's Catholics. Unlike Phelim, when he was a teenager, Gary felt that he was as much British as Irish, and this, he believes, points to one of the fatal flaws in the British state's approach to its counter-insurgency operations in the north of Ireland: the people they were fighting were not Kenyan, or Cypriots or Adenis. They were British citizens.

They never quite realised that they couldn't fight this war the same way as they had elsewhere around their empire, and not because we were Irish, but because in law we were full British citizens. We weren't going to put up with the things they had done elsewhere.

You have to bear in mind that we didn't just wake up one day as bad people, and decide that we were going to start murdering people, and travel over to England and blow places up. We weren't all bad people. And we didn't decide to go to war: the war came to us. We were just the generation that wasn't going to take it any more.

When he was a teenager, maybe fourteen, no older than fifteen, Gary was asked if he would like to join the Fianna. He leapt at the chance: it would mean he was only one step away from joining the IRA.

For a secret organisation, the Fianna was a curiously public affair. In the late 1970s, at Catholic schools in Belfast and Derry, most pupils knew – or at least had a shrewd idea – who was a member. So did some teachers and parents. And so too, no doubt, did some detectives of the RUC Special Branch.

It was, Gary recalls, 'a bit like the Boy Scouts'. The boys were organised by age – juniors up to fourteen, seniors aged fourteen to seventeen. At that time the Fianna's organisation was still based upon the British army's structure of battalions and companies. Gary started in the juniors. 'It would be mainly gathering information, hiding stuff, being the eyes and ears. Petrol bombing the army, that sort of thing.'

When Gary turned eighteen, he was asked by someone within the organisation whether he would be prepared to move from the Fianna to join the IRA. He was honoured. 'One day I was invited over,' he recalls. 'He just asked me, well, would you? It was a natural progression to move over from the Fianna to the Army, but it didn't always happen. I was tremendously proud. I was joining this tradition, this protective grouping, this force that was all around you. It was tremendously prestigious, being asked to join the IRA.'

In places like Andersonstown, there was always stronger backing for the IRA than either the Unionists or the British army would acknowledge. 'There was great support at this time — there was also fear of the IRA, and this should be acknowledged — but there was a tremendous level of support.'

Gary had some doubts, but it was a decision he had to make alone.

> Yes, sure, of course I had reservations. But who could I talk to? I couldn't ask my mother for advice. You can't ask your friends: 'Should I, or shouldn't I, join the IRA?' But once you've put yourself in a position where you are going to be asked, you must have let your sympathies be known. You must have made it clear that the answer may well be yes.[8]

If he'd said no, One Batt would have had no difficulty recruiting another volunteer. But Gary said yes.

There appears to have been no trace of Gary on the security force's files when he joined the IRA. He had been granted a shotgun licence, served as a St John Ambulance volunteer, and had clearance to enter government buildings and even military compounds to work as a plumber.

He was assigned to his first ASU in early 1978. As a consequence of the previous year's Staff Report reorganisation, he was informed that he would be expected to be involved in operations across a wide area. 'The ASUs covered the whole One Batt area — Lenadoon, Andersonstown, Twinbrook, Dunmurry — even Lisburn. There would be four or five members, sometimes six, with people coming and going.'

On 16 March, members of Gary's ASU attempted a sniping attack on an army patrol in Andersonstown. The previous evening, two men, one of them an auxiliary, had concealed two loaded firearms behind a three-storey block of flats overlooking the Glen Road. One of the weapons was an American ArmaLite assault rifle with a full magazine; the other was a Soviet-made Simonov, with nine rounds in its magazine.[9]

When the ASU returned and attempted to fire the weapons, they discovered that both had been tampered with: it appeared to them that the live ammunition had been switched for dummy rounds. The volunteers hid the weapons inside one of the flats, but as they started to make their escape, they encountered a number of British soldiers in plain clothes. Shots were exchanged, and the two members of the ASU and one of the soldiers were wounded.[10]

Within seconds, the area was flooded with uniformed troops, officers and men of the 3rd Battalion, Parachute Regiment, who had been posted the previous month to Fort Monagh Barracks and other bases in the area. The two members of the ASU were arrested, and soldiers recovered the two weapons from the flats, where they had been hidden in a bedroom.[11]

With two members of his ASU in hospital and facing imprisonment – and the unit effectively defunct – Gary was moved to another One Batt ASU: the one to which Harry also belonged. Another member of this ASU was Anne Laverty, who had volunteered a short time before Gary's own recruitment. Anne was aged twenty-one, the youngest child in a large family. She lived with her widowed mother and an elder brother in a terrace house on the Twinbrook estate, just across the park from Bobby Sands and Phelim Hamill.

When Anne volunteered to join the IRA early in 1978, she was asked to think carefully about her decision. In line with the Staff Report recommendation, she was not enrolled into the Women's Council, Cumann na mBan, but was placed in an ASU. In the spring of 1978, she was working at Strathearn Audio, the factory whose debts had been written off by the British government the previous year.

Gary hadn't seen Anne before, but he instantly recognised Harry as one of the two men who had ambushed the driver of the red Allegro outside the Lake Glen Hotel. He told Harry that he had witnessed that operation. Harry tore a strip off him: 'I told him that no IRA volunteer ever spoke like that – I told him that he should never again mention anything that he saw or heard that might damage army security or cause problems for another volunteer.'

Gary came to greatly admire Harry as a Protestant who had joined the Republican movement:

> Other Protestants joined, but always because they had been living in a Nationalist area, and they were maybe married to a Catholic, and stayed where they were when other Protestant families moved away. Harry was completely different. Harry crossed over the divide, he moved to a Nationalist area, and he then joined the IRA: that's a big thing to have done.

Despite the incident on the Glen Road, Gary concluded that there were fewer casualties among One Batt volunteers than there were at Two Batt in the Lower Falls. 'There were more open spaces and fewer gun battles. And Two Batt used to do more of the bombings. And perhaps One Batt was better managed.'

Easter fell early in 1978. As usual, the Provisionals arranged marches to commemorate the 1916 Rising. Provo supporters wound their way around the Glen Road, Andersonstown Road and the Falls, following banners depicting Brian Boru, the tenth-century Irish king; Hugh O'Neill, the seventeenth-century leader of the rebellion against the English invasion; and Theobald Wolfe Tone, the Protestant leader of the eighteenth-century insurrection by the United Irishmen. They paraded past graffiti, plastered on any available wall, reading '7 years is enough 700 IS TOO MUCH!', 'para bastards', and 'brits out peace in'. A number of marchers had brought along their Irish wolfhounds, and draped them in green.

Surreptitiously, the army photographed the marchers, trying

to capture as many faces as possible. One of the photographers was hidden in a covert observation point on the Glen Road, while a second was flying high overhead in a Puma helicopter, using a camera with a 48-inch lens attached to the side of the open door: a device the army nicknamed 'Super Snoopy'.

The endless security-force surveillance kept some of the volunteers on edge. The ASUs were sometimes moving weapons from one location to another several times in a day. That month, 3 Para's companies competed with each other to locate and seize IRA weapons. A soldier from B Company found 1,500 rounds of ammunition and a telescopic sight in a well-constructed hide behind the bottom stair of a house he was searching, for example, while C Company recovered two rifles and a quantity of ammunition. These finds were considered to be good for the soldiers' morale. Some of the soldiers reported that while they were on patrol, members of the public had smiled at them, and one or two had actually exchanged a few words.

Most people were hostile, however, and on Twinbrook there were complaints of homes being ransacked during searches, youths being beaten up by Paras and teenage girls being molested. A local priest complained that he had woken to find a couple of Paras in his bedroom, an incident that some officers of the battalion regarded as highly amusing.[12]

With an unknown number of informers working for the police and the army, and with men and women being broken at Castlereagh and the other holding centres – and with the British military enjoying hugely superior technical surveillance capacity – it was inevitable that some volunteers would be prone to paranoia and suspect their fellow volunteers. Anyone living in a Nationalist area who fell under suspicion of being an informer – a loathed *tout* – was in a very perilous place indeed. They could expect to be interrogated, possibly tortured, and, if found guilty, they could expect that they would be found trussed and hooded beside a road near the border, with a bullet or two in their brain.

Or they could simply vanish, like Brendan Megraw.

On 8 April that year, a Saturday, Brendan's wife, Marie, was at home in her flat on the Twinbrook estate. Marie was waiting for her husband to return from shopping with his mother. Marie and Brendan were both aged twenty-three and she was pregnant with their first child. After a period of unemployment, Brendan had just found work in the British merchant navy. 'Things were looking good,' Brendan's brother Kieran says, 'amid all the badness that was going on, things were looking up.'

Marie heard a knock at the front door, and on opening it was confronted by a man with a stocking mask over his head and transparent rubber gloves on his hands. He brushed past her and into the flat. Eight other men, dressed the same way, followed.

The men searched the flat for Brendan and, finding he was not at home, told Marie to sit on her settee. One of them said: 'We're going to give you an injection.' She explained that she was pregnant, and was told that it would not harm her baby, it would calm her down.

> Two of the men held me down, and he stuck it in my arm. After a couple of minutes or so I felt drowsy. One of them came in with a photograph album that had been in the broom cupboard. They had two photographs of Brendan and me. 'Who's that fellow?' they asked me. But when I told them it was my husband, they told me it wasn't.

When Brendan returned home, he was brought in to see Marie. 'They hadn't hit him and there still wasn't any sign of any guns.' Marie heard Brendan agree to go with the men, saying: 'I've nothing to hide.' Marie was told not to alert anyone, as her husband would soon be home.

Brendan did not come home. Marie spoke to her mother-in-law, the doctor was called, and the police alerted. 'It's a big mystery to me,' Marie told a BBC reporter later that week. 'Brendan never does anything. All he's interested in is motorbikes and cars. And clothes. He's loves his clothes. It baffles me. They've got the wrong person.'

Through intermediaries, Brendan's mother asked for information from the IRA. She was told that the IRA knew nothing whatsoever about Brendan's disappearance.[13] All of west Belfast knew that to be untrue. Rumours spread: some said Brendan had been targeted because he had provided information to the police about an incident in which a well-known west Belfast Republican had been shot dead, apparently during an exchange of gunfire between the IRA and the army. Others wondered if there was a connection with the strange incident on the Glen Road when two IRA weapons had been tampered with.

Such disappearances were devastating for the family and friends of those who vanished, but they also served as a reminder that the IRA was capable of complete ruthlessness in dealing with members of the Nationalist community thought to have threatened its interests. They also reinforced the message to volunteers such as members of Harry's ASU that whatever they say, they should say nothing.

The following week started much like any other across One Batt's area of responsibility. It seems that late on the Monday evening, a girl aged around sixteen called at Michael Culbert's home. Michael is said to have answered the door, and been handed a piece of paper sealed with Sellotape, and a magazine. The magazine was a copy of the *Pigeon Racing News and Gazette*, dating from January 1971. It was open at page twenty-two, which carried a racing report from Northern Ireland. The author's black-and-white photograph appeared at the top left of the page – a handsome, earnest-looking man, wearing a shirt and tie and staring calmly into the camera – and next to it was his byline: 'The Copper'.

Michael opened the sealed note. It is said to have instructed him to inform a number of people that they should 'go on standby', and to await further instructions later in the week. It contained the name of the man in the magazine's byline picture, who was described as a Special Branch officer. It also contained the man's address. This was to be a close-quarter assassination. Michael is alleged to have burned the note and put the magazine to one side.

That night, Michael met Harry, handed him the magazine, and told him to be on standby.[14] The targeting of a policeman in Lisburn was intended to send a clear message to the security forces: that the IRA could strike wherever it pleased. Nowhere, not even the Citadel, was safe. But there was that other, more symbolic rationale behind the attack. Leading members of the IRA in west Belfast knew that their secret army had not killed a policeman in Lisburn since District Inspector Oswald Swanzy had been gunned down in the doorway of a bank almost six decades earlier. They knew this and, perhaps, were feeling a little ashamed of their inaction. They knew too that if they were successful they would be following in the footsteps of a squad operating under the authority of the legendary Michael Collins. 'It had historical resonance,' as Michael Culbert would say.[15]

That week continued as normal on One Batt's patch – or what passed for normal, after almost a decade of conflict. On the Wednesday morning, a patrol from 3 Para's A Company discovered twenty-seven rounds of ammunition in a ditch near the Twinbrook estate, concealed behind a drainpipe. That afternoon two armed men held up a security van delivering cash to a branch of the Allied Irish Bank on Andersonstown Road. Later that night the teenage girl is alleged to have called at

Michael's home once more, and said that an ASU should be ready for an operation the following Saturday. On the Thursday, an army patrol on Twinbrook fired a shot at a youth thought to be carrying a weapon; when the boy was apprehended, the weapon was found to have been a stick.

Elsewhere in the north of Ireland, the vicious war was grinding on at a glacial pace. A policewoman was wounded in a gun attack on an RUC station north of Belfast; on the border, in County Tyrone, soldiers discovered several milk churns packed with explosives: the command line stretched across the border into the Republic.

At Friday lunchtime, Harry approached Gary at the Suffolk Inn on the outskirts of Andersonstown, and asked him to call at his home later that afternoon. Gary came at 5.30 p.m., and Harry told him that they were to meet in Lenadoon Avenue at 11 a.m. the next day. It appears that he also gave Gary instructions as to what he would be doing after they met.

About two hours later, a man called at Anne Laverty's home. After she let the man in, he gave her a hand-drawn map and instructions. The man explained that she was to travel to Lisburn the following day and wait at the junction of Moira Road and Ballinderry Road from 12.30. The place was marked on the map. A car would pull over, and she would be handed a package. She was to take it to a house that was also marked on the map, a house with blue curtains and a TV aerial over the front door. She would hand the package to the man who would answer the door. She would return to Twinbrook on a bus to await further instructions.

Elsewhere that evening, the province was fairly quiet. In beautiful Murlough, at the foot of the Mourne Mountains in County Down, a sniper fired nine low-velocity shots at a passing police car. They missed. A few hours later, in the Markets district just south of Belfast city centre, a group of youths hurled stones at police Land Rovers. One stone cracked a windscreen.[16]

There were diversions, entertainment; there was culture. At Whitla Hall at the Queen's Film Theatre, the Northern Ireland Opera Trust would be spending Saturday preparing for that evening's performance of *La Traviata*, while at the Arts Theatre, the cast was rehearsing Noël Coward's *Blithe Spirit*. The New Vic cinema was showing *Close Encounters of the Third Kind*, while at the Queen's you could see *New York, New York*. For those hoping for a slightly more torrid viewing experience, the crumbling Avenue cinema on Royal Avenue was screening a film entitled *Yellow Emmanuelle*: 'All Week, doors open at 1.45 – Adults Only!'

That evening, the Eurovision Song Contest would be shown live from Paris on BBC1, and then there was *Match of the Day*: a draw at Coventry that afternoon would be enough to clinch a first-ever League Championship for Nottingham Forest, the season after winning promotion from the Second Division.

At Ballycastle, on the north-east coast of the island, an organisation called the Northern Ireland Mixed Marriage Association, established four years earlier to support couples in inter-Church marriages, was holding its annual conference: delegates decided to extend its advice and information service, and also voted to welcome the changing attitudes of the Catholic Church.

In Andersonstown, meanwhile, a Private Bell from B Company of 3 Para shot himself in the foot while climbing over a fence during an attempt to halt and search a car. And in Ballymurphy a young man armed with a revolver relieved a bus driver of his takings and his wallet.

The usual mayhem. But not too much. And so far that weekend, nobody had been killed.

But it was all coming together: the bitter history; the reorganisation of the secret army and its new strategy to strike up close, avoiding unintended casualties; but above all, the determination to kill a member of the security forces in Lisburn and the opportunity to do so.

★

A few minutes past eight on the morning of Saturday 22 April 1978, Millar McAllister said goodbye to Nita, left their bungalow, climbed into his small blue hatchback and drove to Belfast. It had been a chilly month so far, heavy with rain, but this Saturday was shaping up into a clear day and the sun was making a weak effort to shine. Millar had just a few hours' work to complete before returning to his weekend.

And today, as he drove to start his early shift at Knock, he was excited: it was the first day of the racing season.

Around three hours after Millar left home, Gary slipped away from work and went to meet Harry, who was waiting near his home in Lenadoon. Harry had possession of two handguns: a .45 automatic pistol, and a .455 revolver with black tape wound around the handle. During the week, one or two visitors to Harry's home had watched him sitting in an armchair, cleaning the revolver. He had decided that the revolver would be the weapon he would use. 'I knew it would be less likely to jam when I came to fire it.' He handed the automatic to Gary. 'I told him not to shoot anyone, just to show it.'

Slipping the weapon into the pocket of his anorak, Gary walked back down Lenadoon Avenue and turned left along Stewartstown Road. He had been instructed to wait outside a nearby shop until joined by another teenager whose description he had been given the night before. Together they were under orders to acquire a car for that day's operation – 'any car will do' – along with the owner's driving licence. They should check the vehicle carefully for any defects before leaving the keys in a hallway at the entrance to Rice's, the bookmaker's on the Andersonstown Road.

Gary soon saw the other youth. He was as described: tall, thin, sandy-haired. After the briefest of greetings, they made their way to the Andersonstown Road. Standing across the street from Rice's, they watched as a number of cars pulled up and the drivers clambered out, locked up, and climbed the stairway on the left of the building, entering the first-floor bookmaker's to place a bet. The young volunteers didn't fancy any of the cars so far: each, in its own way, was far too dilapidated.

Then a yellow Fiat 127 with Belfast number plates pulled up. Despite a rusty roof rack, it looked reliable enough. Gary and the other youth watched as the owner fitted a steering lock to the wheel, locked the door, and walked up the stairs. 'Right,' said Gary, 'let's go.' To his surprise, the other youth said he needed to go and do something – 'Just wait a minute,' he said, over his shoulder, and walked off down Andersonstown Road. Gary waited, his heart beginning to pound. After a few moments the youth returned with a newspaper. Instead of walking across the road to Rice's, however, he opened the newspaper and began to read. 'What are you doing?' Gary demanded, pulling on a pair of white gloves. 'Let's get on with it!'

They crossed the road and walked up the stairs. The door opened and the Fiat's owner walked out, squeezing past them on his way down. 'Hey, mate,' said Gary. 'Provisional IRA. We want the lend of your car. Give me the keys.' The driver turned, looked at the two young men, and immediately handed over his car keys.

Gary asked the man which one was the ignition key, and he showed him. He then asked for the man's name, address and occupation, and asked if he had his licence with him. The man gave his name and address, told Gary that he was a civil servant, and said that he did not have a licence with him.

Gary took the keys while the other youth escorted the civil servant back into Rice's. Gary returned to the Fiat, but found that he could not open the door. After dashing up the stairs for a brief conversation with the owner, he went back down, opened the car door and then left the keys in the hallway, where they could be picked up by another person, as arranged. Gary asked the other youth to go to see if the Whitefort, a pub a few doors away, was open for business. By now, the civil servant, who had been looking apprehensive, appeared terrified, although he had not been threatened, and Gary had not produced the .45 automatic. 'Don't be nervous, mate,' Gary said. 'You'll be OK. You'll have your car back in an hour.'

The youth returned to report that the bar was open. 'Right,' said Gary, 'come down the 'Fort for a drink.'

The civil servant explained that he did not want to have a drink. 'But I quickly understood that I was going for a drink and walked towards the Whitefort Inn. These two men followed behind. There were quite a few pedestrians about and I didn't see them hand the keys to anyone.'

Inside the 'Fort they took a seat beneath an archway, just inside the door, with the car owner sitting between the two youths. The sandy-haired teenager asked what he would like to drink. 'A beer please.' The youth went to the bar and returned with three beers. The civil servant took in Gary. He noticed his brown-faced watch with a gold-coloured bracelet strap. 'He had shoulder-length, unkempt dark hair, one day's growth of beard, about 5 foot 11 inches tall, well built – good shoulders – well educated and definitely not labourer's hands.'

Gary explained to the civil servant what he should say if he was brought in for questioning by the police. He should say that after his car was hijacked, he had been ordered into the back of a white van and a hood placed over his head; that he was ordered to lie down and a coat thrown over him. He should say that after being driven around for a few minutes, the car did a sharp right turn, and that he was brought out and taken into a house – 'tell 'em you saw a bit of carpet under the hood' – and that after a while he was put back into the van, driven around, then set free.

Gary bought three more beers, and the men sat and chatted about the books they were reading, and about world politics. At one o'clock the Downtown Radio news came on the transistor behind the bar. Gary instructed the civil servant not to pay any attention, and not to listen to any news before he collected his car. The two young men then stood up and instructed him to remain in his seat for five minutes. He could then go and collect his car from the car park of the Crazy Prices store in Lisburn. The keys would be either up the exhaust or in the ignition.

Gary went home and hid the gun under some old carpet on a shelf at the back of his garage. Two hours later a teenage girl called at his home to take it away.[17]

At around the time Gary was meeting Harry that morning, Anne was saying goodbye to her mother at their home on the Twinbrook estate. She stepped out and pulled the front door shut behind her. Anne must have been anxious. She had, perhaps, slept poorly, wondering about this package that she was to collect. It was clearly a gun. What would it have been used for? A robbery? A hijacking? An attack on Crown Forces? There were a number of scenarios that kept pressing themselves upon her.

She walked over to the Stewartstown Road, where she caught a bus to Lisburn. The journey flew by and she was in the town centre by 11.30 a.m. 'I just dandered around for a while, and walked around Crazy Prices.' She looked for a pipe, a birthday present for her brother, and bought a pack of 200 Player's No. 6 King Size cigarettes. Furtively, praying that nobody would notice, she unfolded the map that she had been given the night before. Following its directions, she walked down Chapel Hill and turned onto Longstone Road. She stopped to watch a funeral, and then saw the aftermath of a road accident: two elderly women had been struck by a car. She may well have been thankful for any distraction, even in the form of a funeral and an accident. Then she steeled herself for her task.

Arriving at the junction of Moira Road and Ballinderry Road, Anne could see how busy it was: the traffic never appeared to let up. She felt awkward; she was certain that the people driving past were staring at her, eyeing her up and down, wondering what she was playing at. So she ventured a little way up Ballinderry Road, and waited outside St Patrick's School. 'I waited for a right wee while . . .'[18]

Meanwhile, Harry had handed the automatic to Gary and gone home to dress for the occasion, choosing a blue pin-stripe suit, white shirt with a blue check, no tie. His shoulder-length hair had been carefully combed and brushed back. He wanted to look respectable: beyond reproach; above suspicion. He looked a little out of place on the bus, of course: people didn't usually wear pin-stripe suits on the Lisburn bus, not on a Saturday morning. Well, not at any time, really. Harry hoped that nobody was looking at him too closely; that they were not taking in too many details.

On the right, the fields where the new Poleglass estate was to be built rolled by. The bus picked up a couple more passengers in Dunmurry. Harry put his hand inside the string bag, and touched the old blue scarf that was wrapped around the revolver. He felt the handle, wrapped around with black tape. Sure, he'd taken the better gun, but Gary had been ordered not to shoot anyone in any case. He was just to show it, if he really needed to. *Besides*, Harry thought, *this is all about what I'm going to do: this is my op.*

Harry rang the bell and got off the bus near Christ Church Cathedral. As he made his way along Market Square, towards the car park where he was to meet his driver, he walked past the doorway where Oswald Swanzy had been shot dead. Not that Harry was conscious that he was following the beaten path of Ireland's violent political history: he was concentrating on remaining calm. He was nervous. Excited, too, but definitely jittery. It was natural, he told himself. He had never killed a man before. Although Lord knows he'd tried.

A yellow car pulled into the car park, a Fiat 127 with a rusty black roof rack. It had a Belfast number plate: JOI 5595. At the wheel was the person who had picked it up from Rice's. Harry climbed in. 'Ready?' asked the driver. 'Ready.' They set off, heading south. The driver knew where to go, having recced the location. They drove slowly along the A1, past the hospital, and turned right into Woodland Park. It was a quiet street, an *upright* street: a place of semis, bungalows, well-kept gardens, washed-and-polished family saloons. Harry took it all in, hyperaware.

The driver slowed down as they approached number 106, a small whitewashed bungalow on the right-hand side of the road. The car mounted the kerb on the opposite side of the road and came to a halt with the two left-hand wheels on the pavement. The driver yanked on the handbrake, but kept the engine running.

Harry had already made clear to the driver that he was going to go alone: this man would never open the door to two visitors. As he climbed out of the Fiat he pushed the revolver into his waistband at the back of his trousers and crossed the road. To his left, a couple of hundred yards away, he could see a young woman and two teenage girls walking in his direction. He was breathing fast now and his heart was thumping: he could hear his pulse in his ears. The venetian blinds at the front of number 106 were drawn. To the right of the house, at the end of the drive, a small blue car was parked. Someone was at home. Harry walked quickly up the drive and along the side of the bungalow.[19]

Millar had arrived home after a few hours' work at headquarters. He had said goodbye to his colleagues, made his way back to his car, and set off for Lisburn. He called on a neighbour, and then went home to look after the boys while Nita went to work: she was a nursing domestic at a home a few minutes' walk away. Mark was by now aged eleven, and Alan was just a month short of his eighth birthday. Mark was able to look after himself.

Charlie Chaplin was on BBC1, while Ulster TV was showing *Sesame Street*; Alan hovered around his father, however, watching the things he did. Millar made a sandwich for his lunch and drank some tea. He placed the plate and empty mug in a plastic bowl in the kitchen sink. Then he turned to his left. Through the patterned glass of the back door, he saw a figure moving in his back garden.

Thinking that on the first day of the racing season Millar would probably be tending his beloved pigeons, Harry had walked down the side of the bungalow, looking for the pigeon loft. There was no sign of it. Behind him, he heard a noise. The back door had opened a little, and he could see a man in a brown V-neck sweater and brown leather jacket peering at him. Harry could see immediately that it was Millar, looking exactly as he did in his byline picture in *Pigeon Racing News and Gazette*: the same dark hair, the same slightly sombre expression.

'Are you Mr McAllister?' asked Harry.

'I am.'

'My father sent me up.'

'Who's your father?'

'Mr Lavery of Duncairn Pigeon Club.' He made that one up on the spur of the moment.

The two men stared at each other. *Now*, thought Harry. *Now!*

A small boy appeared at Millar's side and looked up at Harry. The boy stood there, staring at him through the few inches of opened door, not saying a word.

'I'm here about photographs,' said Harry.

'What sort of photographs?'

'Of birds.'

'What birds?'

'Pigeons, of course.'

Both men laughed. Harry put his hands on his hips, pulling his jacket back a little so that Millar could see that there was nothing tucked into the front or sides of his waistband. He looked ever so smart in his pin-stripe suit.

'If you phone my father, he'll give you the details.'

Millar opened the door a little more and stepped into the back garden. So did the boy, staying close to his father.

Will I do it now? thought Harry. *Will I shoot him now, with his boy watching?*

'Why don't you ask your boy to fetch a pencil and paper, so I can write down my father's telephone number?' The boy disappeared into the house.

Harry pulled the gun out and took aim. He looked at Millar's face.

Millar didn't look frightened. He just looked a little disappointed. Irritated, even. Harry could see that he didn't like being tricked.

'Aah,' said Millar, quietly.

Harry held the revolver in both hands and pointed it at Millar's lower chest. Then he squeezed the trigger, felt the recoil, and watched, mesmerised, as a hole appeared in Millar's brown sweater. Millar appeared to fly backwards in slow motion. As he tumbled half in, half out of the kitchen, Harry fired again, aiming at his head. He leaned into the kitchen and fired another shot into Millar's chest. Years later, Harry would say that he was trying to make the sign of the cross, attempting to shoot Millar in his forehead, sternum, the left side of his chest and then his right. 'We used to try to bless 'em,' he claimed, despite his Protestant background. Then he leaned in still closer, the barrel of the revolver almost touching Millar's sweater, and pulled the trigger a fourth time. The sound of the shot thundered around the tiled kitchen with an ear-numbing crash; cordite began to drift across the room.

Harry looked up. There, just inside the kitchen door, stood the little boy, his face frozen in a blind, confused horror. For a moment, man and boy stared at each other. Alan opened his mouth. 'Daddy!' he screamed. And then he screamed again. 'Mummy!'

Harry turned and fled.[20]

Mark raced into the kitchen, where he saw Alan standing, and his father lying on the floor, his feet poking out of the back door. He ran back to the telephone by the front door, dialled 999 and shouted that his father needed an ambulance; please, he begged, come quickly. The call was put through to the Ambulance Control switchboard at the Lagan Valley Hospital. 'At 12.52 p.m. a call came in on the switchboard which I answered,' the operator later told police in a statement. 'As a result of what he said I asked this boy his address and he told me it was 106 Woodland Park, Lisburn. I immediately dispatched an ambulance to the scene.'

As Harry dashed back to the Fiat, the young woman and two teenage girls he had seen as he crossed the road to the bungalow were just a few feet away. They were two sisters and their older cousin, on their way to the shops on an errand. 'I saw a yellow car with a roof rack and black insert in the bumper,' the young woman said.

> There was one person in this car, the driver. The engine was running. Just then I heard three bangs and a man came running out of the gate of a white bungalow on the other side of the street. As the man came running out of the gate, he appeared to be tucking something into his waistband of his trousers. This man came around the back of this yellow car and got into the front passenger's seat. The car then drove off at fast speed.

One of her cousins recalled that the Fiat mounted the pavement to avoid a car coming the other way. She said: 'The person in the driving seat of the yellow car had dirty fair hair and I thought it was a woman.' The third girl said that she knew it to be gunshots that they had heard: 'I have heard shooting in the country before.' The man running from the house was wearing a dark suit and his hair was long onto his shoulders, she said. 'There was a yellow car sitting on the same side of the road as we were walking. There was a girl sitting in the driver's seat. She had fair hair. She started to drive off when the man had only one leg in the car. It drove very fast down the street.'

The ambulance was on the scene within two minutes of Mark's call, but it was already too late. 'I went to the kitchen at the rear of 106 Woodland Park where I discovered the body of a male person,' the ambulance driver said. 'On seeing that this person was dead, I immediately notified our Control to contact the RUC. We stayed at the scene until arrival of police, when we left.'

A nearby police patrol car was alerted at 12.58 p.m., and the driver came to an abrupt halt outside the bungalow at 1.02 p.m. He knew Millar.

An ambulance crew was already at this location, and as a result of what they told me I went to the rear of 106 Woodland Park where I saw the body of a person whom I know to be Constable Millar McAllister. He was lying on his back, the upper part of his body was in the working kitchen, and his feet were protruding through the open rear door. I then went to the front door of the house and spoke to a small boy. I then secured the scene until the arrival of CID and other police officers.

By now, several neighbours were milling around outside the bungalow. They had heard what they thought were three shots, and it did not take long to piece together what had happened: Mark was able to talk, but little Alan was in profound shock.

Nita arrived shortly afterwards and found her husband dead on their kitchen floor. A local GP was called at 1.30 p.m. 'I went to the kitchen at the rear of the house. There I saw the body of a male person. After examination I pronounced life extinct in this person.'

Nita was sedated. A few days later she would be asked to give a statement to the police. 'I am the widow of the late Laird Millar McAllister,' she said. 'I last saw Millar alive on the morning of the 22 April 1978. At approximately 8.00 a.m. he was in his usual good health. Later that day I identified the body of Millar.'[21]

The yellow Fiat sped away down Woodland Park, turned right into Warren Gardens and skirted around the Loyalist Old Warren estate, Union flags fluttering in the spring breeze. Harry was getting his breath back. He felt like he'd run a mile. He began hurriedly wiping down the gun with a handkerchief. The driver turned hard left into Drumbeg Drive, just before a petrol station, past long rows of bungalows, then into Killarney Avenue. The Fiat accelerated hard up a hill and around a slight left-hand bend, past a Presbyterian church on the left, and then took a sharp right, into a road of slightly older terrace houses. They were zigzagging around the western side of the town, attempting to drive as fast as they could without drawing too much attention to themselves. At the end of the road they turned left, back into Warren Gardens, and came to a halt at traffic lights. Red. *Change*, Harry thought, *CHANGE!* Then they were off again, turning left and looking for Anne. Harry was no doubt desperate to get rid of the gun. After polishing it for days, cherishing the thing, he was desperate to be rid of it.

At the junction with Ballinderry Road they could see Anne, a hundred yards from where they expected her to be standing. The driver turned right and slowed down alongside her while Harry wound down the window. Harry passed out the revolver, wrapped in the scarf inside the string bag. 'You're on the wrong fucking road!' he shouted at Anne. The driver then did a U-turn as Harry wound up the window, and the pair sped back towards the town centre.

Anne looked again at her map and started walking up Ballinderry Road. She turned into Causeway End Road, crossed a railway bridge, and turned into a side street on the left, Ardane Gardens. She approached a pebble-dashed terrace house, one with blue curtains and an aerial over the door, and rang the doorbell. Within seconds the door was opened, and Anne was looking at a man in his twenties with reddish receding hair. She recognised him immediately: they both worked at Strathearn Audio. The man nodded. She handed over the gun, turned on her heel, and walked away before he had a chance to say anything.[22]

Harry and the driver abandoned the Fiat at the Crazy Prices car park on Chapel Hill, leaving the keys in the driver's-side footwell, and took separate buses back to Belfast. Harry alighted at the edge of the city and walked through a police roadblock that had been set up in a bid to apprehend the killers. On the way back into the centre of Lisburn, Anne crumpled up the map and threw it in a rubbish bin. Then she too waited for a bus that would take her to Twinbrook.

In Andersonstown, Gary sat in the kitchen of his family's home, looking at the transistor radio. About half an hour after the young girl had called to take away the gun, he switched it on for the news. On the hour, Downtown Radio broadcast a report that a policeman had been shot dead at his home in Lisburn. 'I knew straight away that this was us, that this was what the car had been used for. My stomach immediately started churning and churning. I felt sick. It wasn't good.'[23]

Back at Woodland Park, police were already making door-to-door inquiries. The small bungalow was starting to fill with people going quietly about their work. A team of RUC scene of crime officers was at work in the kitchen and backyard. One of them, John Carlisle, said in a later statement: 'I saw the body of a man, whom I now know to be Millar McAllister, lying face upwards in the doorway of the working kitchen. There were gunshot wounds in the abdomen and there was a pool of blood at the back of the head.'

John found a strike mark on the back wall of the kitchen, opposite the door, and a corresponding hole in the glass in the back door, next to the lock. With the help of colleagues, he moved Millar slightly and found a second strike mark on the floor beneath the constable's body. It corresponded with a third mark on the bottom of the fridge. John could see that two bullets had passed through Millar and ricocheted around the kitchen. One spent bullet was found in the backyard. John drew a chalk mark around it, and took out his tape measure: it was precisely 4 feet and 8 inches from the back door through which it had passed before coming to rest. John and his colleagues began dusting down any area that might yield fingerprints. Then, looking in the sink, one of the officers spotted the bullet that had ricocheted off the fridge. A police photographer took a black-and-white picture of it, lying alongside the plastic bowl that held the plate and the still-warm mug that his Photography Branch colleague had set down a short while before. More pictures were taken of Millar's body, from several angles, as well as of the front and back of the house, and the strike marks.

The two outstanding bullets were recovered when Professor Thomas Marshall, State Pathologist for Northern Ireland, carried out a post-mortem examination at Craigavon Hospital in County Armagh. One was found nestling inside Millar's vest, while the second was recovered from his lumbar region. Professor Marshall concluded that Millar had been a 'healthy, normal young man' of thirty-six years, and recorded the cause of death as bullet wounds to the trunk. There were no other injuries, he wrote, and 'death would have been rapid'.

John Carlisle delivered the two bullets that he had discovered to the Northern Ireland Forensic Science Laboratory in south Belfast, along with Millar's V-neck sweater and brown leather jacket, and the two bullets recovered by Professor Marshall. A scientist established that all four bullets had been discharged from the same .455 revolver. Tests on the clothing showed that far from being given a ballistic sign of the cross, as Harry suggested, all four bullets hit Millar in the chest, with one exiting his left shoulder and one punching a hole in the collar at the back of his jacket.[24]

Eventually, the scene of crime officers and photographers completed their work. Millar's body was lifted gently onto a stretcher, covered, removed, and driven away.

Like the family of the civil servant in Michael Longley's poem, shot dead in his own kitchen with a bullet that pierced not only his body but 'the books he had read, the music he could play', and with the departing police leaving 'only a bullet hole in the cutlery drawer', Nita and the boys were left with three strike marks in their kitchen and a hole in their back door. Nita was widowed, suddenly, awfully, at the age of thirty-five. And her boys would never recover fully from the loss of their father, and the horror of what they saw that day.

After getting off the bus on the outskirts of Belfast, Harry walked quickly: he was expected to be back in Lisburn by three o'clock, to play a game of football. He made his way to a pool hall above a garage in Andersonstown where his football teammates were gathering. One of them gave him a lift home, where he quickly changed his clothes. Harry made arrangements for his pin-stripe suit to be taken to the local dry cleaner's. Then he joined the rest of the team for the journey to Lisburn, for the match at Wallace Park, a little over a mile from Millar's home.

Around the same time, soldiers from 3 Para stopped the yellow Fiat as it was being driven back into Belfast from Lisburn. At the wheel was its owner, the civil servant, who had recovered it from the place where Gary said it would be, at Crazy Prices' car park. After being taken to Dunmurry police station for questioning, he followed Gary's instructions and told a police sergeant that he had been hijacked, hooded and driven away in a van. On realising the seriousness of the crime for which his car had been taken, he began telling the truth.

The killing made a splash in the final edition of that evening's *Belfast Telegraph*: RUC MAN SHOT DEAD AT HOME. 'The killer spent a couple of minutes chatting with his victim before he produced a gun and opened fire,' the newspaper reported. 'It is understood the RUC man's two children were inside his bungalow home at that time.' The dead man, the report added, 'was said to be a pigeon fancier'.

Returning to Belfast after his match, Harry checked out the football results: Forest had secured the draw they needed at Coventry, with their goalkeeper Peter Shilton pulling off two stupendous saves to help them win the English First Division for the first time.

Michael Culbert had spent the day working with the boys at St Patrick's Training School, but at 5 p.m. he nipped out to meet Harry: the pair had agreed to rendezvous near Michael's home off the Stewartstown Road. Harry reported that all the members of the ASU were safe, well and back at home, and that the job had gone smoothly.

'No it didn't,' replied Michael. 'You were followed.'[25]

5

The Consequences

Gary Smyth was first to be arrested. At 5.25 a.m. on the Monday morning, at not yet dawn, there was a series of sharp knocks on the front door of his family's home in Andersonstown. When it was opened, a small army of uniformed RUC officers swarmed inside. Outside, a platoon from 3 Para took up defensive positions. A police constable told Gary that he was being arrested under the Prevention of Terrorism Act. His parents were shocked, appalled. And frightened for their son.

He was driven across the city centre and over the river to east Belfast, to Castlereagh. As he was taken out of the car and across the yard, Gary had his first chance to study, close up, the facility that had acquired such a fearsome reputation. The three-storey brick building, completed just a year before, looked mundane enough. But Gary had heard both Republican and Loyalist paramilitaries' accounts of what went on there. The terrifying stories of being kicked and beaten by teams of plain-clothes interrogators, big men who worked shifts, rotating around the clock. He was filled with a deep, churning sense of dread.

Inside Castlereagh, Gary was booked in by a uniformed RUC sergeant before being led up a narrow stairway and through a door made of white-painted steel. He was then taken into a cell, and the door locked. There was a bed, a rather flimsy plastic chair, the overhead light, and a small steel ventilation grille set high in the wall. There were thirty-eight such cells at Castlereagh, and twenty-one rooms known as 'interview rooms'. Gary knew that it would not be long before he was taken from his cell to an 'interview room'.

His mind began to turn over the bewildering speed with which the police had identified him: barely thirty-six hours had passed from the time of the hijacking at Rice's the bookmaker's to his arrest. Inevitably, Gary started to think about the tall, thin, sandy-haired youth who had accompanied him when he had hijacked the yellow Fiat.

Why had the youth briefly disappeared shortly before they approached the car's owner and demanded his keys? The previous month, the same youth had also been involved in some way in the concealment of the ArmaLite and Simonov rifles behind the block of flats overlooking the Glen Road, in advance of a sniping attack: the attack that had failed because someone had interfered with the weapons. *The common denominator*, Gary said to himself.[1]

Gary ended up waiting in his cell for several hours. It was a little after one o'clock in the afternoon when the door finally opened and he was instructed to stand up and step outside. He was led to a room where three large men in suits were waiting for him. There was a table and chairs. One of the men introduced himself as a detective sergeant, and told Gary that the other two men were a detective constable and a detective chief inspector. The sergeant cautioned Gary, and made a note that he replied: 'You've got the wrong man, I would have nothing to do with killing anyone.'

The detective chief inspector was Roy Cairns, the head of the Regional Crime Squad at Castlereagh. Roy wrote a statement some weeks later, in which he gave his account of what happened during the interrogation of Gary. This is what he wrote:

I was accompanied by Detective Sergeant [redacted] and
Detective Constable [redacted]. Detective Sergeant
[redacted] introduced us all to Smyth and told him that
we're making inquiries into the murder of Constable
Millar McAllister at Lisburn on 22 April 1978.

Detective Sergeant [redacted] asked him to give an
account of his movements on the 22 April 1978. Smyth
then gave a detailed account of the times and places of his
whereabouts between 8.20 a.m. and 1 p.m. that day.
This interview terminated at 3.10 p.m. when Smyth was
returned to his cell.

Later on that same date at 8 p.m. accompanied by
Detective Sergeant [redacted] and Detective Constable
[redacted] I again saw Smyth. He was aware of our
identity and I reminded him that he had previously been
cautioned. He was told that we had good reason to
believe that he had hijacked a vehicle on Saturday, 22
April 1978 and that the vehicle was subsequently used in
the murder of Constable McAllister.

Somewhat improbably, Roy added:

Smyth strenuously denied any connection with the
hijacking and during the course of the interview stated
several times: 'Look, believe me, I didn't know that man
was going to be killed.' He asked several times how
Constable McAllister's family were taking it and appeared
to be distressed about the murder. He appeared to be
thinking deeply and asked at one stage, 'What would I
get for hijacking?' He was told that that was a matter for
the court to decide. He remained silent for a further
period and then said, 'I know nothing about that murder.'

He lapsed into silence once again and then eventually
said, 'All right get your scribbler.' Detective Sergeant

[redacted] asked him if he wished to make a statement, he nodded his head and said, 'Yes, I don't want to know about any murder.' Detective Constable [redacted] asked if he wished to make the statement or have it written for him. He replied, 'No, you write it.' Detective Constable [redacted] then wrote out the heading and the caution, which Smyth then signed. Smyth then dictated a statement to the Detective Constable beginning the statement at 10.50 p.m. and ending at 11.20 p.m. At this time Smyth wrote out and signed the certificate at the bottom of the statement. The statement which was taken by Detective Constable [redacted] was witnessed by myself and Detective Sergeant [redacted]. This interview ended at 11.25 p.m. when Smyth was returned to his cell.[2]

In the event, Gary was not subjected to the full-on 'slap and tickle' that the Regional Crime Squad had come to specialise in, but he would doubtless question the detective chief inspector's version of events. He would regard the claim that he had uttered the words 'All right get your scribbler' as being absurd. He says that while being questioned at Castlereagh he was abused rather than tortured. 'I wasn't beaten,' he says.

I was slapped; there was a bit of slapping and hair pulling, that sort of thing. And I wasn't allowed to sleep: they used sleep deprivation.

But the main thing was that I was being intimidated. These were very big, grown men, and I wasn't much more than a boy. They knew that they were frightening me, by their size, their presence. At one point one of the detectives put a gun on the table in front of me. Just that: he just put a gun there. That was very intimidating.[3]

As with other suspects taken to Castlereagh for interrogation at that time, there was never any question of Gary being granted access to a solicitor until the process had been completed. Sitting in his cell, he continued to obsess about the youth who had accompanied him to the Whitefort pub, and wonder whether this was how he – and perhaps other volunteers involved in the operation – had been betrayed.

At One Batt, however, a number of people had realised that the operation had been compromised even before Harry had walked down the drive at the side of Millar's home. A short while after the hijacked yellow Fiat 127 had pulled away from Rice's the bookmaker's, the IRA had begun to detect signs that the car was being followed.

Coolnasilla Park East is a quiet and pleasant street in a middle-class corner of Andersonstown. One house on the east side of Coolnasilla Park East, a modern, brick-built detached affair with double bay windows, was the headquarters of one of the IRA's most secret initiatives of that time: its signals intelligence operations.

It was one of three houses in the Belfast area from which the IRA had been tracking, unscrambling and decoding the radio traffic of various undercover police and army units, including the SAS. The other two houses were located on the outskirts of Lisburn and in Dunmurry. The loft space of one had been turned into a command post, equipped with transmitters, monitors and position-fixing devices. Some of the equipment came from dismantled television sets and retuned transistor radios, and some had been acquired from Ulster Polytechnic and the Strathearn hi-fi factory.

It wasn't long before the security forces realised their radios may not have been secure, and as a precaution some used codes, which one army officer says led to them 'tying ourselves in knots'. An aide-memoire issued to army unit commanders in 1978 contained a list of code names, but they were so crude that it did not take long for the IRA to understand them. 'Rucksack' was the code name for a male RUC officer, for example, while female officers were code-named 'Ruckbird'. 'Hawkeye' was the Army Air Corps, and army padres were all code-named 'Brimstone'. The IRA also listened out for accents, in order to distinguish between officers and other ranks, and to help identify the army's infantry battalions, many of which recruited their numbers from specific British counties and cities.

One of the other houses, which was owned by a Post Office engineer, was also at the heart of a sophisticated telephone interception operation. The police had encountered evidence of IRA phone-tapping operations once before, following a raid on a house in an affluent south Belfast suburb in 1974, but this was a far more ambitious enterprise: one of the lines being tapped was the unlisted number at the residence of the commander of British land forces in the north. The third house held an archive of IRA files, containing names of targets, addresses and car numbers, surveillance photographs, and page after page of transcripts of conversations over telephone lines and radio frequencies that the security forces believed to be secure.

The IRA had also established a monitoring station in a half-empty office block in Belfast which had a number of spare telephone lines into the local telephone exchange. Inside the exchange, a telephone engineer had placed 'jumpers' to connect the intercept targets with the circuits that linked with the spare lines being monitored from the office block.*[4]

---

* The operation centred on Coolnasilla Park East was eventually discovered in June 1979 after the arrest of a senior IRA man who was carrying a number of notebooks with coded entries. He was also carrying half of a Lebanese banknote with a signature written on it, thought to have been a sign of recognition. After the codes were cracked, all three houses were raided and eleven people arrested. The police discovered evidence that the security breach stretched back almost six years. A court was later told that the raids had uncovered 'sophisticated electronic equipment, including decoders'. They also found material suggesting that the IRA had been spying on police surveillance operations.

That Saturday morning as the hijacked Fiat headed east along Andersonstown Road, one of the receivers at Coolnasilla Park East picked up crackled communications that made clear that the vehicle was being followed, by either the police or the army. Senior figures in One Batt were alerted but decided that there was little they could do. After the Fiat turned right onto Kennedy Way, the security force followers could be heard saying that they too were about to turn right. The next roundabout was a junction of the M1 motorway, and here the Fiat driver had a stroke of luck. The roundabout was planted with dense bushes, hampering the view of his followers, and when the driver turned off towards Lisburn, the pursuers could not see the Fiat and continued ahead. The driver was able to pick up Harry and deliver him to Millar's home – the killing went ahead as planned – but the IRA listeners now knew the operation had been compromised.

After the shooting, some thought was given at One Batt to ordering the members of the ASU to 'go offside' – flee south to the Irish Republic – but a decision was made that they should sit tight and hope for the best. Perhaps the IRA did not wish to alert the security forces to its signals intelligence operation. A few hours later Gary was under arrest.

Gary was interrogated twice that afternoon and again that night, for three-and-a-half hours. At the end of the night-time session, the police had taken a statement in which he admitted to having hijacked the car, but denied knowing that the vehicle was to be used in a shooting. 'I did not know what the car was to be used for,' the statement records him as saying.

The following day he was questioned for two hours in the morning, three hours in the afternoon, and ninety minutes in the evening. The interrogators, detective constables and sergeants, were working in rotating teams. Gary was on Castlereagh's conveyor belt.

The next day was the same: two hours in the morning, four

in the afternoon, and again at night.[5] At the end of this session, he signed a different statement, which said: 'I arrived at Lenadoon Avenue and met the man who then gave me my instructions, and handed me an automatic pistol. I then asked him what was the job. He said we are going after a peeler.'

The police recorded that interview as having started at 4.55 p.m. and terminated at 6.05 p.m. 'Smyth was returned to his cell.' On his way there, he was walked past Phelim Hamill from Twinbrook, who was being taken from his cell to an interview room. The police wanted each man to know that the other was under arrest. They also wanted to observe how they reacted on seeing each other.

Phelim was the second person to be arrested for questioning about the murder of Millar. He had been detained late the previous evening, near his home, by soldiers of the 3rd Battalion, Parachute Regiment, who hauled him roughly into the back of a Land Rover and drove him to Fort Monagh. Police arrived in the early hours of the morning, formally arrested and cautioned him, and drove him to Castlereagh.

He too was interrogated by teams of detectives: two hours that morning, and four-and-a-half hours that afternoon. Phelim says that during each session he was beaten around the face and the back of his head, and that his head was banged against the wall.

His third session began at 6.30 p.m. and ran until around 2.30 the following morning: eight hours. Phelim had been questioned at Castlereagh before, and knew plenty of others who had passed through the interview rooms. Nevertheless, he was shocked at what happened next.

Two detectives shouted at me: 'If you don't make a statement, we will send in the hoods.' Five other detectives arrived. A detective grabbed me by the right leg, another by the left leg, another by the left arm and another by the right arm. Whilst I was held in this position, I was grabbed by the privates and by the throat and was raised off the ground and thrown over the table a few times.

I was stretched across the table and a detective would press down on my shoulders whilst another would press down on my arms. My arms and legs were pinned down and a light-coloured towel was put over my head obstructing my vision. They tied the towel around my neck and choked me. Whilst the towel was tied around my face, a cup of water was poured down my throat and nose giving me a drowning feeling.*

This was repeated on a number of occasions, and terrified Phelim. He thought he was going to die. 'I remember thinking, how far are they going to go? Are they going to kill me?'

This was not the only form of torture to which he was subjected.

My wrists were bent back. My arms were bent up my back. My hair was pulled. I was raised off the ground by my ears. I had hair loss. I was ordered to strip. I refused. The detectives tried to tear my shirt off. It started to rip

---

* This description of his mistreatment, which Phelim first gave shortly after his arrest, is an accurate description of the torture technique that became known as water-boarding when used by the CIA in the years after 9/11. Phelim was giving this statement 23 years before 9/11, however, and many people who had passed through Castlereagh were initially sceptical of his account: it is possibly the only account of water-boarding being used at that holding centre. It is now known that British troops and air crew who were engaged in 'prone to capture' roles had been instructed in water-boarding techniques, to help them prepare for the possibility of it being used against them. A significant number of British soldiers joined the RUC on leaving the army.

underneath the arms. Another detective said 'Leave it', and appeared worried by the fact that it was ripped. My upper lip was bleeding. A detective brought toilet paper dipped in water and made me put it to my mouth to prevent bleeding.

I vomited during the interview. I was told that if I vomited again, they would make me lick it up. I vomited over my shirt and they cleaned it off. They said: 'You think you're being a clever bastard.' I was kicked on the legs whilst on the ground. My ankles were twisted. I was punched on the stomach and back.

Detective Chief Superintendent Bill Mooney, the head of Belfast CID – who usually stayed out of the interview rooms, preferring to prowl the corridors outside, berating his interrogators – came in and allegedly pointed a pistol at Phelim's groin. 'I was tortured because I refused to say anything.' Eventually, he was taken back to his cell and his captors recorded that he was given a cup of tea.

The following day he was again interrogated three times, for a total of ten hours. He was slapped and threatened, but there was no repeat of the water torture.

The next day he was questioned again, and says he was grabbed by the throat by a detective who said that he could kill him if he wished. He was told that if he admitted to a lesser charge of hijacking the car, they would leave him alone; if he did not, he would be charged with murder.

His final interview that afternoon was with two pipe-smoking detectives, who made no attempt to hurt him. 'They hinted that they had forensic evidence to connect me with the murder and also evidence of identification.' Phelim told them that he had been at his family home until midday on the day of the killing, and arrived at Maguire's Bar on the Falls Road at 1 p.m. – around ten minutes after Millar was being gunned down, nine miles away. No doubt he could find patrons who would be prepared to support this alibi.

Phelim asked to see a solicitor, but this was refused. He asked also to see a doctor. A man arrived and examined him: Phelim suspected that he was not a real doctor.

In fact, this man, a Dr Alexander, was not only a real doctor, he was also one of three physicians who had been persistently complaining about the mistreatment of terrorism suspects at Castlereagh and other RUC interrogation centres. Phelim was literally covered in bruises. Dr Alexander recorded that they were around his left eye and on his throat, neck, arms, legs, chest and upper back, and that his right knee and left cheek were cut. Phelim informed him that he had not been bruised on arrival at Castlereagh, but nevertheless did not wish to make a complaint; he feared further beatings.

On the Friday evening, Gary and Phelim were driven from Castlereagh back to Lisburn, where they were both charged with Millar's murder. They appeared briefly in court and were remanded in custody, to appear before magistrates in Belfast four days later. The following day, both young men were examined by Gary's family doctor, whose report on Phelim concluded: 'Has many bruises and injuries which are consistent with his allegations of assault and ill-treatment.'[6]

Millar's murder had been big news in Northern Ireland, but only for a few hours. The following day, few Fleet Street newspapers showed much interest. There was a paragraph in the *Sunday Telegraph*, and the *Sunday Express* carried a seventy-nine-word report on its front page, under the headline SONS SEE PC FATHER KILLED. The newspaper noted that Millar had been the eightieth policeman to die during the Troubles. But there was no mention of the killing in the *Sunday Times*, the *Observer* or the *Sunday Mirror*. News editors were bored with these distant tragedies, and assumed that their readers were too.

On the Monday, *The Times* and the *Guardian* both relegated the news about the killing to a single paragraph, tucked away at the foot of their reports about funding arrangements for the Peace People. There was no mention whatsoever in that evening's *Belfast Telegraph*, which splashed on a story about a survey that suggested that some resilience and confidence remained among Northern Ireland's business community. The IRA's armed struggle was, for some, an incessant background hum: annoying, but something that one learned to live with.

While Gary and Phelim were being interrogated, the police and Millar's family were making arrangements for his funeral. It was held on the Thursday, five days after his death. There was a brief funeral service at Millar's home. Hundreds of people followed Millar's coffin as it was taken from his home to Lisburn New Cemetery, where there was a second service at the graveside. The local newspaper, the *Ulster Star*, reported that the mourners included the Chief Constable, Sir Kenneth Newman, the Mayor of Lisburn, Alderman Mrs Elsie Kelsey, and several local clergy. The RUC band was playing. The newspaper published a picture of the funeral cortège. A Union flag was draped over Millar's coffin, and on that had been placed his RUC cap and a wreath. Millar's sons Mark and Alan could be seen walking behind their father's coffin, between an elder relative and a uniformed police officer. Mark looked angry. Alan's face was blank. There was no sign of Millar's wife, Nita.[7]

The killing of Millar had the desired impact on Lisburn: it immediately generated fear. Police patrols were increased, sales of locks and bolts rose sharply, members of the security forces and their wives and husbands talked to their children about the need to never talk to strangers. 'And never, ever, talk about your da's job!' People questioned their faith in God. The Lisburn Borough Community and Tenants' Associations called on Roy Mason to introduce hanging and birching.[8]

Elsewhere in Northern Ireland, life went on. At Belfast City

Commission, as the city's main criminal court was known at that time, two men were jailed for life for the murder of Harry Cobb, an RUC inspector and father of three children who had been shot dead by the IRA in Armagh the previous July. In Turf Lodge, a seventeen-year-old joyrider, John Collins, was shot dead by soldiers. The Samaritans announced that they had set up help lines in eight towns, to try to talk the depressed and the desperate out of taking their own lives. From his office in Queen's House in central Belfast, Charlie Stout sent a telegram to the State Department, with information about a Gallup poll of 1,295 adults conducted in the Irish Republic: apparently, an overwhelming number wanted the British to leave the north, but even more were opposed to IRA violence, and only 2 per cent supported the IRA.

The investigation into the killing of Millar began to gather pace. Harry Murray was the next to be arrested, on the Wednesday evening after Gary and Phelim were charged with Millar's murder. When he was stopped at a checkpoint manned by police and troops from C Company of 3 Para, he gave a false name. He then heard an officer report over the radio: 'I've got Murray.' He was taken to Fort Monagh, where shortly after 10 p.m. a Parachute Regiment medic asked whether he wished to be seen by a doctor or a nurse. The army was already wary of handing prisoners over to the police without some proof that its troops were not responsible for whatever injuries the prisoner might subsequently be shown to have suffered. 'I asked him to sign the form at the certificate of refusal and watched him sign,' the medic said in a subsequent statement. 'I then checked that everything had been filled in on the form and noticed that he had signed as H. Murray. I made the Captain aware of this fact.'

Anne Laverty was picked up thirty-six hours later. Police officers from Lisburn raided her family home on Twinbrook at 2.55 a.m. while paratroopers took up positions outside. She too was driven across the city to Castlereagh, arriving at 3.20 a.m. Like Gary, she was utterly terrified.

Michael had gone to spend a couple of days on the coast with his family. They returned to their home on the day after Anne's arrest, a Saturday, and a few minutes later soldiers came to take him away. He too was taken first to Fort Monagh, where a police sergeant formally arrested him at 8.20 that evening. He was then ferried across town to Castlereagh.

By his own account, Harry was not beaten while at Castlereagh; the worst mistreatment he suffered consisted of the threats, shouted through the door of his cell at night.

After being allowed a few hours' rest in a cell he was taken to one of the interview rooms, where he was questioned first about the attempted murder of Brian McKee the previous February. A detective constable recorded that Harry gave a full account of his role in the attack but refused to name anyone else involved. Harry then agreed to sign a statement.

He was questioned about his whereabouts on the day that Millar was killed. He told the detectives that he woke around 11 a.m., had a bath and then went to McGrannigan's book-maker's on the Suffolk Road. He chatted about football with a man he met there, placed a bet, then went home for his lunch. Later, he said, he met up with the other members of his football team and they all went to Lisburn for a match that kicked off at 3 p.m. One of the detectives told him that he had been a good friend of Millar, and had seen Millar's body. According to Harry, he was told that he could be thrown down the stairs and killed: 'That they could fucking well do what they liked with him here at Castlereagh.'

Harry was then taken back to his cell and given some lunch. That afternoon he was questioned again about the murder of Millar, and this time offered a full confession. He described the moment that he and Millar chatted at the back door of the bungalow.

He then sent his son in for a pencil. I pulled out the gun, a .45 revolver and shot him at close range. The first one hit him about the stomach. I saw the hole in his pullover. As he went flying backwards, I fired again and hit him around the head. He fell onto the kitchen floor and I fired two more into his chest. The wee boy came running out into the kitchen, he was shouting for his Mummy and Daddy . . .

Harry would later say that he had seen little point in denying his involvement. 'They knew it was me,' he says. Whenever the detectives questioned him about matters in which he was not involved – such as the La Mon House bombing – he was quick to deny them. But he seems to have been ready to confess to Millar's killing.

During a subsequent interview Harry said that he had been sworn into the IRA the previous October, but had been involved with the organisation for around five-and-a-half years. 'Some of his previous Protestant mates had given him a rough time because of his marriage to a Catholic,' one of the police questioners noted.

The following day a detective inspector, Joe Meeke, questioned Harry about his motives for shooting Millar. Harry replied that it was pointless him joining the IRA if he was not prepared to take orders. 'The police and the Brits are the enemy,' he said. 'Look, there's a war on. You don't think it's a war, but we do and I do what I'm told.' The police officer would not have been aware that the man who was insistent that he would do as he was told in the IRA had, a decade earlier, been kicked out of the RAF for refusing to follow an order.

Asked if he had any regrets, the police recorded Harry as saying: 'I was ordered to do it and that was it. I'm not sorry about shooting the policeman but I didn't like the wee lad seeing it.' Joe then asked Harry if he would have been prepared to shoot Nita. Harry replied that he had asked about this before travelling to Lisburn, and had been told that he should shoot Millar's wife if necessary. Harry told Joe that he would have done so, but that he would never have shot the boy. Asked who gave him his orders, he replied: 'No names, I'm not touting.'

In his statement, Joe recorded asking Harry, 'Did he agree with all that the Provies were doing?' Harry then made perhaps his most illuminating comment from the entire series of interviews. 'He said they should ease off the Peelers and Brits and concentrate on killing Prods. Asked did he want a united Ireland or what he was fighting for? He said he was trying to get back at the Prods and would continue fighting until he was either dead or the war was over.'

Harry, it seems, was still burning with hatred of the Loyalists who had driven Kathleen and himself out of their home in north Belfast six years earlier.[9]

Harry was told that he was being charged: 'That you at Lisburn in the County of Antrim on 22 April 1978 did murder Laird Millar McAllister, contrary to Common Law.'

Down south in Portlaoise, the All-Ireland Senior Football Championship was about to get under way, with Carlow playing Westmeath. The championship would end with Kerry beating reigning champions Dublin in a match that the sports journalist Con Houlihan would hail as 'surely the most extraordinary final' the game had ever seen; one in which a goalkeeper's distribution 'was as cool and unerring as the dealing of a riverboat gambler', in which a disconsolate player collapsed 'like a fireman who had returned to find his station ablaze', and in which the spectators, 'in the grey drizzle . . . saw the twilight of the gods'.[10]

In Weybridge, 20 miles south-west of London, a detective was taking a statement from the editor of the *Pigeon Racing News and Gazette*, who confirmed that Millar had contributed a

monthly article to the magazine since 1970; that he had used the
pen name 'The Copper'; and that each piece appeared under his
photograph.

At Castlereagh, detectives were preparing to question Anne.

First, two detective constables took her from her cell to be
fingerprinted. She was then taken to interview room BF10,
where she was cautioned, and informed that she was going to be
questioned about Millar's murder. Asked to account for her
movements on the day of the killing, she said she had done some
shopping in Lisburn and had bought 200 cigarettes before going
home and cleaning the house.

'We kept asking her about the minor part she had played in
the murder of Constable McAllister,' one detective noted. 'At
times she appeared to be deep in thought, and her eyes became
very red, but she continued to deny having played any part in
this incident. We told her to think it over during lunch.'

When she was questioned again, one of the detectives noted
that 'she sat quiet and appeared very nervous, staring at the
floor'. On this occasion, Anne was recorded as saying that she
had agreed to carry a weapon from Lisburn to Andersonstown,
and claimed that it had been handed to her by a boy who had
approached her in the town centre. The detective recorded that
Anne was sitting at a table throughout the interview, and
that she smoked seven cigarettes. He also felt it necessary to
add in his statement, twice, that 'at no time was she ill-treated
in any way'.

That evening, Anne was subjected to two more rounds of
questioning, for a total of around two hours. By now she was
prepared to admit taking the gun after Millar had been shot, and
agreed to give a signed statement. 'I was told to wait for a car
that would give me a package,' she said. 'I waited out in the
Ballinderry Road for a right wee while then a yellow Fiat car
pulled up beside me and a man in the car handed me a package
wrapped up in a scarf. I knew it was a gun as I had been told the

previous night what it was.' Anne insisted that she did not know the identities of the people in the Fiat, however. Asked where she had taken the weapon, she said she could not recall the exact address, and said she had handed it to a woman who had answered the door. She even drew a map, marking with an 'X' the approximate location of the house where she said she had handed it to this woman. It was nowhere near the house where she had actually handed over the revolver.

Twenty-four hours later, Anne agreed to be driven to Lisburn in an unmarked police car, to point out the house where she had taken the gun. The officers who accompanied her reported that she had been unable to identify the correct house. She did point out the rubbish bin where she had dumped the crumpled hand-drawn map, but it turned out to have been emptied. 'She was then conveyed back to Castlereagh, arriving at 12.30 p.m., and returned to her quarters.'

The following day, Anne admitted to IRA membership, and was recorded as saying she did not hear about Millar's death until the day afterwards. 'She felt terrible because she knew it had to do with the gun she collected,' one of the detectives wrote. She also began to give a fuller account of her role in the killing.

Two days later, a Tuesday, a detective inspector and detective sergeant visited Anne. The sergeant drew her attention to a bruise on her right forearm. The inspector made a note that 'Laverty told us that she had received this when she slipped and fell on the toilet'. Anne was then driven to Lisburn police station, where she was told that she was to be charged with possession of a firearm 'with intent by means thereof to endanger life'. Asked if she wished to say anything, she replied: 'Nothing.' She was then told that she was also to be charged with assisting an offender, to which she replied: 'No.'

At this point, Anne appears to have suffered a fairly complete physical and psychological breakdown.

★

Within minutes of his arrival at Castlereagh, Michael Culbert was being questioned by Roy Cairns and a detective constable. 'Culbert denied that he was involved in any way with the murder,' Roy noted. Then:

> We then put it to Culbert that we believed that he was a
> member of the Provisional IRA, but he strongly denied
> this. He went on to say that he disagreed entirely with
> what the PIRA were doing and that he was very moderate
> in his views and claimed that he had no time whatsoever
> for the violence of the Provisional IRA.

After a short break, Roy questioned Michael again, this time with a detective superintendent, Des Browne, and told him that he believed he had planned the killing. Again, Michael denied this, and the conversation turned to Michael's work and his family.

After the complaints Michael had raised following the last time he was held at Castlereagh, the police were being very careful with him: they didn't want to give any cause for fresh involvement with Amnesty International. They maintained a body chart, a sheet of paper which contained an outline drawing of an adult male's front and back, which showed no injuries. The officers also scrupulously recorded each time Michael requested a lavatory break or a shower, recording the word 'granted' against each request. They even made a note of his meals. At 7.50 on the morning after his arrest, for example, they recorded that his breakfast – egg, sausage, toast and tea – was 'part eaten'.

Michael was then fingerprinted, reminded that he remained under caution, and questioned about the killing. A detective constable later gave his account of this:

> I explained to Culbert how Murray had pretended that
> he was interested in pigeons, which was Constable

McAllister's hobby, in order to gain the Constable's confidence, and then when the Constable's attention was diverted, shot him, at close range. I went on to tell Culbert how Constable McAllister's young children had found their father lying dying on the kitchen floor.

Again, Michael denied any involvement, and the police recorded the conversation as turning to the general situation in the north. At one point the Castlereagh custody inspector entered the interview room, asked Michael if he wished to see a doctor, and recorded that Michael had declined. The officers also recorded that a lunch of mince, potatoes, peas and tea was all 'eaten', tea at 6 p.m. of sausage, chips, beans and tea was only 'part-eaten', and then at 1.17 the following morning he was given a cup of milk and biscuits: 'All eaten.'

That evening he was questioned again, with a detective sergeant pointing out the similarities between himself, Michael and Millar: the three of them were all in their late twenties or mid-thirties, all were married, all with young boys. One father dead.

Culbert appeared to be close to tears and sniffed a couple of times. I found it very difficult to get him to make conversation, although he answered all questions put to him. During this interview he continually wrenched his hands and interlocked his fingers and also kept biting the inside of his mouth with his teeth.

The interrogators' subsequent statements claimed that Michael was seated while being questioned. He denies this: he may not have been beaten, he says, but he was forced to stand for very long periods. He also says he was not well fed. As with the others, the interrogation was relentless, with pairs of detectives relieving each other every two and a half hours. The police records show that he was repeatedly told that the detectives knew he had not shot Millar, but that they were certain that he had planned the killing.

The following day, 8 May, the police noted that Michael was remaining silent for long periods while being questioned. They questioned him about the civil rights movement, and recorded him as saying he had not been involved. 'He claimed he had never personally witnessed any violence nor had he even seen the body of any person who died violently. He claimed he had nothing against the police or the Army and had no time for politics.' Asked whether he expected to be convicted if he was charged, Michael is said to have replied: 'Yes.' That night he was questioned again, from 10.35 p.m. until 1.15 the next morning. 'Culbert remained silent for very long periods and gave the impression of being very worried and to be thinking deeply.'[11]

A few hours later, shortly after dawn, police went to the pebble-dashed house off Ballinderry Road in Lisburn and arrested the man in his twenties with receding hair who had taken Harry's revolver from Anne.

His name was Brian Maguire, he was twenty-seven, and he was an electrical engineer and trade union representative at Strathearn Audio. He was also a highly strung young man, punctilious about his appearance: it was not unknown for him to change his shirt several times a day. A few years before, he had paid a considerable sum of money to have his teeth crowned. He was due to be married in a few months' time.

Four years earlier, Brian had spent ten months on remand in prison awaiting trial on armed robbery charges; he was convicted but received a suspended sentence. According to his mother, he was anxious to avoid another spell in prison.

The police believed Brian to be a member of the IRA. According to members of Harry's ASU, Brian had once been involved with the Official IRA, but was not an active member of the Provisionals. He was, however, prepared to help out from time to time. On this occasion, he was asked to take the weapon because he lived in Lisburn with his mother and his uncle, who was a prison officer. 'The gun was left there because we knew the house wouldn't be searched,' says Michael.

On arrival at Castlereagh, a police doctor gave Brian a Valium tranquilliser, and directed that a further two tablets should be taken each day. He also examined Brian, and noted that he had no marks on his body. Brian was taken to cell F2 on the first floor. Again, police arranged for Brian and Michael to pass each other in a corridor.

Brian was questioned from 10.10 a.m. to 10.45 p.m., with a forty-minute break from 5.50 p.m. The interrogators knew what his role had been, and were determined that he would sign a statement admitting to it.

In another interrogation room in Castlereagh, Michael was still being subjected to the conveyor-belt treatment. He is said to have told the officers that he had had little sleep, and had been praying. A detective constable noted: 'I told him that it should be obvious to him by now in view of what he had been told that we knew everybody who had been involved in the murder, and the actual part he played in it.' He went on: 'We continually related to him the circumstances of this crime, the viciousness of it, murdering the Constable in front of his two youngsters. He continued to hang his head and refused to talk.' The officer noted that in between the silences, Michael said that he was confused, that he didn't know what to do, and that he needed time to think. At one point he is said to have told the police that he was worried about his wife and children.

After questioning Michael again that night, a detective constable wrote a statement in which he said Michael had asked how long a sentence he would receive if he admitted IRA membership. He also wrote that Michael had described being sworn in to the IRA after a series of meetings:

Stated his job at this stage was collecting intelligence on everything, even family rows in the area. After that he was made Intelligence Officer in that area. He stated he took timings of army patrols and tried to get the registration of unmarked police cars operating in the area. The details he took down were collected by a girl on a Monday or Wednesday night at his house.

The detective recorded that Michael admitted that the girl had brought him a copy of the *Pigeon Racing News and Gazette*, with Millar's photograph, and that inside the magazine had been a piece of paper, folded and Sellotaped, on which were written Millar's name and address. Michael refused to sign a statement himself, the detective wrote.

At 7 the following morning, Brian Maguire asked to be taken to the lavatory. He was returned to cell F2 ten minutes later, and the light in the cell was switched on. A constable spoke to him, and then at 7.30 a.m. returned to the cell carrying his breakfast on a tray. On opening the cell door, the officer found Brian hanging, with one end of a torn bedsheet tied to a tiny opening in a ventilator grille and the other formed in a noose around his neck. Attempts at resuscitation produced no response and a doctor pronounced Brian dead. A post-mortem examination carried out at the Belfast City Mortuary found that he had been a healthy man – apart from having 'slightly congested' lungs – and the pathologist concluded that 'there was nothing in the findings to suggest that any other person was involved in the death or to suggest manual strangulation'.

Later that morning, two detective constables and a detective superintendent, Billy Hylands, interrogated Michael yet again. Both of the constables made a note of what they would later allege Michael said, and subsequently swore statements in which they said that over a period of an hour and three quarters Michael had given a very full account of his activities in the

IRA and his role in the murder of Millar.

Michael was charged with murder. Two hours later, he was handed a piece of paper and told that it was a form upon which he could register any complaint against any police officer during the ninety-four hours that he had been held and interrogated at Castlereagh. He appears at this stage to have been utterly exhausted, demoralised, defeated. He wrote 'no' and signed at the bottom.

A police officer called at the home of Brian Maguire's mother. She recalled him saying: 'Brian killed himself, Mrs Maguire. He couldn't face you or his girlfriend, so he killed himself.' At home, Michael's wife Monica heard on the radio that a man aged twenty-seven had been found dead in Castlereagh. Michael was twenty-eight. When Monica heard a little while later that Michael had appeared in court, charged with the murder of Millar, she was deeply relieved.[12]

None of those charged with Millar's murder would accept that Brian had hanged himself. 'They went too far and killed him,' is Gary's explanation. 'You couldn't get your little finger into that grille. You certainly couldn't get a bed sheet into it.' Michael is convinced that Brian had died while being water-boarded. 'The police were determined to wipe the squad out,' he says.

At army headquarters in Lisburn, a lieutenant colonel noted in the Intelligence Corps' monthly intelligence assessment: 'The quick arrest of those involved in the killing of Constable McAllister, the Castlereagh photographer, has placed a further damper on ASU activity.' He also concluded that recent arrests had left Sinn Féin with 'a weak second eleven' which had 'bungled the propaganda opportunities of the McGuire [sic] suicide at Castlereagh'.

In Dublin and Derry there were demonstrations over Brian's death. In west Belfast a march that attracted five hundred people ended in rioting, with vehicles hijacked and set ablaze. At

Strathearn Audio, Brian's workmates staged a walkout in protest. One man carried a placard that read 'Newman – Hangman'. There were questions asked in the Commons and the Dáil, and after the police issued a statement in which they said that Brian had admitted to taking the gun that was used to kill Millar, Gerry Fitt's SDLP joined the protests, condemning the statement as 'unseemly and shameful'.[13]

Arrangements were quickly made for a senior officer with Merseyside Police, Peter Rawlinson, to be flown to Belfast to investigate Brian's death. Superintendent Rawlinson questioned all the uniformed police officers who had been on duty at Castlereagh at the time. All were 'sensible, mature men', he reported, and 'none of them is aware of any brutal, inhumane or psychological pressures being brought to bear on prisoners'. The detectives who had questioned Brian were also interviewed: they had clearly subjected him to 'lengthy, intense, rigorous and often repetitive questioning'.

He then interviewed five Loyalists and three Republicans who had been held in cells on the same floor as Brian. Six said they had no complaint. One said he had been beaten and held against the wall while his arms were twisted. Another said that he had been beaten and forced into stress positions, and that he had been suspended in the air with a detective's tie around his neck.

Rawlinson concluded that Brian would have been able to slip a strip of bed sheet through the grille, and that the sheeting could bear his weight. 'I have no doubt whatsoever that Brian Maguire took his own life through hanging,' he reported. He could not be sure whether Brian had intended to die, however, or wished only to generate sympathy for himself. 'If Maguire did intend to end his own life there is nothing in my enquiries so far to indicate what led him to do this.' He speculated that one factor could have been a fear of reprisals from Millar's killers. In an oblique acknowledgement of what was happening in the so-called holding centres, Rawlinson added that Brian could have hanged himself in 'fear of further interrogation at Castlereagh by the Royal Ulster Constabulary'.

At Stormont, a senior civil servant wrote a memo to Roy Mason in which he confidently predicted that the Director of Public Prosecutions would quickly determine that there were no grounds for anyone to be prosecuted over Brian's death, and that it was reasonable to assume it was due to suicide or misadventure. There would be no jury at the inquest, he assured Mason, 'and the Belfast Coroner has a record of sound judgment'.

In the event, there was a jury, of six men and one woman, who concluded that Brian hanged himself.

In June the following year, a Loyalist named Norman Earle, who had been held in the cell opposite Brian, went on trial at Belfast Crown Court. Norman was accused of the murder of a young Catholic man who had been shot four years earlier while sitting in a car beside his pregnant wife. He told the court that during his fourth interrogation at Castlereagh he had been punched repeatedly in the stomach and that his arm had been twisted. The following morning, Norman said, after Brian's body had been cut down, the detective constable who was questioning him had asked what he thought of 'their handi-work'. He added that the officer had said of Brian that they had 'got him' because he had murdered a fellow policeman, and added that they could get away with anything at Castlereagh. Whether they had 'got' Brian or whether the detective was opportunistically making use of a suicide was not clear.[14]

After being charged and making a first appearance in court, Michael, Harry, Gary and Phelim were remanded to Crumlin Road Gaol in Belfast, just across the road from the court where they were to go on trial. Gary and Harry shared a cell for a period, and Gary began to see another, gentle side to Harry, the tough tattooed man whom he once saw opening fire on a passing car. He began to understand why the taciturn Harry was nicknamed the Crab.

The jail had been built in the 1840s and was modelled on Pentonville Prison in north London. The design of Pentonville was inspired by an idea that Jeremy Bentham, the utilitarian philosopher, had developed for a 'panopticon', a house of detention in which a central hall looked out along radiating wings and, in theory, created discipline by inducing uncertainty in prisoners about whether or not they were under surveillance.

In practice, by 1978 the Crum, as it was universally known, was a dark, dirty and malodorous establishment with no end of nooks and crannies in which deals could be done, contraband exchanged, and scores brutally settled. Former prison officers recall it as being so filthy that their shirt collars were always badly soiled by the end of each day. A small number of officers would regularly be inebriated while on duty.

Soldiers assisted in guarding the prison, and would man search-lights on sangars at night. Inside one of the sangars there was a cautionary notice about the strength of the searchlights' beams.

> There was a warning not to shine the lights at a certain degree because they'd dazzle the observation post on the top of the Divis flats in the Falls Road three quarters of a mile away. That's how fucking strong the light was. So, we'd be there at night, and at maybe three in the morning we'd pick a cell, shine it in and leave it on.

One former prison officer recalls the moment at eight o'clock each morning when the cell doors would be opened: 'Never have I experienced such a tangible atmosphere of hopelessness, drudgery and despair, laid bare by the expressions on the inmates' faces and those of their keepers.' From that moment, the prison was alive. He goes on:

> The jail when full of cons and screws was almost like a living organism, with the people in it the lifeblood surging through its veins. From the moment it awoke in the morning at unlock, it lived and breathed, and only slumbered when the last light was turned off by the night guard. It had its own personality.

He added that many of his fellow prison officers not only were from a Protestant and Unionist background, but displayed 'emblems, badges or tattoos that could be construed as sectarian . . . they made no attempt to mask their bigotry and narrow-mindedness'.[15]

While at the Crum, Phelim began to teach an Irish language class for fellow Republican prisoners. Michael, Harry and Gary also worked on their Irish and took other classes. Later that year, Phelim was informed that he would not be facing trial – the Director of Public Prosecutions had withdrawn the murder charge. There was no case for him to answer. Although the prosecution would not publicly concede the point, it was clear that the well-documented injuries that Phelim had suffered at Castlereagh – and the description of water-torture that he was prepared give from the witness box – could also mean that Brian's death would become a central issue of the trial. There was a risk, from the prosecution's point of view, that all four men could be acquitted. Phelim was quietly set free. Back at his father's home on Twinbrook, he is said to have become withdrawn for a while, almost reclusive. Friends wondered whether he had suffered a breakdown following his experiences at Castlereagh.

Anne was remanded to Armagh Gaol, the women's prison 40 miles south-west of Belfast. On arrival at Armagh, remand prisoners were expected to strip and, quickly bathe in a large enamelled tub, and were given a towel and taken to an office where their belongings were recorded in a ledger and then packed away. Once dressed, they would be ordered to sit while their photograph was taken. Then they would be taken to an eight-by-ten-foot cell, with a high window, a metal bed, a plastic chair and table, a plastic chamber pot and a small locker. Outside, in the corner of the exercise yard, the remains of a wooden platform were still visible along the wall, around nine feet from the ground. This was where the gallows had once stood.

Remand prisoners who were members of the IRA would be introduced to two fellow inmates: the IRA officer in command, or OC, and her adjutant. Each morning, prisoners would 'fall in', standing outside their cell doors while the OC carried out an inspection. They would parade briefly again each evening. Because this was in breach of prison regulations, each time this happened, the OC lost a day's remission of sentence. The IRA had their own rules: no communicating with the governor other than through the OC, no aggression towards the 'screws' – the prison officers – no noise after midnight and no public arguments between Republicans. These were known as Standing Orders. There were other, unwritten rules: Síle Darragh, who was serving a five-year term for IRA membership at the time Anne was charged with possession of the firearm, later wrote: 'We couldn't show any emotion in front of the screws. We never let our guard down.'[16]

The prison officers at Armagh, as well as the inmates, were under the most tremendous pressure. While Anne was awaiting trial, one of the prison officers, a forty-year-old woman with six children, was killed in a grenade and gun attack that was launched after she walked out of the front gate to go to a local cafe for lunch. Three of her colleagues were injured.

By this stage, Anne appears to have been depressed and anxious, traumatised by her experiences in Castlereagh and deeply worried about what the future held for her. She was also very upset about the way Millar had been shot dead in front of one of his boys; about the devastation that had been wrought on

Millar's family, and about her role in this. At some point, Anne decided that she wanted nothing more to do with the IRA.

Outside the prison gates, the cycle of war continued: shootings, bombings, security checks, raids, arrests, interrogations, beatings. Mothers in Andersonstown worried that their boys were 'getting involved'. Mothers in Lisburn worried that their boys in the police and army reserves were going to be shot on their post rounds, or while delivering the milk. Mothers in Barnsley and Dundee worried that their boys were going to come home from Northern Ireland in coffins. And the rest of the world tried, for the most part, to look the other way.

The findings of the Northern Ireland Attitude Survey conducted that summer among members of the two communities appeared to shed new light on the divisions in society. They suggested that Protestant attitudes towards Catholics were essentially religious in nature, and were rooted in fears and concerns about the Catholic Church. Catholics, on the other hand, were not concerned with Protestantism, as such, but were anxious about Protestant attitudes towards religion. On reading the results of the survey, one senior British army officer concluded: 'Protestants object to Catholics as Catholics, but not as people. To some extent Catholics object to Protestants as people and not as Protestants.' Perhaps, he speculated, Protestants might one day cease to regard Catholics as a threat; and if this happened, Catholics would feel less threatened, and would then withdraw their support for the IRA.[17]

In the middle of May, two men from Andersonstown were kidnapped by the IRA. Aged eighteen and twenty-two, John McClory and Brian McKinney were blindfolded and beaten while being interrogated about a robbery at a west Belfast bar. They are said to have carried out the robbery while armed with a pistol that was the property of the IRA. On that occasion, the two young men were released. Two weeks later, they were again abducted by the IRA as they walked to work. This time, they simply disappeared without trace.

The following month, Amnesty International published its damning report about the beatings at Castlereagh. Although Roy Mason and Kenneth Newman denied that it was happening, the Amnesty report concluded that prisoners were being mistreated 'with sufficient frequency to warrant the establishment of a public inquiry to investigate it'.

After the report was discussed at the British government's Cabinet committee on Northern Ireland, Bernard Donoughue noted in his diary that Roy Mason was 'reactionary and inflexible'. Callaghan, on the other hand, was being quite liberal, 'and seems to have got the message about Mason being totally a "Prod"'. Once again, it was going to be a difficult summer. Later that month Charlie Stout, the US Consul General in Belfast, discreetly took delivery of an inconspicuous-looking armoured car.[18]

It was going to be hard to resist the establishment of the inquiry that Amnesty was demanding, with its risk that the police brutality that underpinned the government's crimin-alisation policy would be exposed. If that happened, it would give the IRA another means to question the legitimacy of the Northern Ireland state, and to open a new front in its war against it.[19]

That summer, the *Daily Mirror* became the first Fleet Street newspaper to announce support for a phased withdrawal of British forces from Northern Ireland. In a leading article, the newspaper said it had come to the conclusion that the English were part of Ireland's problem; that they were therefore not in a position to solve it, and should leave within five years. A senior editor said that 'if Ireland had been up the coast of Africa, we would have been out generations ago'. In Belfast, however, an army officer briefed defence correspondents, flown over from London, that the military expected to be in the province for the

foreseeable future. Mason and the Conservatives' Northern
Ireland spokesman Airey Neave issued statements saying that
there would be no British withdrawal.

At the end of the year, the Strathearn Audio plant closed with
the loss of 130 jobs, and during six days in November the IRA
detonated more than fifty bombs across the province, targeting
businesses and shopping centres. 'The war to liberate and unify
this country will be a bitter and long drawn out struggle,' it said
in a statement. 'Mason has been forced to eat his arrogant words
of victory, his foolish claims of having defeated the IRA.'[20]

In London, the Treasury announced that inflation had finally
fallen to single figures, but Labour's pact with the Liberals was
breaking down, and Callaghan turned to the Ulster Unionist
Party for the parliamentary support that would enable his
government to limp on. Sensing that an election was imminent,
the advertising agency Saatchi & Saatchi began working on a
series of campaign posters for the Tories, including one under
the banner LABOUR ISN'T WORKING, above a photograph of what
appeared to be a long queue of unemployed people. In fact, all
the people in the 'dole queue' were members of the Young
Conservatives from Margaret Thatcher's constituency.

Shortly before Christmas, a series of IRA bombs exploded in
Liverpool, Manchester, Bristol, Coventry and Southampton.
Bernard Donoughue noted in his diary that London's streets
were quiet. The Thursday before Christmas, he wrote, 'was a
cold and foggy night, not too much traffic because people have
been scared off by the IRA bombing'.

By now the series of strikes that led the winter of 1978–9 to be
called the Winter of Discontent was under way. Callaghan's
government had attempted to persuade the unions to agree to
another pay cap, this time of 5 per cent, at a time when Ford car
workers were demanding a 30 per cent increase. Ford's management were inclined to break the pay cap, not least because

their British operations enjoyed a £246 million profit in 1977. After a nine-week strike the company agreed a 13 per cent deal, and the government's pay cap was dead.

Ambulancemen, traffic wardens, local newspaper reporters, sewage workers, dinner ladies, British Airways pilots and gravediggers: all now began demanding higher wages in the face of rising prices. Many of the strikes that followed were unofficial, mounted by workers who were defying union leaders who for years had collaborated with the government in agreeing to the pay caps.

It was the biggest series of labour stoppages since the General Strike of 1926, and the UK has not seen anything comparable since. In 1979, around 30 million working days were lost. On 22 January that year, 1.5 million public-sector workers were out on strike.

On farms in the south-west of England there were reports of unfed pigs turning to cannibalism. In Liverpool, a strike by gravediggers led to corpses being stored in a factory; the city's medical officer speculated that they might need to be buried at sea. Worried that Callaghan might seek to call in the army to dig graves, Sir Clive Rose, head of the civil contingency unit at the Cabinet Office, telephoned Sir Roland Gibbs, Chief of the General Staff, to test the waters. Gibbs told Rose that the government could fuck off. 'I said: "Thank you",' Rose later recalled. "You've given me my brief."'

It did not help that it was the coldest winter since 1963, with weeks of blizzards, hailstorms and freezing fog. Callaghan did little to muster public support when he flew home from a summit in Guadeloupe looking sun-tanned and relaxed. 'I promise you,' he told waiting reporters, 'if you look at it from the outside, I don't think other people in the world would share the view that there is mounting chaos.'

The following day the splash headline in the *Sun* was CRISIS? WHAT CRISIS? The Tories were able to press home attacks that the Prime Minister was out of touch with Britain and the British people. At Number 10, Donoughue noted in his diary that it was all over for Labour: 'Like the Titanic without the music.'[21]

In March 1979, an official report was published into the detention and interrogation procedures at Castlereagh. Its author was Harry Bennett, a Crown court judge from Yorkshire. He had been tasked with the investigation by Mason, under pressure from other members of the Cabinet, in response to the Amnesty International report. Mason had told MPs that the inquiry would 'discern the difference between truth and propaganda'.

While Bennett was taking evidence from fifty-eight police officers, doctors and lawyers, complaints about beatings at Castlereagh actually increased. A number of doctors decided to go public, telling journalists what they had been witnessing.

Bennett's report was not the exoneration Mason might have hoped for. The judge had said he had been forced to conclude that the 'nature, severity, sites and numbers of separate injuries' were such that they could not all have been self-inflicted; it was beyond doubt, he said, that some were not self-inflicted and had been 'sustained during the period of detention at a police office'. In future, he said, solicitors should be given access to their clients twenty-four hours after arrest, and CCTV cameras should be installed inside the interview rooms.

In Westminster, Callaghan's ailing government was facing a motion of no confidence. Frank Maguire, the independent MP for Tyrone and Fermanagh, told Labour ministers that he would not be attending the vote because he could not support a government that condoned torture. Similarly, Gerry Fitt, the SDLP leader and MP for West Belfast – who had always, resolutely, supported Labour – told the Commons that after reading the Bennett Report he too had decided to abstain. 'When the true story emerges of what has been happening in the interrogation centres the people in the United Kingdom will receive it with shock, horror and resentment,' he said.

The government lost the vote by 311 votes to 310. A general election was now inevitable.

Two days later, Republicans struck a blow that shocked Britain and caused deep personal distress to Margaret Thatcher. Shortly before 3 p.m., the Tories' Northern Ireland spokesman Airey Neave climbed into his blue Vauxhall saloon in the car park beneath the Palace of Westminster. As the car climbed the ramp to ground level, a bomb detonated, shattering his legs and severely burning his torso and head. Neave died a short while later in hospital. Responsibility for the attack was claimed not by the IRA, but by the smaller left-wing Republican group the Irish National Liberation Army (INLA). According to one account, the bomb had been fitted to the car with magnets while it was parked outside the MP's home. A two-stage timer and tilt switch ensured that it was detonated only once the car was started up a second time, and began to ascend the ramp at Westminster, some hours later.

Famously, Neave had been a Second World War prison escapee: like the IRA prisoners at Long Kesh, he and his fellow inmates at Colditz Castle had read everything they could lay their hands on, attended education classes, learned how to smuggle items to the outside world, and plotted their escape. His anti-Nazi commitment lived on after the war. In 1979, he and Thatcher had been close, and his violent death came as a terrible shock to her.

On 3 May, the Conservatives, led by Thatcher, won a forty-three-seat lead on a turnout of 76 per cent. It was an election landslide that would transform Britain and British public life for generations to come.

In the north of Ireland, the leadership of the IRA was committed to rolling out its Long War strategy. It was beginning to think through the ways the prisoner population at Long Kesh could best fight on another front in the war against the Brits. Some even considered the establishment of a 4th Battalion of the Belfast Brigade, comprised entirely of the IRA's non-cooperating prisoners.

On 27 August that year, the Provisionals scored what they would see as a stunning success: they killed a member of the royal family and a large number of British soldiers in separate attacks on the same day.

Shortly before midday a remote-controlled bomb was detonated aboard a boat off the coast of County Sligo, killing the Queen's cousin Lord Mountbatten, along with an 83-year-old woman and two boys. The IRA said it wanted to send a message to the English people that it intended to 'tear out their sentimental imperialist heart'. A few hours later, eighteen soldiers died in an ambush near Warrenpoint in County Down. The IRA had never killed so many soldiers in one attack.

In hindsight, it can be seen that this was the high watermark of the ASUs' campaign of violence: the IRA could never again maintain the same level of operations. Relations between RUC Chief Constable Kenneth Newman and army commander Tim Creasey sank to an all-time low.

The following month at Drogheda, midway between Dublin and the border with the north, in an address to around 300,000 people, Pope John Paul II denounced the IRA's campaign as dishonest, un-Christian and inhumane. 'Violence is evil . . . violence is unacceptable as a solution to problems,' he said. 'Violence is unworthy of man . . . I pray with you that the moral sense and Christian conviction of Irish men and women may never become obscured and blunted by the lie of violence, that nobody may ever call murder by any other name than murder.'

The IRA, no doubt greatly troubled by the Pope's intervention, nevertheless rejected his plea for peace. Their campaign was one of self-defence, the organisation insisted. 'In all conscience, we believe that force is by far the only means of removing the evil of the British presence in Ireland.'

The British position was equally entrenched. In its shock over the death of Mountbatten and the Warrenpoint attack, the British government decided that it needed to persuade Maurice Oldfield, the 63-year-old former head of MI6, to come out of retirement and become the coordinator of security in Northern Ireland. Oldfield is said to have been the model for John le Carré's fictional spymaster George Smiley. One of his first jobs would be to smooth relations between Newman and Creasey. Oldfield was reluctant to accept, but told one of his former schoolteachers that he felt it to be his duty to do so.

Tim Creasey was confident that Oldfield would side with the army in the dispute about the best way to tackle Republican violence, but Oldfield, an intelligence officer to his fingertips, concluded that that MI5 and Special Branch, the intelligence-gathering division of Newman's RUC, should have priority over the military. He quickly established a new Liaison Staff, through which MI5 aimed to resolve any disputes between the military and the police. In 1980, he would be recalled to London after someone – possibly from within MI5 – disclosed that he was gay, and he admitted to having lied about this while undergoing vetting for possible security risks. He was already ill, and died the following year, but his transformation of the UK's security strategy in the north became deeply rooted, and for many years the RUC placed a greater emphasis on intelligence gathering.[22]

The trial of Michael, Harry, Gary and Anne began on the morning of Monday 15 October 1979. The three men were escorted, handcuffed, along the damp and narrow underground tunnel that linked the Crum to the Crown court, and brought into the dock. Anne was driven to court and also placed in the dock. Mr Justice John MacDermott – Long John – the judge who is said to have given Harry a lenient sentence when he had admitted hoarding IRA weapons, was presiding. As was always the case in the so-called Diplock courts, he was sitting alone, without a jury.

In the other courtrooms, young men were being prosecuted for burglaries and car thefts. But there were always at least a couple of terrorism cases in progress at Belfast Crown Court. The communal area outside the courts was much like any other Crown court in the UK, with solicitors, barristers, police and witnesses milling around. But here, armed police officers in flak jackets would stare down the friends and supporters of the defendants; young Republicans would in turn study the police officers, sometimes openly making pencil portraits of them.

As well as being prosecuted for the murder of Millar, the three men were also charged with membership of the IRA. Gary and Harry were charged with possession of a firearm. Gary was also charged with hijacking the Fiat 127 and with the unlawful imprisonment of its owner. Taking the man for a pint at the Whitefort may have seemed a fairly civilised way to keep him in custody, but the law did not see it that way: it was a serious criminal offence. Harry was also charged with attempting to murder Brian McKee after setting up the fake roadworks. The three men denied all the charges.

Anne was charged with possession of the firearm used to kill Millar, with assisting offenders and with membership of the IRA. One week into the trial, she decided to abandon her not-guilty plea and admitted all three charges.

The trial of Gary, Harry and Michael lasted twenty-one days, coming to an end in mid-November. The entire case hinged upon the reliability or unreliability of the admissions they were said to have made at Castlereagh. There was no other evidence against them. Any intelligence gathered about the men, through informers and telephone intercepts, would be excluded from the prosecution case in order to protect those sources. Would MacDermott believe the accused, or the RUC detectives? None of the defendants said they had been beaten, but counsel to Gary and Harry argued that they had signed their statements under duress. Gary chose not to give evidence; Harry did, and he raised the death of Brian Maguire at every opportunity.

Michael also gave evidence, and denied having made the oral admissions attributed to him, although he said that he may, in his exhaustion, have nodded his head on occasion. A consultant psychiatrist giving evidence on Michael's behalf said that the length of his interrogation amounted to inhuman treatment, and offered the opinion that it was contrary to the European Convention on Human Rights. At the end of the trial, MacDermott reserved his decision.

On 12 December, the three men were taken back through the tunnel and Anne was again driven to court. In a judgment that took two hours to read, MacDermott found the three men guilty of all charges. He dismissed any suggestion of ill-treatment at Castlereagh. 'Any detective worth his salt knows that to lose his temper or ill-treat a suspect means he has lost control of the interview.' The way to discover the truth, he said, was through 'calm, persistent and probing questioning'.

MacDermott ruled that Gary Smyth had indeed told police that he knew he was hijacking the car so that Harry could 'go after a peeler'. He added that he regretted not being able to see Gary give evidence:

> In the dock he was always well turned out and well behaved . . . he did not appear the type of young man who would be involved in criminal activity but unhappily appearances can so often be deceptive. There is no doubt in my mind that Smyth was distressed by what he had become involved in.

Turning to Harry Murray, MacDermott said:

> Murray is brash and loud-mouthed. He purports to give
> the impression of a hard man but he probably has a soft
> core and is, I think, a realist. He could not be described
> as intelligent but appeared to me to be cute and cunning
> and undoubtedly is now bitterly hostile to the police. As
> he gave his evidence the impression was of a well-
> rehearsed diatribe and this impression increased during
> cross-examination.

MacDermott said he was satisfied that Michael Culbert was an
IRA intelligence officer. 'The anxieties of membership of that
organisation must be enormous,' he said. The judge then
suggested that this might explain the admissions that the police
claimed Michael had made, and which Michael insisted he had
not. And: 'Arrest to some may be an opportunity to obtain relief
by confession.' He went on:

> Culbert is not, in appearance, the type of person one
> would describe as a typical terrorist, but that proves
> nothing as there is no special type which can properly be
> labelled a terrorist type. Many police officers described
> him as intelligent. That is often a vague yardstick, but
> in my judgement a perfectly fair adjective to apply to
> Culbert, having regard to the manner in which he
> answered questions and obviously followed closely the
> entire proceedings. As a witness he was cool, never
> flustered and, rightly, always thoughtful about his
> answers. I have no doubt that by upbringing, background
> and choice he actively practises his religion and has a
> real conscience.
>
> This accused is a person of decent background and
> upbringing and clear record and in normal times would

probably never have troubled the courts. To such a person participation in a senseless and craven act of terrorism must have weighed very heavily on his conscience, and with his religious upbringing and background I have no doubt that Culbert had a conscience.

MacDermott emphasised Michael's conscience not to compliment him, however, but in order to justify the guilty verdict that he was recording. Michael had not signed a confession, and was insisting that he had not admitted guilt while at Castlereagh. MacDermott was finding a man guilty of murder on the word of a number of detectives, despite warnings from both Amnesty International and the Bennett Report that prisoners at Castlereagh were being beaten. MacDermott's thesis, that Michael had been so overcome by guilt that he had confessed to murder, may have been intended in part to ensure that his guilty verdict survived a trip to the Court of Appeal.

The judge told Anne Laverty: 'You had the good sense to admit your part at an early stage. You have pleaded guilty and that takes a certain amount of moral courage.' He sentenced her to three years on each charge, to be served concurrently.

Michael, Harry and Gary knew that the only sentence MacDermott could pass on them was life imprisonment. 'As has been said many times this year, murder is murder,' the judge told them. 'You are here because the IRA exists and you have seen fit to be involved in its evil activities. The result is that you will waste the best years of your lives in prison and your families and friends will suffer greatly.'

He told Gary and Michael that he was not recommending a minimum term that they should serve, although there was an argument that those who murder individuals seeking to do their public duty should remain in prison for the rest of their natural lives. 'In your case, Murray, you killed this constable callously and without mercy and in your case my recommendation is that a period of thirty years should elapse before you are considered for release.'

He then gave Harry a second life sentence for the attempted murder of Brian McKee, and gave all three men a series of concurrent sentences for the lesser offences. From the dock, Harry yelled at MacDermott: 'The Republican struggle will continue! It will go on until Ireland is free!'[23]

Anne, no doubt relieved by the light sentence, was led away to a waiting prison van. Michael, Harry and Gary were handcuffed to prison officers, led down to the tunnel, and taken back to the Crum.

All three lodged appeals against their convictions. Gary and Harry eventually abandoned their appeals, but Michael pressed on, with his counsel arguing that MacDermott's verdict was against the weight of the evidence. Two years later, the Lord Chief Justice, Lord Lowry, spent little time in dismissing the appeal.

As filthy and overcrowded as the Crum was, nothing prepared the three men for the horrors of their next place of incarceration: the H-shaped cell blocks of HMP Maze or, as Republicans termed it, Long Kesh, near Lisburn.

For more than three years, following the removal of the 'special category' status that had allowed Republican prisoners to wear their own clothing, many had been refusing to wear prison uniforms and instead were clad only in blankets. 'Special category' status had offered a partial recognition that they were fighting a war rather than committing a series of criminal offences, and they were determined to recover it.

The regime at the Maze was brutal, with warders frequently beating Republican prisoners. Pay day was said to be the worst time, when some warders would have a few drinks in nearby pubs, and then return to lay into the prisoners. In March 1978, Republican prisoners refused to leave their cells to wash and slop out their chamber pots, for fear of being attacked. This act of self-preservation escalated rapidly into the dirty or 'no wash' protest, with some prisoners smearing excreta, sometimes mixed with food, on the walls of their cells. Their hair and their beards grew long and unkempt. Each day they continued with their protest, the prisoners lost remission on their sentences.

They would agree to wear a uniform only in order to receive visitors, a process described by Bobby Sands, who had developed as a writer and leader behind bars:

> The warning rattle of the lock and the door opened. I rose from the mattress pulling the blankets off me, letting them drop to the ground and wrapping a towel around me. I stepped out of the cell door into the urine-covered corridor of the wing. It was warmer in the corridor than it was in the cells. I trod through the river of urine until I reached the end cell where the prison garb was stored.

After a painful and humiliating strip search, he would put on the uniform. 'I was a sorrowful-looking sight, dirty face, shaggy hair and beard, with the prison uniform that was several sizes too large hanging off me. I didn't give a damn.'

Before long, many of the cells were infested with maggots. Some prisoners, unable to cope, abandoned the protest, and were moved to a new block where they would wear a prison uniform. Any hopes that prisoners held that they would gain sympathy beyond their core Republican supporters was misplaced; some Unionists began to joke that if cleanliness was next to godliness, then to whom were these men close? But hundreds of prisoners continued with the protest, demanding not only the right to wear their own clothes, but the right not to work, free association with other prisoners, weekly visits and letters, and the restoration of lost remission.

In the summer of 1978, Archbishop Tomás Ó Fiaich, head of the Irish Roman Catholic Church, visited the Maze and was appalled by what he saw. 'I was shocked at the inhuman conditions prevailing in H Blocks three, four and five, where over 300 prisoners were incarcerated,' he said.

> One would hardly allow an animal to remain in such conditions, let alone a human being. The nearest approach to it I have seen was the spectacle of hundreds of homeless people living in sewer pipes in the slums of Calcutta. The stench and filth in some cells, with the remains of rotten food and human excreta scattered around the walls, was absolutely unbelievable. I met two of them and was unable to speak for fear of vomiting.

The government insisted that these men were no different from ordinary criminals; Ó Fiaich, however, said that everything about their backgrounds, and the way they were prosecuted, indicated that they were.

The IRA was by now targeting prison warders, in close-quarter assassination attacks at their homes and with under-car bombs. In November 1978, three men burst into the north Belfast home of Albert Miles, the deputy governor of the Maze. One put his hand over Albert's wife's mouth while the other two shot him dead.

Inside the prison, the beatings and the protest continued. Neither side would back down. The Republican prisoners believed they held the moral high ground; the warders saw them as the scum of the earth. Nowhere was the schism of Northern Ireland life more acute, or more poisonous, than inside the H Blocks. Outside the prison, Roy Mason made it clear that he would never grant 'special category' status to IRA prisoners. Following the 1979 general election, and Mason's departure, the Thatcher government was equally intransigent.[24]

When their appeals failed, Michael and Harry went straight onto the blanket protest.

By now, many of the Republican prisoners had come to accept that further escalation was inevitable: they knew that there was to be a hunger strike. Hunger striking to death had a long tradition in Republicanism, but most such protests had happened generations before, and most such protests in recent years had been in English prisons. Most hunger strikes in the north of Ireland had been protests that were not intended to end in death. This time it was different: the prisoners at the Maze knew – given the doggedness of Thatcher and her government – that this hunger strike would result in deaths.

The first hunger strike began on 27 October 1980, with six IRA prisoners, led by their commanding officer, Brendan Hughes, being joined by one prisoner who was a member of the INLA. On 1 December they were joined by three women at Armagh Gaol.

Later that month six Loyalist prisoners also started a hunger strike. They were demanding the same five concessions, plus a sixth: the right not to be housed near Republicans. On 15 December, a further twenty-three Republicans joined the strike.

Forty-three days into the strike, at a press conference in Dublin, Thatcher insisted there could be no 'special category' status for paramilitary prisoners. 'Murder is a crime,' she said. 'Carrying explosives is a crime, maiming is a crime. Murder is murder, is murder. It is not now, and never can be, a political crime. So, there is no question of political status.'

On 18 December, after fifty-three days, one of the original seven men, Sean McKenna, appeared to be close to death. In the belief – despite Thatcher's words – that a British government official was en route to the prison bearing a letter that offered a number of concessions, Hughes ordered an end to the hunger strike.

The document, when it arrived, was considered by many of the prisoners to be inadequate, and Bobby Sands – who had taken over from Hughes as commanding officer inside the prison – began almost immediately to draw up plans for a new hunger strike. It would be staggered, with one man embarking upon it every few days. Bobby would go first. He must have known he was going to die.

It was a grim and depressing time on the H Blocks. While on the blanket protest, Michael began to question his religious faith. Harry and Gary also experienced moments of deep despondency. Harry met a number of volunteers whom he had not seen since they had attended an IRA training camp together. He also encountered anti-Protestant bigotry for the first time since 1972, when he and Kathleen had fled from north to west Belfast. He approached a senior IRA commander in H Block 5 to complain about the conduct of a couple of the other prisoners. 'Can you tell them to stop calling me Harry the Prod?' This was done, and the men were told that if they wanted to use any form of words to describe Harry, they should say 'Harry the IRA volunteer'.

Gary lost part of the sight in his left eye as a result of an accident in the prison. When he was awarded £25,000 in compensation, the Northern Ireland Office took steps to recoup the money, to offset the £35,000 compensation that had been paid to Nita McAllister following the murder of Millar, and the £4,500 paid to Alan for the trauma he suffered on seeing his father shot dead.[25]

Bobby Sands started his hunger strike on 1 March. Three more men joined him that month. During his protest, he contested a by-election for the Westminster Parliamentary seat of Fermanagh and South Tyrone, which he won on 9 April. His election brought international media attention and raised Republican hopes that the British government would concede their five demands. Thatcher's government refused. On the street corners of west Belfast, people gathered and prayed.

Towards the end, Bobby was skeletal and blind in one eye. He was in excruciating pain. He slipped into a coma and died in the early hours of 5 May, after sixty-six days on hunger strike. Five members of his family were at his bedside. Serious rioting erupted across Nationalist areas of the north and outside the British embassy in Dublin. More than 100,000 people lined the route of the funeral procession from Twinbrook to Milltown cemetery. The mourners included Phelim. 'It was massive,' he recalled later. 'I thought nobody could fail to recognise that this man is not a criminal. It broke my heart, as did the deaths of the others. But it made me more determined.'[26]

Three more hunger strikers died that month, and five more men joined the strike. In June, four more men began refusing food. There have been claims – still bitterly disputed – that the British government effectively conceded a number of the prisoners' demands at this point, but that the IRA leadership outside prison wanted to press on with the hunger strike because of the enormous political gains it was bringing. Many people from both communities were appalled at the unfolding human tragedy. Jack Hermon, by now the RUC Chief Constable, and Dick Lawson, the British army's commanding officer in the province, believed it had to be stopped – 'there had to be some recognition of the feelings of the Catholic community,' Hermon later wrote – and the two men flew to Chequers, the Prime Minister's country retreat, to warn that the prisoners were resolved to continue: men would continue to die.[27] From the United States to the Soviet Union there was condemnation of the way the British government had allowed an elected Member of Parliament to starve to death over his right to wear his own clothes in prison.

The strike was finally called off on 3 October, after a number of hunger strikers' families made clear that they would authorise a medical intervention as soon as their menfolk slipped into unconsciousness. By the time the decision was taken, five further volunteers had been lined up to join the hunger strike. The fifth was Harry.[28] By that time, ten men were dead.

Three days later the British government partly conceded to the prisoners' demands, including their right to wear their own clothes. The British press hailed the end of the strike as a resounding victory over the 'H Block terrorists'. The *Daily Mail* celebrated Thatcher's 'magnificent obstinacy'. The *Guardian* welcomed the outcome. 'The Government has overcome the hunger strikes by a show of resolute determination not to be bullied,' the newspaper said. Many British media commentators' only concern was whether the deaths would trigger renewed IRA bombings in Britain.

What Fleet Street and the British government had not grasped was that Britain's intransigence resulted in the hunger strikers being seen, internationally, as the bravest of Davids doing battle against a cruel Goliath.

In Ireland, they were seen to be invoking the traditions of the rebels of 1916. Elsewhere, people were reminded of the way the British had brutally suppressed resistance in every corner of their empire.

What Margaret Thatcher had not seen – but Bobby Sands clearly had – was that the IRA had opened up a new front from within the Maze, and that the Republican movement would emerge much fortified from the hunger strikes, regardless of who 'won' or 'lost' over the issues of clothing and free association.

Although the British government's concessions made no mention of 'political status', Republicans seized upon them as meaning just that. On the H Blocks, IRA commanders ordered their men 'to openly adopt a much more confident or aggressive attitude towards the screws and to make our presence on the wing felt'. Senior prison officers were told by IRA prisoners that they should be in no doubt as to who was running those wings:

it was the IRA. Morale among prison warders plummeted.[29]

Being able to more freely move around the prison gave the prisoners opportunities to assess possible weaknesses in security, and draw up plans for escape. Although the Maze was thought to be the most secure prison in Europe – with each block designed as a jail within a jail – in September 1983, after six months of planning, inmates of H Block 7 mounted the largest jailbreak in British history.

Six handguns and a number of knives had been smuggled into the prison. One of the handguns was given to Harry. At 2.30 on a Sunday afternoon, the prisoners took control of the block by taking many of the prison officers hostage. One was stabbed, another clubbed, and one was shot in the head but survived. A dozen were relieved of their uniforms, and given ponchos fashioned from blankets. The officers were all bound and had pillowcases placed over their heads, and prisoners donned their uniforms.

Meanwhile, seven IRA men were waiting outside the prison in a van, armed with two heavy machine guns and a number of rifles.

When a food delivery truck arrived at the block, the prisoners seized it, climbed into the back and forced the driver to take them to the gatehouse. A small number of prisoners who were due shortly to complete their sentences were left with the hostages.

The truck was allowed through one set of gates when the guards recognised the driver. The prisoners then took control of the main gate complex, where four more prison officers were stabbed. One, James Ferris, was stabbed in the chest with a prison workshop chisel, and collapsed and died of a heart attack.

When two officers blocked the main entrance with their own cars, the prisoners abandoned the hijacked truck and ran to the fence on foot. Harry, wearing one of the uniforms and still armed with a handgun, clambered over the fence but then returned to assist another prisoner who had become entangled on barbed wire. A prison officer, Campbell Courtney, approached him, pointing one of the weapons at him that the escapers had dropped.

Campbell saw Harry turn and point the handgun at him. 'I thought it was an imitation weapon and kept on going,' Campbell recalled. 'It wasn't and he shot me in the leg.'

Harry turned and fled, but had gone just a few yards when he felt a thud in his thigh and found himself lying on his back: Gunner David Lee, a sentry in a watchtower, had held his fire until he saw Harry shoot the prison officer, and then took one shot.

Harry was quickly recaptured and beaten by prison officers, some of whom berated him as a 'turncoat bastard'. The beating was halted when a British army medic arrived to give him first aid. He was then taken to the Lagan Valley Hospital in Lisburn, where he found himself on a stretcher alongside Campbell. The two men traded insults until Harry drifted off.

Thirty-eight men had escaped. Although fifteen were recaptured the same day, and four more over coming days, many made it across the border. Two reached Amsterdam and four made it to the United States. Two were arrested in the Republic, but the courts refused to extradite them on the grounds that they would 'probably [be] targets for ill-treatment by prison staff'.

One prison officer had died, four others had been stabbed, two shot and wounded, and many others beaten. Doctors certified that forty-two prison officers were unfit for work due to nervous disorders brought on by the violence. Some are said to have remained damaged for the rest of their lives. Prison staff say they received no debriefing or support; Courtney Campbell says his wife received no support while he was in hospital. On returning to work, he was placed in the same block as Harry, the man who had shot him.

A number of the escapers were charged with the murder of James Ferris, but were acquitted after the prosecution failed to establish that the stabbing caused his heart attack.

An official inquiry found that the watchtower sentry had not opened fire on Harry earlier because he believed it would have been unlawful to do so. Under the so-called yellow card rules under which soldiers in the province were operating, he believed he could not shoot before Harry had shot the prison officer. He had wanted to shoot him with a rubber bullet, but found that he was unable to unlock the container in which this ammunition was stored.

In 1988, eighteen men appeared at Belfast Crown Court and were sentenced for their roles in the escape. The longest sentence – eight years – was passed on Harry, for a series of offences, including wounding the prison officer.

In the immediate aftermath of the escape, Harry had been questioned by detectives. At one point, he says, a police officer came to him and told him: 'Constable McAllister's widow wants you to know that she's forgiven you.'

'I told him that I didn't care whether she had forgiven me or not.'[30]

6

The Far Side of Revenge

> So hope for a great sea-change
> On the far side of revenge.
> Believe that a further shore
> Is reachable from here.
> Believe in miracles
> And cures and healing wells.
>
> Seamus Heaney, *The Cure at Troy*

Michael's two boys were both young men by the time he was released from prison in late 1993. Harry's four children had been aged between seven and three when he was convicted, and were in their early twenties and late teens when he was finally released.

Gary spent more than twelve years behind bars, during which time he completed an Open University degree in psychology. In early 1985 he married a young Belfast woman he had met through Phelim and who had been visiting him in prison. Following his release, he and his wife had three daughters.

Many released prisoners in Northern Ireland have experienced difficulty finding meaningful work, regardless of how well qualified they may be. Some also experience difficulty obtaining insurance, even decades after their release.

Harry spent a period on the bru, and then helped to run a boxing club. In 2013 he was appointed director of a community interest company, running an amateur sports club in Lenadoon.

Gary enrolled at Queen's University in Belfast to study for a master's degree. Michael was informed that, as a convicted murderer, he was barred from social work. He attempted to enrol at a teacher training college, but was told he could not teach, either.

Many of the families of released prisoners also experienced profound problems: a 1992 Queen's University survey found that most prisoners' partners had financial worries, and were anxious that their partner would not be able to find work. The greatest fear – expressed by 91 per cent of partners – was that they would be harassed by the security forces. Around a fifth said they had suffered depression while their partner was behind bars.

The three men were released into a society that was itself deeply traumatised, a place where significant numbers of people experienced mental health problems as a consequence of the conflict. Attempts have been made to quantify this trauma and its causes. In 1993, for example, a study of the risk of death from political violence found that in Germany the average annual figure for such deaths was 0.1 for each one million deaths. In Italy it was 0.6 per million. In Northern Ireland it was 97.6.

A survey conducted in 2010 by the Northern Ireland Statistics and Research Agency found that 11 per cent of the population had been bereaved by the Troubles, 6 per cent had suffered physical injury and 24 per cent had cared for someone who had suffered trauma.

As one health professional who has both studied and treated victims of trauma in Northern Ireland for several decades observes: 'The deep silence of grief is made worse when the bereavement arises from the active will of others.'

Studies indicated that by the mid-1980s, the conflict had begun inflicting very substantial damage upon the mental health of the population; that women were more likely than men to have poor psychological health; and that most people were still suffering significant emotional distress more than twenty years after they were bereaved. One of the most common psychological problems, of course, is post-traumatic stress disorder.[1]

Released prisoners experienced their own fairly unique set of psychological problems; having been politically motivated did not protect Republican ex-prisoners and their families from substantial and complex emotional pressures.

One study of eighteen Republican ex-prisoners and four family members found that many had become introverted and detached from loved ones. Absence had led inevitably to a degree of estrangement; attempts that had been made during family visits to hide worries – in the mistaken belief that such concealment would help maintain family ties – had sometimes had the opposite effect.

A number of the former prisoners said that they had had plenty of time to read and debate, and had made intellectual gains while behind bars, but had lost out in terms of emotional development. 'When I arrive up home it is all polite, the same old talk,' said one interviewee. 'It is almost like a visit again and the closeness, it's gone, it is not the same. And I have found more and more the distance is getting greater rather than smaller.'

Some of the ex-prisoners experienced delayed mourning over family deaths that had occurred while they were in prison. Most said they had experienced depression. Others said, on release, that they felt guilty about fellow prisoners who had been left behind. Some found themselves overwhelmed by such simple matters as noise and colours and traffic. One former lifer says that he repeatedly tripped over uneven pavements. 'In prison, all the floors are smooth; outside, each time I went out, I damned near broke my neck.'[2]

Nita eventually remarried and moved away from the bungalow in Lisburn. She remained deeply traumatised by the events of 22 April 1978. Decades later, she finds it difficult to talk about the murder of her husband. And the middle-aged man who, as a little boy, saw his father's killer through a crack in the back door, and who Harry saw watching him after he fired the last of his four shots, also remains deeply distressed.

After leaving the British army, Swede Tompkinson was diagnosed as having post-traumatic stress disorder. 'I was asked by the psychologist to name ten incidents which affected/define my life. Ulster was mentioned four or five times. We talked at length about Ulster and my army time and as a result I was treated with Eye Movement Desensitisation and Reprocessing and the treatment worked very well for me.' Like many former British soldiers who served in Northern Ireland, he takes the view that he had been motivated not by any political objectives, but a desire to serve his regiment and his comrades. 'Despite having a couple of relapses since, I look back on my whole army time with pride and satisfaction of serving with such bloody good mates who were always at hand.'

Swede moved back to Sweden, where he rarely talks about the Troubles. 'Nobody understands and really cares. My brother, after the first tour, asked: "How was Ulster?" I replied: "Being shot at is very dangerous." He replied: "What! You were shot at with live bullets?"'[3]

Glen Espie, the plumber and part-time soldier in the UDR who had escaped after being shot at point-blank range, survived a second close-quarter assassination attempt in 1987. While driving to work, three masked men opened fire on him with assault rifles. 'The car was starting to vibrate as the first rounds hit the car,' he recalls. Glen was shot through the wrist but managed to get out of the car and return fire. Some time afterwards, he noticed that his two small children were cowering whenever they travelled in the back of the car. He decided it was time to leave the army.

After surviving Harry's attempt on his life, and being moved from the police barracks at Andersonstown to Portadown, Brian McKee transferred to CID:

In the meantime my marriage fell apart. I would blame the police service, particularly after that incident. My life changed quite a bit. I was drinking heavier. I was spending too much time on the job. Fourteen- or fifteen-hour days. Then you'd go up to the local army camp, somewhere safe, and have a few bevvies.

Some guys became paranoid. I didn't become paranoid, but you'd be more careful about how you checked your car in the morning. You'd be more careful about people coming to the house. My wife had her car, and you'd be checking that for bombs every morning as well.

You'd just become more aware of how vulnerable you were. I suppose it all added up to the break-up of my marriage. The marriage just dissolved. It was my fault.

After a year, Brian left the police, did a few short-term jobs and then joined the ambulance service.

One day, I saw a red Allegro with a black vinyl roof, the same as my old car, in the car park at Craigavon Hospital. That roof wasn't normal on the Allegro. I went over looking at it, and down the side of the door you could see the rust marks where the bullet holes had been patched. It had been bought by a young doctor. He told me that the front passenger door, where most of the bullets had come in, was always rattling. When we took the inside panel off, there was a slug lying there.

Brian remarried, and helped raise two stepchildren.

If I had my life to live again, would I join the police? Perhaps. But maybe not. The regime of Unionism that we were supporting wasn't a particularly good regime; there was all that discrimination, people unable to vote, people unable to work. I can understand better now the rage that came out of those days.

I've ended up more nationalist-minded now. I feel Ireland is too small an island to have two separate countries on it. Financially we would be better off as one place.

The whole constitution of the south has changed so much that a Protestant could live quite comfortably there now. Forty years ago, that might not have been possible. But I spend a lot of time down there now. And I think differently.

In July 2007, the British army's campaign in Northern Ireland finally came to a close. Known within the military as Operation Banner, it had lasted for thirty-eight years – the longest continuous operation by British armed forces. Remarkably, throughout that time the army had never drawn up anything that recognisably resembled a campaign plan.[4]

Marie, the wife of Brendan Megraw, the man who was disappeared in April 1978, gave birth to a girl at the end of that year. She was still hoping that one day her smiling Brendan would walk back through the front door of their home on Twinbrook.

'Nobody knew what was happening,' says Brendan's younger brother Kieran. 'You thought he would come back. Then the baby was born, and he still hadn't come back.' The months became years, the years decades. 'You could never use those words "move on",' says Kieran. 'You couldn't move on, you just had to deal with it as best as you could.'

The family was still holding out hope when, twenty-one years later, the IRA finally admitted it had killed Brendan. He had been, the organisation said in a statement, an 'agent provocateur' for a British army special forces unit called the Military Reaction Force, although that unit had been disbanded several years before his abduction. 'That's when we finally knew he was never coming back,' Kieran says.

As part of the peace process, a series of searches were mounted for Brendan and other men and women who had been 'disappeared' by the IRA. The searchers relied on information that Republicans passed on, often via Roman Catholic priests, about dimly recalled burial sites.

The remains of John McClory and Brian McKinney, who had been abducted as they walked to work, were found in June 1999 in a shallow grave at the edge of a bog, two miles across the border in County Monaghan. Brendan's remains were found eventually in October 2014 in a grave at the edge of a peat bog near Kells in County Meath. He was three feet below the surface, bent at the waist, with his ankles crossed. He had been shot in the head. An inquest in Dublin heard that he had been killed on the day he had been abducted, or very shortly afterwards.

'I don't think we'll ever get to the bottom of the reason why Brendan was taken,' says Kieran. 'We'll never know, we've never been told.' He says Brendan wasn't involved in the Republican movement. 'He had a good job to go to. Things were looking good, amid all the badness that was going on.'

Marie eventually remarried. Brendan and Marie's daughter is now a middle-aged woman. The family does not like to talk about her; they want to protect her.[5]

In 1994, just as Gary, Michael and Harry were getting out of prison, Phelim found himself going back in.

By now he was Dr Féilim Ó hAdhmaill – he had changed his name in the early 1980s – and he had switched to studying social policy and completed a PhD. His thesis, completed in 1990, studied the way people living and working in Nationalist communities in west Belfast organised themselves during the Troubles. He had married, had two sons, and raised them as Irish speakers. Speaking Irish was, for Féilim, a way of asserting his Irish identity: 'The State was denying that there was such a thing as Irishness in that part of the world.' His boys were encouraged not to hate the British people, nor even their armed forces. His elder son Seán says: 'We were told that even though there was a British soldier in your garden or pointing a gun at you when you were playing in the street, they're following orders and it's the British establishment that are the problem, the people in power giving orders are the problem, not the ordinary people.'

Féilim had remained an active member of the IRA. By the early 1990s, he had recognised for some time that the IRA's armed struggle was 'turning off more and more of our potential support bases'. Nevertheless, he believed it should continue, if only to force the British government to consider a political settlement. He had also become increasingly involved in the IRA's operations in England.

He had remained of interest to the police, army and MI5 since the charge of murdering Millar McAllister had been withdrawn in 1979. He is said to have been spotted making contact with an IRA man in central Scotland during 1993, a year in which there had been a number of bomb attacks in Britain. One of these bombings, at Bishopsgate, had devastated the heart of London's financial district, causing damage of more than £1 billion, and had killed a press photographer. It was, on the IRA's terms, an outstanding success. Another, which claimed the lives of two small boys in Warrington, caused widespread shock and revulsion, a horror which was shared by many Republican sympathisers.*

The following January, Féilim travelled from Belfast to take up a post as a lecturer in sociology at the University of Central Lancashire in Preston. He also took up residence in a terrace house a few miles away, on the east side of the small town of

---

* Féilim denies any responsibility for the Warrington bombing.

Accrington. His true reason for moving to England was to take a closer command role over the IRA's activities in Britain.

At this time, the beginning of peace talks was almost inevitable, but the IRA believed that Sinn Féin's then-slender electoral mandate, north and south of the border, would not necessarily justify a place at the table. While there was a growing acceptance that violence had become an obstacle to political change, rather than a means of achieving it, the organisation also believed that only armed force – and attacks in England – would guarantee its full involvement in the political process.

Senior figures in the movement had also accepted that with the end of the Cold War, the UK could no longer be argued to have a strategic interest in the north of Ireland. A few days after Féilim arrived in England, Martin McGuinness was asked by an interviewer about the future of the 'armed struggle'. He replied: 'We're trying to end it.' Nevertheless, violence – and the threat of continuing violence – was one of the few tools at the IRA's disposal.

The British security service was well aware of Féilim's presence in Britain. His house in Accrington was being watched and filmed, and teams of MI5 surveillance specialists followed him as he commuted to and from the university by train, some apparently grumbling with him when the train was late.

MI5 formed the view that Féilim was either the commander of the IRA in England or its chief quartermaster. Either way, the agency concluded, he would be a very important catch.[6]

On 13 February, following a tip-off from Ireland, police watched as a silver Datsun car arrived on the back of a truck at Fleetwood in Lancashire. The truck was driven to West Thurrock, east of London, where the Datsun was unloaded in a car park. Three times over the next week, police and MI5 officers followed Féilim as he travelled by train to London and then took a taxi not to West Thurrock, but to a motorway service station at South Mimms, north of the city, where he would wait for hours, apparently expecting the Datsun to arrive.

There had been a serious breakdown in communications. Féilim travelled from Accrington to Bolton and Blackpool, where he made a number of telephone calls, apparently using code words. Eventually, the car was driven to west London, and then to South Mimms, where Féilim arrived once again to collect it.[7]

Féilim recalls his subsequent arrest as a slightly comical affair:

> I had gone to London to collect a car. It contained a gun and bomb-making material, Semtex, which had been built into the body of the car. It was clear to me that there were problems, probably before I picked up the car, but certainly from the time I picked it up – I had spotted people acting strangely and maybe I was in denial of this. The question I had was, do I go ahead with this or do I not? And if I don't go ahead with it, what are the consequences? Not to me, but to the struggle?
>
> I went ahead and it was obviously a mistake. The car was an absolute bucket, a complete wreck. I was travelling up the motorway at about 35 miles an hour. The British security services had smashed the wing mirror [. . .] so you couldn't even spot the followers.

Féilim arrived back in Accrington and began removing the contents of the car. 'Gunmen just arrived from all over the place – about twenty of them.'

At first he feared that the police were going to shoot him.

> I was told to lie down, and at that point I realised I wasn't going to be killed. I thought: 'Result!' I knew immediately that I was going to prison for a long time, and that was fine. I was genuinely unconcerned about that. You had to accept that either that was going to happen, or that you were going to be killed.

He still thought that he would be beaten. In the event, two detectives lifted him gently to his feet. 'They were really, really polite. I couldn't believe it. I was expecting to get kicked all around the place.'[8]

Féilim refused to say a word to the police when they attempted to interview him. The police were unconcerned: the lengthy surveillance evidence and a search of Féilim's pockets, along with his home and, critically, the car, produced more than enough evidence for a successful prosecution. His comings and goings in Lancashire had all been filmed. He was charged with possession of explosives and conspiring to cause explosions between January 1993 and the point of his arrest in February 1994.

He says that two of the detectives shook hands with him after he was charged. He was then driven to Belmarsh high-security prison in south-east London. On being handed over to prison officers, he refused to give his name and date of birth. When the prison officers insisted that he must, he asked: 'What are you going to do if I don't? Throw me out?' Behind him, he could hear the police chuckling. The prison officers booked him in.

How methods had changed from Castlereagh in 1978.

Féilim's sons, then aged thirteen and ten, were as much astonished as distressed by his arrest. The older boy, Seán, later said: 'I didn't have a clue that my dad was involved. It came as a complete surprise and shock to us. I just thought he went on a lot of business trips. I thought he was a bit of a pen-pusher because he was always wearing a shirt and tie and carrying a briefcase.'[9]

Féilim went on trial at the Old Bailey later that year. The jury was told that police had found 17 kilos of Semtex plastic explosive in the car, along with 17 detonators, 15 power units, two magnetic under-car bombs, and a 9mm automatic pistol and ammunition, all hidden in the seats and under the wheel arches.

The court heard that in his wallet, wrapped in cellophane in a ball smaller than a pea, police found fifteen cigarette papers, on which were written a number of potential targets, marked A for military, P for political or S for strategic. They included details of Cabinet members and backbench politicians with an interest in Northern Ireland; oil and gas installations and reservoirs; RAF bases and government offices; the Post Office Tower in London and the Humber Bridge near Hull, at that time the longest single-span suspension bridge in the world. There were also the dates and locations of the Cruft's Dog Show and a concert due to be given by the band of the Royal Marines, a band that had been bombed by the IRA five years earlier, with eleven marines killed and twenty-one wounded. Also written on the cigarette papers were a number of codes for communicating with active service units in England.

The jury was told that Féilim was by then a 'strategic planner' for the IRA, and it was alleged that he was to have selected the targets and distributed the explosives to active service units based in England and Scotland.

The prosecution was led by Sir Derek Spencer, QC, the Solicitor General. He said that Féilim's post at the university had 'provided him with an admirable cover for the other side of his character – not the academic – but as a very skilled active operator in a major bombing campaign'.

Féilim did not contest the bulk of the prosecution's evidence, and admitted to being a member of the IRA. However, he insisted he had been planning to bury the Semtex explosive in woodland near Accrington, for possible future use by the IRA, and had not been intending to use it. The judge rejected his lawyers' suggestion that the jury should be permitted to consider a charge of unlawful possession of explosives as an alternative to a charge of conspiring to cause explosions.

The jury took less than two hours to convict. In a statement read to the court, Féilim said:

With all due respect, as far as I'm concerned I should not be before a criminal court. The actions I'm accused of are political actions which result from the ongoing conflict which results from your country's colonial conquest of Ireland . . . I'm a political prisoner and that's how I should be treated by your government.

He said that he hoped that the IRA ceasefire, which had been announced ten weeks earlier,

leads to a permanent end to the war in my country and the establishment of a lasting and just peace settlement. Let us hope your government has finally got the message and is prepared to leave us in peace. I don't want my children to grow up in the kind of society I did: one filled with bigotry, racism, bitterness and burnings.

He added: 'I deeply regret being captured, and I suppose congratulations are due to the security services.'

Sentencing Féilim, Mr Justice Rougier showed contempt for his speech about hopes for peace. 'There can be very few people who do not bitterly regret the loss of life during the Troubles and I hope the peace process will ultimately succeed,' the judge said. 'But I do not know how you managed to persuade yourself that the end you had in mind could be justified by the means you wished to use.' He asked how a Doctor of Philosophy could go along with any movement or action that led to the 'maiming and killing of innocent men, women and children'.

He added: 'That is your moral problem, not mine. You are not just criminal but evil. You will go to jail for twenty-five years.'[10]

A number of Féilim's fellow Republicans say that by the time of his arrest he was fully committed to the peace process, and that he had been engaged in operations intended not to cost lives but to force the British government to commit more clearly to peace talks at a time when that process was stalled.

The IRA's attacks in Britain at that time were clearly intended to influence Anglo-Irish talks. A few days before Féilim was arrested, incendiary devices had been planted at eight shops in London just a few hours before the British Prime Minister John Major and the Irish Taoiseach Albert Reynolds had been due to meet to discuss the peace process.

Those attacks continued after his arrest: a few days later, mortar bombs rained down on Heathrow Airport from tubes buried outside the perimeter. A second attack was triggered two days later and a third two days after that; none of the mortar bombs exploded – apparently by design – and nobody was hurt. But the message was clear: we can cause mayhem, if we wish.

In 1996, Féilim's appeal against both conviction and sentence was rejected. During the initial years of his imprisonment he was moved around a number of maximum-security prisons in England. At Whitemoor in Cambridge, he and a number of other IRA men mounted a blanket-and-no-wash protest against being expected to work and over the way in which glass panels separated them from visiting relatives. On a number of occasions his wife was refused permission to visit because she insisted on speaking in Irish. On another occasion, Féilim rang his family on Christmas Day to wish them a merry Christmas. The moment he did so – in Irish – the listening prison officers ended the call.

Féilim's eldest son Seán recalls his visits to English prisons as a surreal experience. They were usually located on the edge of remote villages. 'They'd know as soon as you opened your mouth who you were and why you were there. And it wouldn't take long for it to travel around. There was an atmosphere that wasn't great, for someone to look down at you from a young age.'[11]

After a few years, Féilim was transferred to the Maze. He says:

> Long Kesh was like I was in paradise. You could see the
> sky. You were also among friends and comrades. In
> England there was a lot of solitary confinement, and even
> when you did get out to exercise, the yard was covered
> by walls with metres thick of wire mesh above. In England
> you were treated like public enemy number one.

In Long Kesh, by this time, Féilim found that the prison officers
were treating Republican inmates like political prisoners.[12] He
was appointed commander of the Gaeltacht wing, the Irish-
speaking block, where he helped to run classes. In July 2000,
Féilim was among the final group of seventy-eight inmates to be
released from the Maze under the Good Friday Agreement. A
few years later he moved to the Republic.

He picked up his academic career, and now has a diploma
in European Humanities, a diploma in teaching English as a
foreign language, a postgraduate certificate in Teaching and
Learning in Higher Education from University College Cork,
and a Dioplóma sa Ghaeilge Fheidhmeach – a diploma in
applied Irish. He is also a qualified therapeutic counsellor.

Féilim has dedicated much of his academic life to the study of
conflict and peace processes across the world. At the time of
writing, he is a social science lecturer at University College
Cork, where his responsibilities include coordinating a master's
degree in Conflict, Transformation and Peace Building. There
was some opposition to his appointment to the university post,
which he resents. 'People think we should be cleaning the streets
or emptying bins, doing jobs like that.'

Looking back at the Provisionals' campaign, he says that a
point was reached where Republicans were probably unable to
expand their appeal beyond their 'limited' core support. This
was partly, he says, because of a ban on the broadcast of
Republicans' statements, in both the UK and the Republic, and
because most people living outside Republican areas did not

know any members of the IRA, and saw only their violence.

He says that his own membership of the IRA has been only one small part of a life in which he has also been a husband, a father and a carer, and has worked with asylum seekers. However, reflecting on his role in that campaign he says that he chose to become involved because he believed it was the right thing to do at that particular time.

> I'm not a pacifist . . . the vast majority of people believe in things like a just war, and I believe that in order to bring progress to society, at times you have to engage in conflict, whether it be violent or not. It seems to me that the only reason why any sane person would engage in violence is if they feel there's no other options.
>
> A lot of the injustices that existed when I was growing up, my kids and their kids won't have to go through. I believe that it was necessary for us to go through this process of struggle and suffering in order for us to reach this particular stage that we're at, where people are prepared to sit down and say: 'Look, maybe we can work out our differences.'[13]

Today, Michael is also completely committed to the peace process. After being barred from social work and refused the opportunity to take up teaching, he found a role with a Republican ex-prisoners' organisation. He has made efforts to assist in peace-building overseas, particularly in Colombia. His work towards peace and reconciliation in the north of Ireland has included arranging encounters between former British soldiers and members of the RUC and former IRA volunteers. He has also sat on the Victims and Survivors Forum, a body established to advise on the needs of people who suffered during the Troubles. His appointment was, perhaps inevitably, criticised by some Unionists, but the Victims' Commissioner pointed out that Michael's family had been burned out of Bombay Street at the start of the Troubles, and argued that a range of voices was needed for a worthwhile debate on victims' needs.

Like Féilim, however, Michael believes that the political violence of the Provisionals had been an entirely appropriate response to the violence of first the Stormont government, and then the British state. The options, he says, were extraordinarily limited for Irish men and women seeking political change in the north.

'The narrative about Ireland tends to be very simplified,' he said during a radio interview in 2015. 'The issues of Ireland didn't start with 1969 or 1970, and it didn't start with riots in Derry or Belfast.' To understand why people joined the IRA, you must take a broad historical context of the island being a colony of Britain. 'From my perspective, there was a series of events that led me to believe that political change was not going to be offered by the local Stormont government, and that the British government would not push the Stormont government to make the change we were looking for.' He added that he believes 'the circumstances which led me to believe it was correct to take up arms against a foreign government no longer exist'.

Questioned about the killing of Millar, he said:

> I stand over it, and no apology has or will be offered for actions taken by personnel in the IRA. The IRA apologised as an organisation to people who were killed by the IRA, who were not connected to conflict – let's say innocent civilians. Other than that, IRA activities stand, no apologies offered, no regrets. No sleepless nights at all.[14]

Like other Republicans, Michael would say that he didn't go to war: the war came to him. When he is not being interviewed on the radio as a representative of the Republican movement, however, Michael's views about the impact his actions had on Millar's family appear to be a little more ambiguous. He appears anguished when talking about the dead man, and wrings his hands when he mentions 'those boys'. But he insists they were right to do it. 'He was the enemy.'

Today Harry still lives in the Lenadoon area, where an enormous Republican mural adorns his end-of-terrace house. He is proud of his membership of the IRA and his role in the armed struggle – particularly the Maze breakout – and is particularly gratified by the way he was embraced by the Republican movement, despite his background.

He is even more uncompromising than Michael when asked about the killing of Millar. 'I thought what I did was right.'

And Millar's sons? 'That boy would be about the age of my son now.' He smiles slightly. 'I don't know what effect it would have on him, seeing his father lying there.' And being fatherless? 'It's not for me to say how he feels about that. He was the enemy. It had to be done.'

The Crab, it seems, does not wish to display the slightest hint of remorse.[15]

Looking back, Gary can recall the way his stomach began to churn when he heard on the radio that a policeman had been shot dead in Lisburn. This was not caused by guilt, he insists.

> It wasn't guilt. There was a war on, and I played my part. Would you ask the RAF bomber crews who bombed Dresden whether they felt guilty? I would imagine they would feel pity for the people down below, but they wouldn't feel guilt. It was just the role you had to play, it was your part in it – it was what you had to do.
>
> We had very, very few choices if we wanted to bring about necessary political change.

Millar had been seen at Castlereagh – the hated Castlereagh – and as such was 'part of a cruel and brutal system', Gary says. He could not be targeted at Castlereagh, however, so shooting him at his home was the only option. 'It was not personal.'

Although he did not know that the car he hijacked was to be used in a killing – and his conviction for murder, rather than for hijacking, is still the cause of some bitterness – Gary accepts that he had no reason to believe that the operation was *not* going to end in someone's death. But while he feels no guilt, he does, at times, admit to feeling some shame. Moreover, he questions whether the IRA's Long War strategy could be justified, once it became clear that the British were not going to withdraw under pressure. 'If what you're doing isn't working, do you have a right to carry on doing it?'

He too is completely committed to the peace process, and to reconciliation: the work he has undertaken in recent years has included helping to run a men's health centre in a Loyalist neighbourhood; the clients who have been helped by the centre have included former British soldiers, returning from Iraq and Afghanistan.[16]

Anne does not like to speak about the past. On release from prison, she had no further involvement with the IRA. She still lives in the north of Ireland, but some distance from Twinbrook and Lisburn, in a gaily painted house with a view over parkland.

Today, the infrastructure of war has been largely dismantled from One Batt's area. Andersonstown Barracks has long been demolished and on the site where Fort Monagh once stood there is a smart new housing estate. The gable-end murals are as likely to celebrate peace as to commemorate conflict, and here and there are memorials to the dead. There is one outside Roddy's, a Republican club named after Roddy McCorley, an Irish rebel hanged by the English in 1800 and the great-grandfather of one of the men who shot dead Oswald Swanzy in Lisburn in 1920. Engraved on it are the names of nine volunteers from One Batt and the Cumann na mBan who lost their lives. Four of them were women, the youngest aged eighteen.

Nine miles down the road, Lisburn is enjoying its new status as a city, having lobbied for the designation during the Queen's Golden Jubilee celebrations in 2002. By then, many Catholic families had settled in the area: up to 40 per cent of the population is now Catholic. The new city adopted the motto 'Lisburn – a city for everyone'.

Not everyone saw it that way. A few months after the Jubilee, three masked Loyalists armed with baseball bats attacked a 21-year-old local man, James McMahon, as he walked alongside the Lagan in the city centre. James died shortly afterwards. Police believe he was killed because he was a Catholic. Nobody was convicted of the murder.

Some people in Lisburn appear to be only vaguely aware of The Burnings, and of the way the character of their city was so completely transformed over three days and nights during the summer of 1920. But the city itself cannot erase the memory. The scars have not disappeared; its face remains slightly disfigured, and reconstructed. Dotted here and there around Market Square, wedged between the fine late-Victorian stone-fronted buildings, are a handful of red-brick structures, awkward and out of place, thrown up during the lean days of the 1920s to replace the Catholic-owned business premises that were torched during the riots that followed the murder of Oswald Swanzy.

Today, Lisburn city centre resembles one of those European cities that were bombed during the Second World War: historical buildings are punctuated by affordable replacements. But unlike Groningen or Portsmouth or Munich, this reconstruction is not acknowledged to be a reminder of a devastating conflict.

If you cross the square to Christ Church Cathedral, you will pass the spot where the Catholic-owned confectionery shop once stood. It had been the first building to be attacked. Following the riots, its ruins were razed completely to the ground to provide a wider entrance to the cathedral.

Inside the cathedral, on your left, is a brass plaque. 'In proud and ever-loving memory of Oswald Ross Swanzy, DI, Royal Irish Constabulary who gave his life in Lisburn 22nd August 1920. Erected by his mother and Irene his sister.' Like the other plaques within the cathedral, it receives a regular rubbing from cathedral volunteers armed with Brasso.

Walking out, and turning right, as Oswald Swanzy did, you cross to the north-west junction of Railway Street and Castle Street. The branch of the Northern Bank outside which his killers struck has long since closed; at the time of writing, the premises were occupied by a jeweller's shop. On either side of the recessed doorway where Swanzy died there were glass cabinets: £360 Tissot watches on your right; equally expensive necklaces and bracelets on your left.

A few paces to the west is Bow Street, where the man from the Belfast *News Letter* had watched aghast as shop after shop became 'a seething mass of fire' during the riots that followed Oswald Swanzy's murder, while the air was filled with sparks 'like thick showers of crimson snow'.

In 1978, at the end of Bow Street, by Market Place, on the right, was the Crazy Prices store. That too has been knocked down and the site is the home of the Bow Street Mall. But the car park around the back is still there: the place where Millar's killers agreed to rendezvous.

About half an hour's walk to the south-west, just before the city gives way to farmland, you can find Blaris New Cemetery, one of the traditional resting places for the people of Lisburn: the Irwins, the Crawfords, the Hallidays, the Orrs and the Cuthbertsons; God-fearing Protestant folk. Their headstones are of black marble, unostentatious, with white lettering.

Kenneth Newman attended the funerals of ten murdered

police officers in 1978. There were others the year before, and more to come the year after. Here and there, between the carefully maintained grass paths at Blaris, lie the remains of several police officers who were killed during the Troubles. The inscription on most of their graves reads 'Killed in the Execution of His Duty', followed by the date that they died, and their age. The head of each stone is engraved with the RUC's crown and harp insignia.

Elsewhere are the graves of soldiers and assassinated Loyalists, 'murdered by the enemies of Ulster'.

Millar was buried at Blaris; his grave is in the centre of the cemetery. It is at one side of a double plot. The other side remains vacant, and a small flower holder in the middle bears the message: 'Till We Meet Again.' His headstone reads: 'McAllister, In Loving Memory of a Dear Husband and Devoted Father – Millar, Died 22nd April 1978, Aged 36 Years.' There is no police insignia, there are no crowns or harps – no mention of his having been a police officer, or a victim of the Troubles – and no dark words about enemies or murder or killing. Instead, at the top of the stone is an engraving so small that it would be easy to miss, were you hurrying along the ranks of graves in search of the resting place of a loved one.

At the top of Millar's headstone is an engraving of a racing pigeon.

A Note on Police Interview Records and Other Sources

Those passages of this book that describe the events of the day that Millar McAllister was shot dead in front of his seven-year-old son, the days leading up to that event, and the days that followed rest in part upon documents that are, I hope, uncontentious, such as pathologists' notes, forensic science records and scenes of crime photographs. They rely also upon material such as newspaper articles that would have been produced in hurried and imperfect conditions, written by journalists who may or may not have been fastidious about accuracy. But for the most part these passages rely upon two planks that I have attempted to prop up against each other to see whether they might jointly stand up, withstanding the buffeting of claim and counter-claim, to offer a narrative framework that might be regarded as the truth. These two planks are memory and police records.

Memory has been described as a relative of truth, but not its twin. As unreliable as memory might be, I would suggest that police records from the 1970s – indeed, police documents created almost anywhere during that decade – would on occasion be an even less solid foundation for the reconstruction of events within the interview room.

Records that were created within the so-called holding centres in Northern Ireland towards the end of the 1970s might be considered to be particularly suspect. The Amnesty International report that was being finalised around the time that Millar's killers were arrested had warned that suspects being questioned at Castlereagh and elsewhere were being mistreated, and the accuracy or validity of their statements or confessions must be open to question.

Harry, Gary, Michael and Féilim have given accounts of the way they say they were treated at Castlereagh. Given that a number of former Castlereagh interrogators have also given me unvarnished descriptions of the way they operated, I find the men's accounts to be compelling. Anne has not spoken to me, and so I have no way of knowing whether she would say that the police explanation for the way she suffered bruising after her arrest – that she had slipped in a lavatory – is correct or not.

I respected Millar's family's request not to discuss his death with me.

Other sources of information included declassified British and Irish government files of the time, US diplomatic cables, material acquired under the UK's Freedom of Information Act, memoirs, biographies, academic papers and contemporary maps. Also, of course, a great many books have been published about Ireland and the Troubles.

Harry gave me a very detailed account of the way he had travelled to Lisburn, of the brief conversation that he had with Millar before he produced his weapon and fired four shots, and of his escape from the scene.

When I subsequently acquired the court and police records from the case, including statements signed by Harry, I discovered that his memory and the contemporary police records corroborate each other to a remarkable degree: the description that he had given me matched in *every* respect the account that he had given to detectives thirty-four years earlier.

The police records do not record any threats or assaults, of course. Féilim does not feature in those police records that became part of the court file, as the charges against him were withdrawn.

Nor is there any mention of Brian Maguire in those police notes, although there are separate records of the post-mortem examination conducted after his death, as well as a coroner's file prepared for the inquest and the report of an inquiry by Merseyside Police into his death.

The second youth who, along with Gary, hijacked the yellow Fiat 127 outside Rice's bookmaker's appears only in the witness statement that was taken from the owner of the car. Other than that, he makes no appearance in the court file or police notes: it is as though he has been largely airbrushed from the official record.

Acknowledgements

Once again, thanks are due first and foremost to my family and friends, for their patience.

This book would not have been possible without the enthusiasm, encouragement and diligence of its editor, Laura Barber.

It has been an enormous pleasure to work with my agent Kate Shaw on this book, our third together.

Yet again I am deeply grateful for the assistance of Martin Soames and the advice – both legal and editorial – that he offered after reading the manuscript.

I am also grateful to Susan McKay and Sinéad O'Callaghan for agreeing to read a draft of the book and offer comments and advice.

Thanks are due to the staff of Granta Books, in particular, Pru Rowlandson, Christine Lo, and the copy-editor, Martin Bryant.

I would like to thank Michael Culbert, Harry Murray, Gary Smyth and Féilim Ó hAdhmaill for the initial help that they felt able to give me. They approached the project in a thoughtful and open-minded way, and I quite understand their decision to cease cooperating. Anne Laverty declined to assist – a decision that I respect.

Some people deserve particular thanks for the various ways in which they have assisted me. Brian McKee and Kieran Megraw

agreed to talk about difficult periods from the past. The late
Peter Melchett was generous with his time. I thank Huw Bennett
and Aaron Edwards for their encouragement, and Alan Simpson
for his assistance and advice.

I am thankful to Gordon Ogilvie for permission to quote from
'Suspect Device'.

The extracts from Seamus Heaney's verse are from 'Whatever
You Say Say Nothing', published in *North*, by Faber & Faber, in
1975, and from *The Cure at Troy*, published by Faber & Faber
in 1990. The quotation from Gerald Dawe is from 'Memory',
which was published in *Sheltering Places*, Blackstaff Press, 1978.
The extract from Michael Longley's 'The Civil Servant' is from
the longer poem 'Wreaths', published in *The Echo Gate*, Secker
& Warburg, 1979.

I am grateful for both the work and the assistance of the
Lisburn historian Pearse Lawlor, and for the advice of Ciaran
Toal and Brian Mackey of the Irish Linen Centre & Lisburn
Museum.

I am indebted to various other libraries, archives, museums
and agencies, and their staff, particularly the the Linen Hall
Library, the Public Record Office of Northern Ireland, and the
Northern Ireland Statistics and Research Agency, in Belfast;
the Bureau of Military History, in Dublin; the University
Library, Cambridge; and the National Archives at Kew, the
British Library, the Templer Study Centre at the National Army
Museum, the Imperial War Museum, and the Liddell Hart
Centre for Military Archives at King's College, in London.

Thanks are due also to Jon Baker, John Bew, Owen Bowcott,
David Bolton, Thomas D. Boyatt, Jake Burns, Ciaran Byrne,
Anne Cadwallader, Duncan Campbell, Paul Carson, Patricia
Coyle, Emma Cummins, Martin Dillon, Roseanna Doughty,
Wesley Geddis, Rosa Gilbert, Lynsey Gillespie, Martin Hill,
Alison Houston, Darragh MacIntyre, Ian McBride, Barry
McCaffrey, Eamonn McDermott, Henry McDonald, Paul

McErlane, Kieran McEvoy, Anne McHardy, Tommy McKearney, David McKittrick, Ed Moloney, Claire Murphy, Raymond Murray, Toby Neal, Richard Norton-Taylor, Sarah O'Cathain, Paul O'Connor, Malachi O'Doherty, Pádraig Ó Muirigh, Siobhan O'Neill, David Ramsbotham, Sean Rayment, Chris Ryder, Katy Stoddard, Scott Wilford and Musab Younis.

I apologise to anyone I have inadvertently left out.

Any errors are mine.

Notes

Chapter 1: The People

1. Trotter, *Constabulary Heroes*, pp. 213–14; *Pigeon Racing Gazette*, June 1978.
2. Author interview, Belfast, June 2012.
3. Author interview, Belfast, June 2012; police interview, RUC, Castlereagh, 5 May 1978.
4. Author interview, Belfast, June 2012.
5. Conversations with author, 2012; Horgan and Taylor, 'The Provisional Irish Republican Army: Command and Functional Structure', p. 22.
6. *ISIS*, Vol. 1, April 1981, IRA Interview.
7. White, *Provisional Irish Republicans*, pp. 88–9.
8. Author interview, Belfast, June 2012.
9. Doherty, *The Dead Beside Us*, pp. 271–81.
10. Scarman Report.
11. *Daily Telegraph*, 15 August 2009.
12. O'Brien, *The Long War*, p. 39; conversation with author, Derry, January 2015.
13. MacIntyre, *Conversations*, pp. 310–11; Alonso, *The IRA and Armed Struggle*, p. 56.
14. Author interview, County Kildare, June 2012; Alonso, *The IRA and Armed Struggle*, p. 26; MacIntyre, *Conversations*, pp. 309–13.
15. O'Leary, 'Mission Accomplished?', pp. 233–4.
16. Gill and Horgan, 'Who Were the Volunteers?'
17. Alonso, *The IRA and Armed Struggle*, pp. 13–15; O'Doherty, *The Volunteer*, pp. 13–15, 40; Moloney, *Voices from the Grave*, pp. 29–38.
18. Reich, *The Origins of Terrorism*, pp. 267–8; Silke, *Terrorists, Victims and Society*, pp. 29–51.

19. Lyons and Harbinson, 'A Comparison of Political and Non-Political Murderers in Northern Ireland'; *Independent*, 29 November 1986; Heskin, in Alexander and O'Day, *Terrorism in Ireland*, pp. 103–4; Ryder, *Inside the Maze*, xiii.

20. Silke, *Terrorists, Victims and Society*, pp. 40–1.

21. Collins, *Killing Rage*, pp. 50–80, 238.

22. *Independent*, 6 February 1989.

23. Adams, *The Politics of Irish Freedom*, p. 60; Taylor, *War and Peace*, p. 8.

Chapter 2: The Time

1. *Belfast Telegraph*, 9 September 1977; Belfast *News Letter*, 10 September 1977; Potter, Testimony, p. 195.

2. Statement to Association for Legal Justice, November 1977.

3. Author interviews, Belfast and Antrim, August, September 2010; Bishop and Mallie, *The Provisional IRA*, pp. 320–1; Moloney, *A Secret History of the IRA*, p. 155.

4. *Irish Times*, 22 December 1976; *Sunday Times*, 23 October 1977; TNA CJ 4/1197; Mason, *Paying the Price*, p. 199.

5. Longford and McHardy, *Ulster*, p. 182; Haines, *The Politics of Power*, p. 120; Bloomfield, *A Tragedy of Errors*, p. 48; Donoughue, *Prime Minister*, p. 131; Mason, *Paying the Price*, p. 218; Hayes, *Minority Verdict*, p. 235; Murphy, *Gerry Fitt*, p. 248.

6. Savage, *The BBC's 'Irish Troubles'*, pp. 156–9; Taylor, *Brits*, p. 199.

7. Stout, Northern Ireland and Terrorism: Police Taking Hold Again But Can't Win, 3 April 1978.

8. Ryder, *The RUC 1922–2000*, p. 172; Hayes, *Minority Verdict*, p. 235; Hamill, Pig in the Middle, pp. 220–1; *Daily Express*, 5 December 1977; Murphy, *Gerry Fitt*, p. 263.

9. Hamill, *Pig in the Middle*, pp. 220–1.

10. Donoughue, *Downing Street Diary*, p. 298; *Irish Times*, 30 December 2008.

11. TNA CJ 4/1195.

12. Smith, *Fighting for Ireland?*, pp. 143–5.

13. Ryder, *The Ulster Defence Regiment*, pp. 184–5.

14. Author conversation, County Monaghan, February 2010; Eames, *Chains to be Broken*, p. 174; Loyalism, Republican Lecture Series No. 9, quoted in O'Brien, *The Long War*, pp. 88–9.

15. Healey, *The Time of My Life*, pp. 3–4, 30; Hayes, *Minority Verdict*, p. 246.

16. Rowthorn, 'Northern Ireland: An Economy in Crisis'; TNA CJ 4/1077; Mason, *Paying the Price*, p. 218; *The Times*, 29 December 1979.

17. Report of an Amnesty International Mission to Northern Ireland, London, June 1978.

18. Bailie, *Trouble Songs*, pp. 103–4; Belfast *News Letter*, 19 October 2007; Robb, *Punk Rock: An Oral History*, pp. 253, 306–8.

19. *Observer*, 2 June 2002; Robb, *Punk Rock: An Oral History*, p. 305; Link, *Kicking up a Racket*, p. 63.

20. Bailie, *Trouble Songs*, p. 156; Bradley, *Teenage Kicks*, pp. 78–80.

21. Bailie, *Trouble Songs*, p. 156; Bradley, *Teenage Kicks*, pp. 78–80; Robb, *Punk Rock: An Oral History*, pp. 474–5.

22. *Republican News*, 18 October 1975; 'People's Assembly', undated, *c*.1978, quoted in O'Brien, *The Long War*, pp. 47–9.

23. Moloney, *Voices*, pp. 198–9.

24. Adams, *Before the Dawn*, pp. 245–51.

25. TNA CJ 4/2289; Adams, *Before the Dawn*, pp. 245–51; White, *Provisional Irish Republicans*, pp. 139–41, Bishop and Mallie, *The Provisional IRA*, pp. 311–12; English, *Armed Struggle*, pp. 181–3; Moloney, *Voices from the Grave*, pp. 189–207; Sharrock and Devenport, *Man of War, Man of Peace*, pp. 147–57.

26. Adams, *Before the Dawn*, pp. 252–3; Smith, *Fighting for Ireland?*, pp. 148–9; Kelley, *The Longest War*, p. 265.

27. Associated Press, 6 January 1978; McCollum obituary, *An Phoblacht*, 24 April 2008.

28. *Magill*, August 1978.

29. McKearney, The Provisional IRA, pp. 141–2; Collins, *Killing Rage*, p. 81; Bean and Hayes, *Republican Voices*, pp. 59–60; Bradley and Feeney, *Insider*, pp. 190–1; O'Leary, 'Mission Accomplished? Looking Back on the IRA', p. 228; TNA CJ 4/2289; CJ 4/2171.

30. Author interview, Belfast, June 2012; author conversations, County Monaghan and County Derry, February 2010, County Antrim, June 2012.

31. Author interviews, Belfast, May and June 2012.

Chapter 3: The Place

1. O'Driscoll, *Stepping Stones*, p. 66.

2. Lawlor, *Lisburn*, pp. 27, 37; Lawlor, *The Burnings 1920*, p. 14.

3. Dwyer, *The Squad*, pp. 89–95; BMH WS0746.

4. BMH WSO746.

5. Stewart, *The Narrow Ground*, p. 174; BMH WS0746, WS0389, WS0746.

6. Lawlor, *The Burnings 1920*, pp. 115–43; Belfast *News Letter*, 23 August 1920; Bardon, *A History of Ulster*, p. 472.

7. London *Daily News*, 30 August 1920.

8. Lawlor, *The Burnings 1920*, pp. 126–212; History Ireland, Issue 1, Jan/Feb 2012; Shea, *Voices and the Sound of Drums*, p. 112.

9. PRONI COM/63/1/702; Hansard, 2 December 1976; Mason, *Paying the Price*, p. 218; *Andersonstown News*, 7 January 1978.

10. Hall, *Building Bridges at the Grassroots*, pp. 6–8.

11. Ó hAdhmaill, 'The Function and Dynamics of the Ghetto', Chapters Four and Eight; O'Hearn, *Bobby Sands*, pp. 24–5.

12. Charters, RUSI Journal, September 1977; IWM BFC21.

13. University of Strathclyde, Concurring Majority.

14. Brown, *Into the Dark*, pp. 111–20.

15. Author interview, Lisburn, February 2015; TNA WO 305/5964; *Shropshire Star*, 14 April 1988.

16. Wharton, *Wasted Years Wasted Lives Volume 2*, pp. 39–40; *Independent*, 6 February 1989; Arthur, *Northern Ireland Soldiers Talking*, p. 126.

17. Future Terrorist Trends, TNA FCO 87/976; Adams, *The Politics of Irish Freedom*, p. 63.

18. O'Hearn, *Bobby Sands*, pp. 102–6; MacIntyre, *Conversations*, pp. 312–13.

19. McKittrick et al., *Lost Lives*, pp. 601–2; 719.

20. J. Bowyer Bell, *The Irish Troubles*, pp. 484–90; Sharrock and Devenport, *Man of War*, pp. 136–46; Adams, *The Politics of Irish Freedom*, p. 59.

21. Moxon-Browne, 'The water and the fish'; O'Doherty, *The Trouble with Guns*, pp. 8–11.

22. Singleton, in Boal and Douglas (eds.), *Integration and Division*, pp. 183–4; TNA CJ 4/3201; *Fortnight*, May 1983; TNA CJ 4/1988.

23. (PRONI CAB /1634/1; Operation Playground, September 1972, reproduced in Faligot, *Britain's Military Strategy in Ireland*, p. 216.

24. TNA CJ 4/1982; *Guardian*, 13 March 1982.

25. Author telephone interview, May 2017; Stout, 'The Advantages – and Risks – Of Increased US Investment in Northern Ireland'; Fallon and Srodes, *DeLorean*, pp. 114–43; PRONI CENT 1/10/18.

26. Author interview, Belfast, June 2012.

27. *Irish Times*, 30 December 1977.

28. Charles R. Stout, 'Fire Bombs in Belfast', *Belfast Telegraph*, 12 January 1978.

29. *Irish Times*, 14 January 1978.
30. See, for example, M. L. R. Smith, *Fighting for Ireland?*, pp. 141–7.
31. Glover, 'Future Terrorist Trends', TNA FCO 87/976.
32. Taylor, *Provos*, p. 216.
33. *Irish Times*, 20 February 1978; 26 July 1978; Associated Press, 20 February 1978.

Chapter 4: The Killing
1. Benn, *Conflicts of Interest*, pp. 282–3.
2. McKittrick et al., *Lost Lives*, pp. 749–51; Wharton, *Wasted Years Wasted Lives Volume 2*, pp. 69–72; Stout, 'Shift in Terrorist Tactics in Northern Ireland'; Stout, 'Police Taking Hold Again But Can't Win', *Andersonstown News*, 11 March 1978.
3. Adams, *The Politics of Irish Freedom*, pp. 64–5.
4. Wharton, *Wasted Years Wasted Lives Volume 2*, p. 40.
5. Wharton, *Wasted Years Wasted Lives Volume 2*, pp. 78–81.
6. Author interview, Lisburn, February 2015; Police interview, Springfield Road RUC Station, 4 May 1978.
7. Author interview, Lisburn, February 2015.
8. Author interview, June 2012.
9. TNA WO 305/4817.
10. Murray, *The SAS in Ireland*, pp. 208–14.
11. *Belfast Telegraph*, 6 October 1979; TNA WO 305/4817.
12. *Andersonstown News*, 30 March 1978; TNA WO 305/4817; *Pegasus*, Vol. XXXIII, Number 3, July 1978.
13. McKittrick et al., *Lost Lives*, pp. 752–3; Author telephone interview, July 2016.
14. Police interviews, RUC Castlereagh, 7 and 10 May 1978.
15. Author interview, Belfast, May 2012.
16. TNA WO 305/4817; RUC interview, Castlereagh, 7 May; RUC statement, taken at Castlereagh, 5 May 1978; *Belfast Telegraph*, 22 April 1978.
17. Author interview, June 2012; Witness Statement, 23 April 1978; Police interview notes, RUC Castlereagh, 24 and 26 April 1978.
18. Witness statement, 9 May 1978.
19. Author interview, Belfast, June 2012; witness statement, 4 May 1978.
20. Author interview, Belfast, June 2012; police interviews, RUC Castlereagh, 5 and 6 May 1978.
21. Witness statements, 15 December, 28 April, 17 December, 31 May, 13 December, 22 June, 3 May 1978; *Ulster Star*, 28 April 1978.

22. *Ulster Star*, 28 April 1978; police interview, RUC Castlereagh, 7 May 1978.
23. Author interview, June 2012.
24. Witness statement, 21 May 1978; coroner's inquest records; witness statement, 26 July 1978.
25. Witness statements, 4 May and 24 April 1978; author interview, Belfast, June 2012, RUC interview notes, 10 May 1978; *Belfast Telegraph*, 22 April 1978.

Chapter 5: The Consequences

1. Author interview, Belfast, June 2012.
2. Statement of Robert [Roy] Cairns, 7 June 1978.
3. Author interview, Belfast, June 2012.
4. Ryder, *The RUC 1922–2000*, pp. 215–20; Bell, *The IRA, 1968–2000*, pp. 208–9, 246–7; Doherty, 'SIGINT Used by Anti-State Forces'; Arthur, *Northern Ireland Soldiers Talking*, p.122; Matchett, *Secret Victory*, p.164; Aldrich, *GCHQ*, pp. 498–500; NAM 1994-05-26.
5. Judgment of Mr Justice MacDermott, Belfast, 12 December 1979.
6. Statement to the Association for Legal Justice, undated; author interviews, Belfast, August 2010 and County Kildare, June 2012; Taylor, *Beating the Terrorists?*, pp. 284–5; TNA WO 305/4817; *Irish Times*, 14 August 2017; *Ulster Star*, 5 May 1978.
7. *Ulster Star*, 28 April 1978.
8. *Ulster Star*, 5 May 1978.
9. Police statements, 7 July, 12 and 15 December 1978; TNA WO 305/4817; Judgment of Mr Justice MacDermott, 12 December 1979; author interview, Belfast June 2012; signed handwritten statement, 5 May 1978.
10. *Evening Press*, 25 September 1978.
11. Author interview, Belfast, June 2012; police statements, May–July 1978.
12. *An Phoblacht*, 20 May 1978; Merseyside Police Report, 8 June 1978; Taylor, *Beating the Terrorists?*, pp. 280–4; TNA CJ 4/4222; *Irish Times*, 27 March 1982; author interview, Belfast, June 2012.
13. *Guardian*, 11 May 1978; Kelley, *The Longest War*, p. 289; *An Phoblacht*, 20 May 1978; *Irish Times*, 12 May 1978.
14. Merseyside Police Report, 26 May 1978; TNA CJ 4/4222; *Irish Times*, 27 March 1982; McKittrick et al., *Lost Lives*, p. 755; *Belfast Telegraph*, 12 June 1979.
15. Arthur, *Northern Ireland Soldiers Talking*, pp.106–7; Greg, *The Crum*, pp. 2, 185, 150.

16. Darragh, *'John Lennon's Dead'*, pp. 20–8, 142.
17. Moxon-Browne, *Nation, Class and Creed in Northern Ireland*, pp. 167–78; Dewar, *The British Army in Northern Ireland*, p. 227.
18. Wharton, *Wasted Years Wasted Lives Volume 2*, p. 40; Donoughue, *Downing Street Diary*, pp. 334–5.
19. Report of Amnesty International Mission to Northern Ireland, 28 November–6 December 1977.
20. Hamill, *Pig in the Middle*, pp. 233–4; Bowyer Bell, *The Secret Army*, pp. 441–2; *Republican News*, 9 December 1978.
21. Turner, *Crisis? What Crisis?*, pp. 263–4; Beckett, *When the Lights Went Out*, pp. 464–9, 496; Sandbrook, *Seasons in the Sun*, pp. 736–9, *Sun*, 11 January 1979; Donoughue, *Prime Minister*, p. 183.
22. McKearney, *The Provisional IRA*, p. 143; Bessel, *Violence*, p. 43; Reuters, 2 October 1979; *Guardian*, 26 June 2018; Pearce, *Spymaster*, pp. 312–43.
23. Judgment and Sentence of Mr Justice MacDermott, 12 December 1979; *Sunday Times*, 23 December 1979.
24. Author interview, County Monaghan, February 2010; Taylor, *Brits*, pp. 220–6; White, *Provisional Irish Republicans*, p. 110; Sands, *One Day in My Life*, pp. 69–70; McKittrick et al., *Lost Lives*, p. 771.
25. Author conversations, Belfast, June 2012 and October 2013; *Irish Times*, 26 April and 11 May 1985.
26. O'Hearn, *Bobby Sands*, pp. 368–70; MacIntyre, *Conversations*, p. 315.
27. Hermon, *Holding the Line*, pp. 123–4.
28. *Belfast Telegraph*, 12 March 2005.
29. McKeown, *Out of Time*, pp. 102–3; Hennessy Report, 9.27–8.
30. Hayes, *Break-Out!*, pp. 170–220; Kelly, *The Escape*, pp. 52–150; McKittrick et al., *Lost Lives*, pp.592–3; Hennessy Report, 2.01–2.28; Murtagh, *The Maze Prison*, pp. 452–3; *Evening Herald*, 27 April 1988; author interview, Belfast, June 2012.

Chapter 6: The Far Side of Revenge

1. McEvoy et al., 'The Home Front'; Bolton, *Conflict, Peace and Mental Health*, pp. 1–7, 52–102; Report: 'Trauma, Health and Conflict in Northern Ireland'.
2. Jamieson and Grounds, 'Release and Adjustment'; author conversation, Derry, February 2010.
3. Wharton, *Wasted Years Wasted Lives*, pp. 40–1.
4. BBC NI, *Spotlight on the Troubles*, 1 October 2019; author

interview, Lisburn, February 2015; Bailey et al., *British Generals in Blair's Wars*, p. 27.

5.   Author telephone interview, July 2016; *Irish Times*,
     3 December 2015.

6.   Rolston, *Children of the Revolution*, p. 67; Thomas Leahy, 'The
     Influence of Informers and Agents on Provisional Irish Republican
     Army Military Strategy', pp. 141–2; Holland and Phoenix, *Phoenix*,
     pp. 287–94; O'Brien, *The Long War*, p. 305; Geraghty, *The Irish
     War*, p. 149; Urban, *UK Eyes Alpha*, p. 280.

7.   *Independent*, 9 November 1994.

8.   MacIntyre, *Conversations*, p. 310; author interview, County Kildare,
     June 2012.

9.   Rolston, *Children of the Revolution*, pp. 109–10.

10. *Andersonstown News*, 12 November 1994; *The Times*,
     9 November 1994; *Central News*, 8 November 1994.

11. Rolston, *Children of the Revolution*, pp. 111–16.

12. MacIntyre, *Conversations*, p. 317.

13. Alonso, *The IRA and Armed Struggle*, pp. 178–9; author interview,
     County Kildare, June 2012; MacIntyre, *Conversations*, pp. 318–19.

14. BBC Radio 5 live, 23 March 2015.

15. Author interviews, June 2012.

16. Author interviews, June 2012.

Bibliography

Abbot, Richard, *Police Casualties in Ireland 1919–1922* (Mercier Press, Cork, 2000)

Adams, Gerry, *The Politics of Irish Freedom* (Brandon, Dingle, 1986)

Adams, Gerry, *Before the Dawn: An Autobiography* (Heinemann, London, 1996)

Aldrich, Richard J., *GCHQ* (HarperPress, London, 2011)

Alexander, Yonah, and O'Day, Alan (eds.), *Terrorism in Ireland* (Croom Helm, London, 1984)

Alexander, Yonah, and O'Day, Alan (eds.), *Ireland's Terrorist Trauma: Interdisciplinary Perspectives* (Harvester Wheatsheaf, Hemel Hempstead, 1989)

Allen, Charles, *The Savage Wars of Peace* (Futura, London, 1990)

Alonso, Rogelio, *The IRA and Armed Struggle* (Routledge, Abingdon, 2007)

Arnold, Bruce, *What Kind of Country: Modern Irish Politics 1968–1983* (Jonathan Cape, London, 1984)

Arthur, Max, *Northern Ireland Soldiers Talking: 1969 to Today* (Sidgwick & Jackson, London, 1987)

Bailey, Jonathan, Iron, Richard, and Strachan, Hew (eds.), *British Generals in Blair's Wars* (Ashgate, Farnham, 2013)

Bailie, Stuart, *Trouble Songs: Music and Conflict in Northern Ireland* (Bloomfield, Belfast, 2018)

Bardon, Jonathan, *A History of Ulster* (Blackstaff Press, Belfast, 1992)

Barnett, Joel, *Inside the Treasury* (Andre Deutsch, London, 1982)

Barzilay, David, *The British Army in Ulster, Vol. 2* (Century Books, Belfast, 1975)

Barzilay, David, *The British Army in Ulster, Vol. 3* (Century Books, Belfast, 1978)

Bean, Kevin, and Hayes, Mark (eds.), *Republican Voices* (Seesyu Press, Monaghan, 2001)

Beckett, Andy, *When the Lights Went Out: Britain in the Seventies* (Faber & Faber, London, 2009)

Bell, J. Bowyer, *The Secret Army: The IRA 1916–1979* (Poolbeg, Swords, 1989)

Bell, J. Bowyer, *IRA Tactics & Targets* (Poolbeg, Dublin, 1990)

Bell, J. Bowyer, *The Irish Troubles: A Generation of Violence 1967–1992* (St Martin's Press, New York, 1993)

Bell, J. Bowyer, *The Dynamics of the Armed Struggle* (Frank Cass, London, 1998)

Bell, J. Bowyer, *The IRA, 1968–2000: An Analysis of a Secret Army* (Frank Cass, London, 2000)

Benn, Tony, *Against the Tide: Diaries 1973–77* (Arrow Books, London, 1991)

Benn, Tony, *Conflicts of Interest: Diaries 1977–80* (Arrow Books, London, 1991)

Beresford, David, *Ten Men Dead* (Grafton, London, 1987)

Bessel, Richard, *Violence: A Modern Obsession* (Simon & Schuster, London, 2015)

Bew, Paul, and Gillespie, Gordon, *Northern Ireland: A Chronology of the Troubles 1968–1999* (Gill & Macmillan, Dublin, 1999)

Bishop, Patrick, and Mallie, Eamonn, *The Provisional IRA* (Corgi Books, London, 1987)

Bloomfield, Kenneth, *A Tragedy of Errors: The Government and Misgovernment of Northern Ireland* (Liverpool University Press, 2007)

Boal, Frederick W., and Douglas, Neville H. (eds.), *Integration and Division: Geographical Perspectives on the Northern Ireland Problem* (Academic Press, London, 1982)

Bolton, David, *Conflict, Peace and Mental Health: Addressing the Consequences of Conflict and Trauma in Northern Ireland* (Manchester University Press, 2017)

Booker, Christopher, *The Seventies* (Penguin, London, 1980)

Bradley, Gerry, with Feeney, Brian, *Insider, Gerry Bradley's Life in the IRA* (O'Brien Press, Dublin, 2011)

Bradley, Michael, *Teenage Kicks: My Life as an Undertone* (Omnibus Press, London, 2016)

Brown, Johnston, *Into the Dark: 30 Years in the RUC* (Gill & Macmillan, Dublin, 2006)

Burton, Frank, *The Politics of Legitimacy: Struggles in a Belfast Community* (Routledge & Kegan Paul, London, 1978)

Callaghan, James, *Time & Chance* (Collins, London, 1987)

Campbell, Brian, McKeown, Laurence, and O'Hagan, Felim (eds.), *Nor Meekly Serve My Time: The H Block Struggle 1976–81* (Beyond the Pale, Belfast, 1998)

Clarke, Liam, and Johnston, Kathryn, *Martin McGuinness: From Guns to Government* (Mainstream, Edinburgh, 2003)

Collins, Eamon, with McGovern, Mick, *Killing Rage* (Granta Books, London, 1997)

Compton, Paul A., *Northern Ireland: A Census Atlas* (Gill & Macmillan, Dublin, 1978)

Conway, Kieran, *Southside Provisional* (Orpen Press, Blackrock, 2014)

Coogan, Tim Pat, *The IRA* (HarperCollins, London, 2000)

Curtis, Liz, *Ireland: The Propaganda War* (Sásta, Belfast, 1998)

D'Arcy, Margaretta, *Tell Them Everything* (Pluto, London, 1981)

Darragh, Síle, *'John Lennon's Dead'* (Beyond the Pale, Belfast, 2011)

Dawe, Gerald, *Sheltering Places* (Blackstaff Press, Belfast, 1978)

Dawson, Graham, Dover, Jo, and Hopkins, Stephen, *The Northern Ireland Troubles in Britain* (Manchester University Press, 2017)

Deacon, Richard, *'C': A Biography of Sir Maurice Oldfield* (Futura, London, 1985)

De Baróid, Ciarán, *Ballymurphy and the Irish War* (Aisling Publishers, Dublin, 1989)

DeGroot, Gerard, *The Seventies Unplugged: A Kaleidoscopic Look at a Violent Decade* (Macmillan, London, 2010)

Devlin, Paddy, *Straight Left: An Autobiography* (Blackstaff Press, Belfast, 1993)

Dewar, Michael, *Brush Fire Wars: Minor Campaigns of the British Army Since 1945* (Robert Hale, London, 1984)

Dewar, Michael, *The British Army in Northern Ireland* (Arms and Armour Press, London, 1985)

Dillon, Martin, *The Dirty War* (Arrow, London, 1991)

Dixon, Paul, *Northern Ireland: The Politics of War and Peace* (Palgrave, Basingstoke, 2001)

Doherty, Paul, *The Dead Beside Us: A Memoir of Growing Up in Derry* (Mercier, Cork, 2017)

Donoughue, Bernard, *Prime Minister: The Conduct of Policy under Harold Wilson and James Callaghan* (Jonathan Cape, London, 1987)

Donoughue, Bernard, *Downing Street Diary: With James Callaghan in No. 10* (Jonathan Cape, London, 2008)

Dwyer, T. Ryle, *The Squad and the Intelligence Operations of Michael Collins* (Mercier Press, Cork, 2005)

Eames, Robin, *Chains to be Broken* (Weidenfeld & Nicholson, London, 1992)

Elliott, Marianne, *The Catholics of Ulster: A History* (Penguin, London, 2001)

Elliott, Sydney, and Flackes, W. D., *Northern Ireland: A Political Directory 1968–1999* (Blackstaff Press, Belfast, 1999)

English, Richard, *Armed Struggle: The History of the IRA* (Macmillan, London, 2003)

English, Richard, *Does Terrorism Work? A History* (Oxford University Press, Oxford, 2016)

Faligot, Roger, *Britain's Military Strategy in Ireland: The Kitson Experiment* (Brandon, Dingle, 1983)

Fallon, Ivan, and Srodes, James, *DeLorean: The Rise and Fall of a Dream Maker* (Hamish Hamilton, London, 1983)

Fitzgerald, Garret, *All in a Life: An Autobiography* (Gill and Macmillan, Dublin, 1991)

Foster, R. F., *The Irish Story: Telling Tales and Making it Up in Ireland* (Allen Lane, London, 2001)

Foster, R. F, *Luck and the Irish: A Brief History of Change 1970–2000* (Allen Lane, London, 2007)

Geraghty, Tony, *The Irish War* (HarperCollins, London, 2000)

Glennon, Kieran, *From Pogrom to Civil War: Tom Glennon and the Belfast IRA* (Mercier Press, Cork, 2013)

Graham, Stephen (ed.), *Cities, War and Terrorism* (Blackwell Publishing, Oxford, 2004)

Greg, Patrick, *The Crum: Inside the Crumlin Road Prison* (Glen Publishing, 2013)

Haines, Joe, *The Politics of Power* (Coronet, London, 1977)

Hall, Michael (ed.), *Building Bridges at the Grassroots: The Experience of Suffolk-Lenadoon Interface Group* (Island Publications, Newtownabbey, 2007)

Hamill, Desmond, *Pig in the Middle: The Army in Northern Ireland 1969–1985* (Methuen, London, 1986)

Haseler, Stephen, *The Grand Delusion: Britain After Sixty Years of Elizabeth II* (I. B. Tauris, London, 2012)

Hayes, Maurice, *Minority Verdict: Experiences of a Catholic Public Servant* (Blackstaff Press, Belfast, 1995)

Hayes, Paddy, *Break-Out* (The O'Brien Press, Dublin, 2004)

Healey, Denis, *The Time of My Life* (Penguin, London, 1990)

Hermon, Sir John, *Holding the Line* (Gill & Macmillan, Dublin, 1997)

Hill, George, *An Historical Account of the Plantation of Ulster* (M'Caw, Stevenson & Orr, Belfast, 1877)

Holland, Jack, and Phoenix, Susan, *Phoenix: Policing the Shadows* (Coronet, London, 1997)

Horgan, John, *The Psychology of Terrorism* (Routledge, Abingdon, 2005)

Horgan, John (ed.), *Great Irish Reportage* (Penguin, London, 2015)

Hurd, Douglas, *An End to Promises: A Sketch of Government 1970–74* (Collins, London, 1979)

Jamieson, Ruth, and Grounds, Adrian, *No Sense of an Ending: The Effects of Long-Term Imprisonment Amongst Republican Prisoners and their Families* (Seesyu Press, Monaghan, 2002)

Kelley, Kevin, *The Longest War: Northern Ireland and the IRA* (Brandon, Dingle, 1982)

Kelly, Gerry, *The Escape: The Inside Story of the 1983 Escape from Long Kesh Prison* (M&G Publications, 2013)

Keogh, Dermot, *Jack Lynch: A Biography* (Gill & Macmillan, Dublin 2008)

Lawlor, Pearse, *The Burnings 1920* (Mercier Press, Cork, 2009)

Lawlor, Pearse, *Lisburn: A History of the Catholic Community of the Parish of Blaris (Lisburn)* (Clovercorry, Lisburn, 2014)

Link, Roland, *Kicking Up a Racket: The Story of Stiff Little Fingers 1977–1983* (Appletree Press, Belfast, 2009)

Lodge, Juliet (ed.), *Terrorism: A Challenge to the State* (Martin Robertson, Oxford, 1981)

Longford (Lord), and McHardy, Anne, *Ulster* (Weidenfeld & Nicolson, London, 1981)

Machon, Annie, *Spies, Lies and Whistleblowers* (Book Guild, Lewes, 2005)

MacIntyre, Darragh, *Conversations: Glimpses of Modern Irish Life* (Gill & Macmillan, Dublin, 2005)

Mackey, Brian, *Lisburn: The Town and its People 1873–1973* (Blackstaff Press, Belfast, 2000)

Mac Stíofáin, Seán, *Memoirs of a Revolutionary* (Gordon Cremonesi, London, 1975)

Mason, Roy, *Paying the Price* (Robert Hale, London, 1999)

Matchett, William, *Secret Victory: The Intelligence War that Beat the IRA* (Hiskey, Lisburn 2016)

McEvoy, Kieran, *Paramilitary Imprisonment in Northern Ireland* (Oxford University Press, Oxford, 2001)

McGladdery, Gary, *The Provisional IRA in England: The Bombing Campaign 1973–1997* (Irish Academic Press, Dublin, 2006)

McKay, Susan, *Bear in Mind These Dead* (Faber & Faber, London, 2008)

McKearney, Tommy, *The Provisional IRA: From Insurrection to Parliament* (Pluto, London, 2011)

McKeown, Laurence, *Out of Time: Irish Republican Prisoners, Long Kesh 1972–2000* (Beyond the Pale, Belfast, 2001)

McKittrick, David, Kelters, Seamus, Feeney, Brian, and Thornton, Chris, *Lost Lives* (Mainstream, Edinburgh, 1999)

McKittrick, David, and McVea, David, *Making Sense of the Troubles* (Penguin, London, 2001)

Moloney, Ed, *A Secret History of the IRA* (Penguin, London, 2007)

Moloney, Ed, *Voices from the Grave: Two Men's War in Ireland* (Faber & Faber, London, 2010)

Morgan, Kenneth O., *Callaghan: A Life* (Oxford University Press, Oxford, 1997)

Moxon-Browne, Edward, *Nation, Class and Creed in Northern Ireland* (Gower Publishing, Aldershot, 1983)

Murphy, Michael A., *Gerry Fitt: A Political Chameleon* (Mercier Press, Cork, 2007)

Murray, Raymond, *The SAS in Ireland* (Mercier Press, Cork, 1990)

Murray, Raymond, *State Violence: Northern Ireland 1969–1997* (Mercier Press, Cork, 1998)

Murtagh, Tom, *The Maze Prison: A Hidden Story of Chaos, Anarchy and Politics* (Waterside Press, Hook, 2018)

O'Brien, Brendan, *The Long War* (O'Brien Press, Dublin, 1999)

O'Callaghan, Sean, *The Informer* (Bantam Press, London, 1998)

O'Doherty, Malachi, *The Trouble with Guns: Republican Strategy and the Provisional IRA* (Blackstaff Press, Belfast, 1998)

O'Doherty, Malachi, *Gerry Adams: An Unauthorised Life* (Faber & Faber, London, 2017)

O'Doherty, Shane Paul, *The Volunteer* (Strategic Book Group, Durham, CT, 2011)

O'Driscoll, Dennis, *Stepping Stones: Interviews with Seamus Heaney* (Faber & Faber, London, 2008)

O'Hearn, Denis, *Bobby Sands: Nothing but an Unfinished Song* (Pluto Press, London, 2016)

O'Rawe, Richard, *Blanketmen: An Untold Story of the H-Block Hunger Strike* (New Island, Dublin, 2005)

O'Reilly, Des, *The Rivers of Belfast: A History* (Colourpoint Books, Newtownards, 2010)

Parker, Michael (ed.), *The Hurt World: Short Stories of the Troubles* (Blackstaff Press, Belfast, 1995)

Pearce, Martin, *Spymaster* (Bantam Press, London, 2016)

Reich, Walter (ed.), *The Origins of Terrorism* (Woodrow Wilson Center Press, Washington, DC, 1998)

Richardson, Louise, *What Terrorists Want* (Random House, New York, 2007)

Robb, John, *Punk Rock: An Oral History* (Ebury Press, London, 2006)

Rolston, Bill, *Children of the Revolution* (Guildhall Press, Derry, 2011)

Rolston, Bill, *Review of Literature on Republican and Loyalist Ex-prisoners*

(Transitional Justice Institute, University of Ulster, 2011)

Ryder, Chris, *The Ulster Defence Regiment: An Instrument of Peace?* (Methuen, London, 1992)

Ryder, Chris, *Inside the Maze: The Untold Story of the Northern Ireland Prison Service* (Methuen, London, 2000)

Ryder, Chris, *The RUC 1922–2000: A Force Under Fire* (Arrow Books, London, 2000)

Ryrie, Alec, *Protestants: The Radicals Who Made the Modern World* (William Collins, London, 2017)

Sandbrook, Dominic, *Seasons in the Sun: The Battle for Britain, 1974–1979* (Penguin, London, 2013)

Sands, Bobby, *One Day in My Life* (Mercier Press, Dublin, 2001)

Savage, Robert J., *The BBC's 'Irish Troubles': Television, Conflict and Northern Ireland* (Manchester University Press, Manchester, 2015)

Sharrock, David, and Devenport, Mark, *Man of War, Man of Peace* (Macmillan, London, 1997)

Shea, Patrick, *Voices and the Sound of Drums: An Irish Autobiography* (Blackstaff Press, Belfast, 1981)

Shirlow, Peter, Tonge, Jonathan, McAuley, James, and McGlynn, Catherine, *Abandoning Historical Conflict? Former Political Prisoners and Reconciliation in Northern Ireland* (Manchester University Press, 2010)

Silke, Andrew (ed.), *Terrorists, Victims and Society: Psychological Perspectives on Terrorism and its Consequences* (Wiley, Chichester, 2003)

Simon, Ben, *By the Banks of the Lagan* (Laganscape and Lagan Valley Regional Park, Belfast, 2011)

Simpson, Alan, *Duplicity and Deception: Policing the Twilight Zone of the Troubles* (Brandon, Dingle, 2010)

Smith, M. L. R., *Fighting for Ireland? The Military Strategy of the Irish Republican Movement* (Routledge, London, 1995)

Sounes, Howard, *Seventies* (Simon & Schuster, London, 2006)

Stevenson, Jonathan, *'We Wrecked the Place': Contemplating an End to the Northern Irish Troubles* (The Free Press, New York, 1996)

Stewart, A. T. Q., *The Narrow Ground: Aspects of Ulster 1609–1969* (Blackstaff Press, Belfast, 1997)

Sweeney, Eamonn, *Down Down Deeper and Down: Ireland in the 70s and 80s* (Gill & Macmillan, Dublin, 2010)

Taylor, Peter, *Beating the Terrorists?* (Penguin, London, 1980)

Taylor, Peter, *Provos* (Bloomsbury, London, 1997)

Taylor, Peter, *Loyalists* (Bloomsbury, London, 2000)

256   *Anatomy of a Killing*

Taylor, Peter, *Brits: The War Against the IRA* (Bloomsbury, London, 2001)

Tomlinson, Jim, *The Politics of Decline* (Routledge, London, 2000)

Tonge, Jonathan, *Northern Ireland* (Polity, Cambridge, 2006)

Toolis, Kevin, *Rebel Hearts* (Picador, London, 1995)

Townshend, Charles, *Political Violence in Ireland* (Clarendon Press, Oxford, 1983)

Townshend, Charles, *Easter 1916: The Irish Rebellion* (Penguin, London, 2005)

Townshend, Charles, *The Republic: The Fight for Irish Independence* (Penguin, London, 2014)

Trotter, Sam, *Constabulary Heroes 1826–2009* (Impact, Coleraine, 2010)

Turner, Alwyn W., *Crisis? What Crisis? Britain in the 1970s* (Aurum, London, 2008)

Urban, Mark, *Big Boys' Rules: The SAS and the Secret Struggle Against the IRA* (Faber & Faber, London, 1992)

Urban, Mark, *UK Eyes Alpha: The Inside Story of British Intelligence* (Faber & Faber, London, 1996)

Van De Bijl, *Nick, Operation Banner: The British Army in Northern Ireland 1969–2007* (Pen & Sword, Barnsley, 2009)

Von Tangen, Michael, *Prisons, Peace and Terrorism: Penal Policy in the Reduction of Political Violence in Northern Ireland, Italy and the Spanish Basque Country 1968–97* (Macmillan Press, Basingstoke, 1998)

Wharton, Ken, *Wasted Years Wasted Lives Volume 1: The British Army in Northern Ireland 1975–77* (Helion, Solihull, 2013)

Wharton, Ken, *Wasted Years Wasted Lives Volume 2: The British Army in Northern Ireland 1978–79* (Helion, Solihull, 2014)

Wheen, Francis, *Strange Days Indeed: The 1970s: The Golden Age of Paranoia* (Public Affairs, New York, 2009)

White, Robert W., *Provisional Irish Republicans: An Oral and Interpretive History* (Greenwood Press, Westport, CT, 1993)

White, Robert W., *Out of the Ashes: An Oral History of the Provisional Irish Republican Movement* (Merrion Press, County Kildare, 2017)

Whitehead, Phillip, *The Writing on the Wall: Britain in the Seventies* (Michael Joseph, London, 1985)

Whyte, John, *Interpreting Northern Ireland* (Clarendon Press, Oxford, 1990)

Journals and pamphlets:

The Lagan Valley, Department of the Environment, Northern Ireland, 1977

Pegasus, Journal of the Parachute Regiment & Airborne Forces, Vol. XXXIII, No. 3, July 1978

Trade Unions & H Block, Trade Union Sub-Committee of the National H Blocks Committee, Belfast, 1980

Articles:

Aveyard, Stuart, '"We Couldn't Do a Prague": British Government Responses to Loyalist Strikes in Northern Ireland 1974–77', *Irish Historical Studies*, 39:153, May 2014

Bosi, Lorenzo, 'Explaining Pathways to Armed Activism in the Provisional Irish Republican Army, 1969–1972', *Social Science History*, 36:3, Fall 2012

Charters, David, 'Intelligence and Psychological Warfare in Northern Ireland', *RUSI Journal* 123:3, September 1997

Dawson, G. M., 'Defensive Planning in Belfast', *Irish Geography*, 17:1, 27–41, 2009

Doherty, Frank, 'SIGINT Used by Anti-State Forces: A Case Study of Provisional IRA Operations', in *War and Order*, Bledowska, Celina (ed.) (Junction Books, London, 1983)

Drake, C. J. M., 'The Provisional IRA: A Case Study', *Terrorism and Political Violence*, Vol. 3, 1991

Edwards, Aaron, 'A Whipping Boy If Ever There Was One'? The British Army and Politics of Civil-Military Relations in Northern Ireland, 1969–79', *Contemporary British History*, 28:2, 166–89

FitzGerald, Garret, 'The 1974–5 Threat of a British Withdrawal from Northern Ireland', *Irish Studies in International Affairs*, Vol. 17, 2006

Gill, Paul, and Horgan, John, 'Who Were the Volunteers? The Shifting Sociological and Operational Profile of 1240 Provisional Irish Republican Army Members', *Terrorism and Political Violence*, 25:3, 435–56, 2013

Horgan, John, and Taylor, Max, 'The Provisional Irish Republican Army: Command and Functional Structure', *Terrorism and Political Violence*, 9:3, Autumn 1997

Ilardi, Gaetano Joe, 'IRA Operational Intelligence: The Heartbeat of the War', *Small Wars & Insurgencies*, 21:2, June 2010

Jackson, Harold, 'The Two Irelands: The Problem of the Double Minority – A Dual Study of Inter-Group Tensions', Minority Rights Group, London, May 1973

Jamieson, Ruth, and Grounds, Adrian, 'Release and Adjustment: Perspectives from Studies of Wrongly Convicted and Politically Motivated Prisoners', in *The Effects of Imprisonment*, Liebling,

Alison, and Maruna, Shadd (eds.) (Routledge, Abingdon, 2006)

Leahy, Thomas, 'The Influence of Informers and Agents on Provisional Irish Republican Army Military Strategy and British Counter-Insurgency Strategy, 1976–94', in *Twentieth Century British History*, 26:1, 122–46, March 2015; https://academic.oup.com/tcbh/article-abstract/26/1/122/1664379

Lyons, H. A., and Harbinson, H. J., 'A Comparison of Political and Non-Political Murderers in Northern Ireland, 1974–84', *Medicine, Science and the Law*, 26:3, 1986

Matchett, William Roy, 'Security: Missing from the Northern Ireland Model', *Democracy and Security*, 11:1, 2015

McBride, Ian, 'Provisional Truths: IRA Memoirs and the Peace Process', in *Uncertain Futures*, Senia Paseta (ed.) (Oxford University Press, Oxford, 2016)

McEvoy, Kieran, O'Mahony, David, Horner, Carol, and Lyner, Olwen, 'The Home Front: The Families of Politically Motivated Prisoners in Northern Ireland', *British Journal of Criminology*, 39:2, 1999

McEvoy, Kieran, Shirlow, Peter, and McElrath, Karen, 'Resistance, Transition and Exclusion: Politically Motivated Ex-Prisoners and Conflict Transformation in Northern Ireland', *Terrorism and Political Violence*, 16:3, 2004

McLoone, Martin, 'Punk in Northern Ireland: The Political Power of "What Might Have Been"', *Irish Studies Review*, 12:1, 29–38

Moxon-Browne, E., 'The Water and the Fish: Public Opinion and the Provisional IRA in Northern Ireland', *Terrorism: An International Journal*, Vol. 5, 1981

Ó hAdhmaill, Féilim, 'Equal Citizenship for a New Society? An Analysis of Training and Employment Opportunities for Republican Ex-prisoners in Belfast', Cork Open Research Archive, 2001

O'Leary, Brendan, 'Mission Accomplished? Looking Back on the IRA', *Field Day Review*, 1:1, 217–48, 2005

Rose, Richard, McAllister, Ian, and Mair, Peter, 'Is There a Concurring Majority about Northern Ireland?' Centre for the Study of Public Policy, University of Strathclyde, 1978

Rowthorn, Bob, 'Northern Ireland: An Economy in Crisis', *Cambridge Journal of Economics*, 5, 1–31, 1981

Todd, Jennifer, 'Two Traditions in Unionist Political Culture', *Irish Political Studies*, 2:1, 1987

White, Robert, 'I'm Not Too Sure What I Told You Last Time:

Methodological Notes on Accounts from High Risk Activists in the Irish Republican Movement', *Mobilization: An International Quarterly*, 12:3, 287–305, September 2007

Reports:

Operation Banner, An Analysis of Military Operations in Northern Ireland, UK Ministry of Defence, 2006

Police Report, Brian Maguire, Deceased, Merseyside Police, 26 May 1978

Report of an Amnesty International Mission to Northern Ireland, 28 November to 6 December 1978, pub. 13 June 1978

Report of the Committee into Police Interrogation Procedures in Northern Ireland (Bennett Report), Cmnd. 7497, HMSO, March 1979

Report on the Interchange of Intelligence between Special Branch and CID (Walker Report), Royal Ulster Constabulary, 1980

Report of an Inquiry by HM Inspector of Prisons into the Security Arrangements at HM Prison, Maze, (Hennessy Report) HMSO, January 1984

Trauma, Health and Conflict in Northern Ireland, The Northern Ireland Centre for Trauma and Transformation and the Psychology Research Institute, University of Ulster, 2008

Violence and Civil Disturbances in Northern Ireland in 1969, Report of Tribunal of Inquiry (Scarman Report), Cmnd. 566, HMSO, April 1972

Selected newspaper and magazine articles:

Browne, Vincent, 'There Will Be No More Ceasefires Until the End', *Magill*, August 1978

Doherty, Frank, 'How the IRA Survives', *The Phoenix*, 23 September 1988

McCloskey, Conor, 'How Writers Sought to Make Sense of the Troubles', *Irish Times*, 1 December 2016

Thomas, Christopher, 'Hopes Fade, Targets Change', *The Times*, 29 December 1979

Unbylined, IRA Interview, *Iris*, 1:1, April 1981

PhD thesis:

Ó hAdhmaill, Féilim, 'The Function and Dynamics of the Ghetto: A Study of Nationalist West Belfast', University of Ulster, 1990

Index

Abigail's Party, 50, 52

Adams, Gerry, 31, 61–8, 70, 96, 99, 119–20, 124

Adams, Gerry (senior), 61

Aden counter-insurgency, 5

Alexander, Dr, 172

All-Ireland Senior Football Championship, 177

Amnesty International, 4, 54, 180, 192, 195, 202, 236

Andersonstown News, 88, 97, 101, 124

Antrim, 87

Ardboe, 126

Ardoyne, 12

Armagh Gaol, 189–90, 206

Army Air Corps, 167

Arts Theatre, 146

Association for Legal Justice, 54

B Specials, 6, 47

Ballycastle, 146

Ballymurphy, 30, 61, 66, 146

Bangor, 87, 92

Battle of the Boyne, 19

BBC, 17, 18n, 31, 39–40, 49–50, 109, 143

Beattie, Rev. William, 101

Behan, Brendan, 22

Belfast City Commission, 173–4

Belfast City Mortuary, 184

Belfast Crown Court, 187, 198–9, 212

Belfast Lough, 107

Belfast Telegraph, 84, 131, 161, 173

Bell, Ivor, 62

Bell, Private, 146

Belmarsh Prison, 223

Benn, Tony, 121

Bennett Report, 195, 202

Bentham, Jeremy, 188

Bewley, Neil, 94

Bishopsgate bombing, 220

Bloody Sunday, 13, 23, 30

Bodenstown cemetery, 67

Bombay Street, 16–18, 229

Bourn, John, 43

Bradley, Gerry, 11n, 72–3

Bradley, Michael, 60

Brian Boru, 140
Britain
  economy, 50, 53, 193–4
  general election, 196
  mainland bombing campaign,
    193
  social and political attitudes,
    47–50, 191–3
  Winter of Discontent, 193–5
British army
  end of campaign, 218
  former soldiers, 216
  relations with RUC, 73, 197–8
  signals intercepted, 166–7
  soldiers' experiences, 93–6,
    141
  support for phased withdrawal,
    192–3
  surveillance operations, 140–1
'Britishness', Loyalist sense of, 46
Brown, Johnston, 91–3
Browne, Des, 180
Bureau of Military History, 82n
Burgess, Paul, 57–8
Burns, Jake, 58–9

Cairns, Roy, 163–4, 180
Callaghan, James, 19, 47, 101,
  108–9, 121–3, 192–5
Carlisle, John, 159–60
Carrickfergus, 110
Carryduff, 2
Caruso, Enrico, 57
Castlereagh holding centre, 3–4,
  32–7, 53, 63, 76, 108, 119, 141,
  223, 231
  Amnesty International report,
    192, 195, 202, 236

Anne Laverty and, 174–5,
  178–9, 190
Bennett Report, 195, 202
Brian Maguire and, 182–7
Gary Smyth and, 162–6, 199–
  200, 236
Harry Murray and, 174–7,
  199–200, 236
Michael Culbert and, 175,
  180–5, 199–200, 202, 236
Phelim Hamill and, 169–72,
  189, 236
Chaplin, Charlie, 153
Clash, the, 57, 59–60
Coalisland, 112
Cobb, Harry, 174
Collins, John, 174
Collins, Michael, 82, 144
Control Zone, 102, 108–9, 123
Conway, Sir Fulke, 78
Cooke, Judith, 42
Coolnasilla Park East, 166, 167n,
  168
Corden-Lloyd, Lieutenant Colonel
  Ian, 117
Corrigan, Mairead, 98–9
Costello, Elvis, 59
Courtney, Campbell, 211
Coward, Noël, 146
Craigavon Hospital, 159
Crawford, Laura, 97–8
Creasey, Lieutenant General
  Timothy, 41–2, 44, 47, 73, 197
Cromwell, Oliver, 78
Cruft's Dog Show, 224
Crumlin Road Gaol, 187–9, 203
Cubbon, Sir Brian, 42–3, 47, 73
Culbert, Michael, 16–19, 32–5, 37,

46, 53–4, 75–6, 143–5, 161
  arrest and interrogation, 175,
    180–5, 236
  imprisonment, 187, 189, 203, 207
  later life, 213–14, 219, 228–30
  and Maguire hanging, 185
  trial, 198–203
Culbert, Monica (née Higgins), 18,
  185
Culhane, Sean, 82–3
Cumann na gCailíní, 65
Cumann na mBan, 65, 139, 232

Daily Mirror, 192
Darragh, Síle, 190
Dawe, Gerald, 55–6
death penalty, calls for restoration,
  119
defensive planning, 102, 104
DeLorean Motor Company, 107
Derry Gaol, 21
Dhofar counter-insurgency, 42
Dickens, Charles, 57
Diplock courts, 4, 35, 37, 43, 199
Doherty, Tony, 13–14
Donoughue, Bernard, 42–3, 47,
  108, 123, 192–3, 195
Downtown Radio, 149, 158
Drabble, Margaret, 48–9
Drogheda, 197
Drumm, Jimmy, 67–8
Duffy, Paul, 122
Dundalk, 84–5
Dunmurry, 89, 138, 151, 161,
  166

Eames, Archbishop Robin, 46
Earle, Norman, 187

Elizabeth II, Queen, 106–7
Elliott, James, 112
Espie, Glen, 126–9, 216
European Convention on Human
  Rights, 200
Eurovision Song Contest, 146
Ewart-Biggs, Christopher, 42

Falklands War, 134
Fall and Rise of Reginald Perrin, The,
  49–50
Falls Road, 87–8, 120, 130
Faul, Father Denis, 54
Ferris, James, 210, 212
Finaghy, 32
Fitt, Gerry, 38–9, 186, 195
Football League Championship,
  146, 161
Fort Monagh, 93, 95, 125, 139,
  169, 174–5, 231
Front de Libération du Québec, 27

Gaelic football, 9, 16
Garda Síochána, 68–9
General Motors, 106
Gibbs, Sir Roland, 194
Glen Road incident, 138–40, 143,
  163
Glover, Brigadier Jimmy, 113–17,
  122
Good Friday Agreement, 11n, 227
Gorman, Tommy, 72
Graigavon, 111
Grills, cecil, 112–13
Guevara, Che, 21

Haines, Joe, 38
Hamill, Molly, 19

Hamill, Phelim, 19–22, 25, 46, 97, 136, 139, 169–72, 174, 187, 189, 208, 213, 236
  later life, 219–28
Hamill, Sean, 19–22, 220, 223, 228
Harbinson, Helen, 27
Hardy, Thomas, 31
Harland & Wolff, 4, 134
Harman, Paul, 108
Haskell, Dr Philip, 103
Hayes, Maurice, 39, 41
Healey, Denis, 47
Heaney, Seamus, 55, 78, 213
helicopter, downed by IRA, 117
Hermon, Jack, 102, 104, 208
HMP Maze, *see* Long Kesh prison
Houlihan, Con, 177
housing policy (West Belfast), 88–90, 100–5
Hughes, Brendan, 62, 206–7
Humber Bridge, 224
hunger strikes, 24, 206–9
Hylands, Billy, 184

Imperial Contribution, 51
International Monetary Fund, 50, 53
IRA
  active abstentionism policy, 62
  Active Service Units (ASUs), 70–1, 114–16
  arsenal, 115
  auxiliaries, 65
  bombing campaign, 109–13
  ceasefire (1975), 43, 61
  close-quarter assassinations (CQA), 120, 122–33
  creation of Northern Command, 63, 70–1, 73

economic war, 33, 106, 109
  Glover assessment, 113–17
  Green Book, 13–15, 19, 46, 55
  intelligence officers, 18
  level of support in Republic, 174
  Long War strategy, 66, 114, 116, 196, 231
  mainland bombing campaign, 193
  origins, 80–1
  payments, 11n
  and peace movement, 98–9
  peace process, 225–6
  recruitment and training, 10–15, 65
  reorganisation and politicisation, 61–73, 113–14
  resentment against, 99–100
  role of prisoners, 61–3, 196–7
  signals intelligence, 166–7
  snipers, 115
  suspected informers, 141–3
  under surveillance, 140–1
  volunteers, community involvement, 96–7
  volunteers, demobbed, 72–3
  volunteers, numbers and profiles, 23–6
  volunteers, Protestant, 11–12
  volunteers, psychology, 26–31
  volunteers, women, 24, 65
  weapons shortages, 75–6
  wearing of balaclavas, 21
Irish Free State, 86
Irish Home Rule, 85
Irish language, 15, 189, 219–20, 226–7

Irish National Liberation Army
    (INLA), 196, 206
Irish Republican Brotherhood, 61
Irish war of independence, 80
'Irishness', Republican sense of, 46,
    219–20

James II, King, 19
John Paul II, Pope, 197

Kearney, Michael, 37
Kelly, Matthew, 7
Kelsey, Elsie, 101, 173
Kenya counter-insurgency, 42
Kingsley, Robert, 68–9
kneecapping, 12
Knock, 2, 77, 147

La Mon House bombing, 117–22,
    124, 126, 176
Lagan Valley Hospital, 211
Lagan, river, 77–8, 84, 103, 232
Lambeg, 84
Laverty, Anne, 139, 145, 150,
    157–8, 174–5, 178–9, 182,
    189–91, 231, 236
    trial, 198–200, 202–3
Lawson, Dick, 208
le Carré, John, 198
Leach, Edmund, 48n
Lee, Gunner David, 211
Leigh, Mike, 50
Lenadoon, 8, 32, 88–91, 97–8, 138,
    145, 147, 169, 213, 230
Liberty, 96
Lisburn
    anti-Catholic riots (The
        Burnings), 83–7, 232

history, 77–80
housing policy, 87–8, 100–5
McAllister murder, 143–58, 173
New Cemetery, 173, 233–4
reconstruction and memorials,
    232–4
Swanzy murder, 81, 83–7
Lisburn Standard, 86
Lloyd George, David, 81
Lombroso, Cesare, 26
Long Kesh (Maze) prison, 31, 61,
    66, 72, 196, 203–12, 226–7
    breakout, 210–12, 230
    dirty protest, 203–4
    hunger strikes, 24, 206–9
    Hut 11 think tank, 61–3, 66
Longley, Michael, 56, 160
Lower Falls, 20, 74, 90, 104, 140
Lowry, Lord, 203
Lowry, William, 134
Lynch, Jack, 47, 123
Lyons, Alec, 27

McAllister, Alan, 2, 152–6, 173,
    207, 215–16, 230
McAllister, Hugh, 1–2
McAllister, Mark, 2, 152, 155–6,
    173, 230
McAllister, Millar, 1–4, 6, 44, 51,
    77, 93, 108
    funeral and burial, 173, 234
    murder, 147, 152–7, 159–60,
        190–1, 229–31
    murder investigation, 164, 166,
        168, 171–2, 174–86, 220
    murder trial, 198–203
    press coverage, 172–3
McAllister, Nita (née Corry), 2–3,

77, 147, 152, 157, 160, 173,
177, 207, 212, 215
McBirney, Martin, 56
McClory, John, 191, 219
McCollum, Seamus, 69, 70n
McCorley, Roddy, 231
McCorley, Roger, 82–3
MacCurtain, Tomás, 81–2
MacDermott, Mr Justice John, 10,
198–203
McDonald, Henry, 58
McGuinness, Martin, 41, 221
McKearney, Tommy, 71–2
McKee, Brian, 93–4, 129–33, 175,
203, 216–18
McKenna, Sean, 206
McKinney, Brian, 191, 219
McMahon, James, 232
Maguire, Annie, 98
Maguire, Brian, 182–7, 189, 200,
237
Maguire, Frank, 195
Major, John, 226
Marshall, Professor Thomas,
159–60
Mason, Roy, 37–41, 47, 73, 88,
101, 105–6, 108, 111, 113,
117–19, 122–3, 173, 187, 192–3,
195, 205
Meeke, Joe, 176–7
Megaw, Brendan, 142–3, 218–19
Megaw, Kieran, 218–19
Megaw, Marie, 142–3, 218–19
Melchett, Lord, 105
MI5, 198, 220–1
Miles, Albert, 205
Military Reaction Force, 218
Mills, James, 118

Milltown cemetery, 10, 33, 208
Mooney, DCS Bill, 35, 37, 171
Morris, Joseph, 118
Mountbatten, Lord, 197–8
Mountjoy Prison, 67
Murlough, 145
Murphy, Dick, 82–3
Murray, Denis, 17
Murray, Harry, 4–14, 16, 61, 74–6,
95, 107, 129–31, 133, 139–40,
143–5
arrest and interrogation, 174–7,
236
imprisonment, 187–9, 203, 207,
209–12
later life, 213, 219, 230
McAllister murder, 147, 150–5,
157–8, 160–1, 166, 168, 180,
182, 216
trial, 198–203
Murray, Henry, 4, 7
Murray, Kathleen (née Kelly), 6–9,
76, 177, 207
Murray, Margaret, 4

Na Fianna Éireann, 65, 137
Neave, Airey, 193, 196
Newman, Kenneth, 35–7, 40–1,
44, 47, 73, 118, 173, 186, 192,
197, 233
Newry, 112
News Letter, 84, 101, 233
Newtonards, 87
Newtownabbey, 92
Nicholson, James, 106
Nobel Peace Prize, 99
Northern Ireland
casualty figures, 36, 44, 91, 124

creation of state, 86
domestic murder rate, 27n
economy, 51–3, 105–6
entertainments, 146
firefighters' strike, 109, 112
internment without trial, 7, 30, 43
memorials, 231–2
mental health problems, 214–15
mixed marriages, 7, 146
'Night the Troubles Began', 17
'normalisation', 45–7
power sharing, 116
punk rockers, 56–60
released prisoners, 213–15
royal visit, 106–7
unemployment, 52, 134–5
writers, 54–6
Northern Ireland Attitude Survey, 191
Northern Ireland Development Agency, 107
Northern Ireland Forensic Science Laboratory, 160
Northern Ireland Opera Trust, 146
Northern Ireland Police Federation, 41
Northern Ireland Statistics and Research Agency, 214
Nowasad, James, 123

O'Callaghan, Brendan, 97–8
O'Doherty, Malachi, 99–100
Ó Fiaich, Tomás, 205
Official Irish Jokes, 48
Ogilvie, Gordon, 59
Ó hAdhmaill, Féilim, see Hamill, Phelim

Oldfield, Maurice, 198
O'Neill, Hugh, 140
Oman counter-insurgency, 42
Orange Order, 4

Palestine Liberation Organization, 69
Peace People, 98–9, 173
Peel, John, 60
Pentonville Prison, 188
Pigeon Racing News and Gazette, 3, 108, 143, 153, 177–8, 184
Poleglass, 100, 102, 104–5, 151
Post Office Tower, 224
Prevention of Terrorism Act, 162
Proclamation of the Irish Republic (1916), 14–15

Queen's University, 22, 37, 40, 214
Rag Week killings, 123–4
Quigley, George, 51
Quinn, Gordon, 109

racism, 135–6
Rawlinson, Peter, 186–7
Red Army Faction, 27
Rees, Merlyn, 38
Regional Crime Squads, 35–6, 54, 165
Republican News, 62, 116
Reynolds, Albert, 226
Rice's bookmakers, 147–8, 152, 163, 166, 237
Rogers, Hugh, 32–3
Rose, Sir Clive, 194
Rougier, Mr Justice, 225
Royal Irish Constabulary (RIC), 80–1

Royal Marines, 94, 102, 224
RUC
    intelligence-gathering role, 198
    morale, 92–3
    Police Primacy policy, 43–5, 51,
        73, 107
    policing style, 8–9
    recruitment, 51
    relations with army, 73, 197–8
    split with Catholic community,
        17
    use of torture, 35–7, 53–4,
        169–72
    see also Castlereagh holding
        centre
RUC band, 173
RUC Photography Branch, 2–3, 6,
    159
RUC Special Branch, 4, 35, 72,
    117, 137, 144, 198

Sacred Heart of Mary convent,
    83–4
St Patrick's Training School, 18
Samaritans, 174
Sands, Bobby, 62, 96–7, 139, 204,
    207–9
sangars, 102, 133, 188
SAS, 166
Scott, Sir Walter, 79
SDLP, 53, 186, 195
Shakespeare, William, 13
Shankill Butchers, 20, 136
Shankill Road, 16, 88, 98, 109
Sharkey, Feargal, 60
Shea, Patrick, 86
Shilton, Peter, 161
Short Strand, 74

Simpson, Charles, 122–3
Sinn Féin, 46, 53, 61, 65–6, 80,
    185
Smyth, John Garrett (Gary),
    133–40, 145, 147–51, 158, 161
    arrest and interrogation, 162–6,
        168–9, 172, 174–5, 236
    imprisonment, 187–9, 203, 207
    later life, 213–14, 219, 230–1
    and Maguire hanging, 185
    trial, 198–200
Smyth, Pat, 133
Somerset Light Infantry, 83
Spence, Norma, 123
Spencer, Sir Derek, 224
Stiff Little Fingers, 58–60
Stormont Castle, 38
Stout, Charlie, 40, 109, 111–12,
    119, 123, 174, 192
Stout, Laura, 112
Strathearn Audio, 105–6, 139, 158,
    166, 182, 186, 193
Strummer, Joe, 60
Swanzy, Elizabeth, 86, 233
Swanzy, Henry, 82
Swanzy, Rev. Henry, 83
Swanzy, Irene, 83, 86, 233
Swanzy, Oswald, 81–7, 134, 144,
    151, 232–3

Thatcher, Margaret, 121, 193, 196,
    205–9
Thiepval Barracks, 77
Tiger's Bay, 4–8
Tolstoy, Leo, 31
Tompkinson, Private Jonathan
    ('Swede'), 95–6, 125, 216
Trelford, Guy, 58, 60

Turf Lodge, 93–5, 102, 108, 125, 174

Twomey, Seamus, 66–7, 70

Tyrone Democrat, 112

Ulster Defence Association (UDA), 109

Ulster Defence Regiment (UDR), 32, 44–5, 51, 77, 113, 126, 129, 132, 216

Ulster Hall, 56, 59

Ulster Polytechnic, 166

Ulster Star, 173

Ulster TV, 153

Ulster Unionist Party, 46, 193

Ulster Volunteer Force (UVF), 8, 85, 102, 109

Undertones, the, 60

United Irishmen, 140

University College Cork, 227

University of Central Lancashire, 220

US State Department, 40, 106, 123, 174

vengeance, psychology of, 29–31

Vengeful vehicle tracking system, 90

Victims and Survivors Forum, 228

Vietnam War, 21

Wallace Park, 160

Warrenpoint, 197–8

Warrington bombing, 220

water-boarding, 170n, 185, 189

Way Ahead, The, 43, 61

Westlink, 102

White, Robert, 11

Whitefort Inn, 148–9, 166, 199

Whitemoor Prison, 226

William III, King, 19

Williams, Betty, 98–9

Williams, Shirley, 121

Wolfe Tone, Theobald, 67, 140

World Council of Churches, 42

Yom Kippur War, 48

Young, Brian, 57

CRUEL BRITANNIA

A Secret History of Torture

WINNER OF THE PADDY POWER TOTAL POLITICS DEBUT BOOK OF THE YEAR AWARD

'A fine study of the role Britain has played in the business of torture' *Sunday Times* 'Must Read'

'In one of the most shocking and persuasive books of the year, Ian Cobain details not just British complicity in torture but the longstanding practice of the thing itself, and the lies British politicians have always told, and are still telling, to cover it up' David Hare

'Ian Cobain's particularly fine book [shows] . . . what's been done under the aegis of the British state [and] will shock anyone who cherishes civilised values' *Metro*

'*Cruel Britannia* makes it clear that a culture of secrecy doesn't just serve to protect the elite but is also the soil in which the worst aspects of humanity can take root and grow. This is a shocking book that deserves a wide readership . . . to ignore its findings would be to grant impunity to actions that reveal the worst of human behaviour' *New Statesman*

'Utterly gripping . . . I will not forget what I have learnt from this book, and I will be telling others about it for years to come' PJ Harvey

'A dramatic challenge to official dishonesty and public complacency, past and present' *Independent*

'A genuine contribution to history' *Daily Telegraph*

'Absorbing and devastating' *Observer*